Maryland Revolutionary Records

Data obtained from 3,050 Pension Claims
and Bounty Land Applications, including 1,000 Marriages of Maryland
Soldiers and a List of 1,200
Proved Services of Soldiers
and Patriots of other
States

By
HARRY WRIGHT NEWMAN

Author of
ANNE ARUNDEL GENTRY
THE SMOOTS OF MARYLAND AND VIRGINIA
THE STONES OF POYNTON MANOR
THE LUCKETTS OF PORTOBACCO

Southern Historical Press, Inc.
Greenville, South Carolina

This volume was reproduced from
An copy located in the
Publishers private Library

All rights reserved. No part of this publication may be reproduced,
stored in a retrieval system, transmitted in any form, posted
on to the web in any form or by any means without
the prior written permission of the publisher.

Please direct all correspondence and orders to:

www.southernhistoricalpress.com
or
SOUTHERN HISTORICAL PRESS, Inc.
PO BOX 1267
375 West Broad Street
Greenville, SC   29601
southernhistoricalpress@gmail.com

Originally published: Washington, D.C. 1938
Reprinted by:
Southern Historical Press, Inc.
Greenville, SC
ISBN #0-89308-772-6
All rights Reserved.
Printed in the United States of America

Foreword

The data contained in this publication taken from the applications of Maryland veterans of the Revolutionary War, their widows and their heirs for Federal pensions and bounty land are about as complete as it is possible to obtain from official sources. They include the rejected claims as well as the approved. The only exception is the elimination of identified colored veterans and of several native Europeans who had contracted marriages with women not of their race. The information was obtained from the original applications, all facts stated under oaths with affidavits.

In the preparation of this work, a complete digest of the claim, including all facts pertaining to genealogy or clues for the genealogist and to history, was made. Many valuable and interesting items were collected, among which were over 700 Bible records and several militia muster rolls, copies of which were not among the public or official papers of the State of Maryland.

HARRY WRIGHT NEWMAN

Table of Contents

		Page
1	Brief Resumé of Maryland Revolutionary Pensions . . .	7
2	Brief Resumé of Maryland Federal Bounty Land Warrants.	57
3	List of Maryland Soldiers (Non-Pensioners) Proved Through Pension Claims	85
4	Marriages Proved from Maryland Revolutionary Pensions	109
5	Miscellaneous List of Non-Maryland Revolutionary Soldiers Established from Pension Claims	127

Part I

MARYLAND REVOLUTIONARY PENSIONERS

*Indicates that the widow applied for pension

NOTE: Complete information on the following veterans may be secured for a reasonable fee by addressing the compiler.

Name of Veteran	Birth	Rank	Establishment	Miscellaneous facts and other State services
Ackbright, Isaac	1738	Pvt.	Militia	Wounded
Acre, Cornelaus	1760	Pvt.	Maryland Line	Prisoner
Acton, Henry*	1755	Pvt.	Flying Camp	Militia
Acton, Smallwood*	1758	Pvt.	Militia	Wounded
Adams, John	1760	Pvt.	Militia	
Adams, John*	1764	Pvt.	Militia	Pa. Service
Adams, John*	1763	Pvt.	Sea Service	
Adams, Mark*	1755	Pvt.	Maryland Line	Prisoner
Adams, Richard	1755	Pvt.	Militia	
Agens, James	1751	Sergt.	Maryland Line	N. Y. Service
Ahl, John Peter	1748	Surgeon	Continental Line	Wounded
Alcock, Robert	1759	Pvt.	Maryland Line	Wounded
Alder, George*	1756	Pvt.	Militia	Prisoner
Alder, James	1760	Pvt.	Militia	
Aldridge, William	1757	Pvt.	Continental Line	Ky. Service
Alexander, James*	1756	Surgeon	Militia	N. C. Service
Alexander, William*	——	Lieut.	Maryland Line	Killed in action
Allbaugh, Zachariah	1758	Pvt.	Militia	
Allen, Alexander*	——	Pvt.	Maryland Line	Prisoner
Allen, Jacob*	1751	Pvt.	Maryland Line	Prisoner
Allen, John*	——	Pvt.	Maryland Line	
Allen, Nathan	1755	Pvt.	Sea Service	
Allen, Patrick	1740	Pvt.	Militia	Penn. Service
Allison, Burch	1764	Pvt.	Militia	
Allison, Robert*	——	Corpl.	Flying Camp	Prisoner
Allsop, Joseph*	——	Pvt.	Flying Camp	
Alvey, Josias	1757	Pvt.	Maryland Line	
Alvey, Thomas Green	1750	Pvt.	Maryland Line	Wounded

Amos, Mordecai	1753	Lieut.	Militia	
Anderson, Alexander	1761	Pvt.	Militia	Va. Service
Anderson, Richard	——	Capt.	Maryland Line	Invalid
Andrews, William	1754	Pvt.	Maryland Line	
Armstrong, James F.*	——	Chap.	Maryland Line	
Arnaud, John Peter	1753	Pvt.	Naval	Prisoner
Arnett, Samuel*	1746	Pvt.	Militia	
Arnold, George*	1751	Pvt.	German Regiment	
Arthur, James*	——	Lieut.	Maryland Line	
Ashley, William*	1757	Corpl.	Continental Line	
Austin, Richard	1756	Pvt.	Militia	
Ayer, Darius	1755	Pvt.	Militia	
Ayres, John	1750	Pvt.	Maryland Line	Del. Service
Ayres, Thomas*	1755	Pvt.	Maryland Line	Wounded
Azelip, Richard	1753	Pvt.	German Regiment	
Babbs, John	——	Pvt.	Maryland Line	Wounded
Backenbaugh, Leonard*	1760	Pvt.	Militia	
Badger, Charles	1754	Pvt.		
Baer, Henry	1758	Pvt.	Militia	
Baggerly, David*	——	Pvt.	Militia	
Bagum, Henry	1761	Pvt.	Militia	
Bailey, James*	1741	Pvt.	Maryland Line	Wounded
Bailey, James*	1761	Sergt.	Maryland Line	
Bailey, Josephus	1755	Pvt.	Maryland Line	
Bailey, Thomas	1752	Pvt.	Maryland Line	Wounded
Baker, Absalom	——	Pvt.	Maryland Line	Wounded
Baker, Isaac	1758	Pvt.	Militia	
Baker, John	1761	Pvt.	Militia	Also War of 1812
Baker, John	1758	Pvt.	Militia	Penn. Service
Baker, Worsley	1762	Pvt.	Militia	
Balch, Stephen	1748	Capt.	Militia	
Baldwin, John	1757	Pvt.	Militia	
Baldwin, Samuel	1760	Pvt.	Militia	
Ball, Amos	1756	Pvt.	Militia	
Ball, James	1751	Sergt.	Militia	
Ballard, Jonathan	1758	Pvt.	Maryland Line	Wounded
Ballerson, William	1733	Pvt.	Maryland Line	
Bandfield, James	——	Pvt.	Maryland Line	
Bantham, John	1756	Sergt.	Maryland Line	Wounded

Bantham, Peregrine	1756	Pvt.	Maryland Line	
Barber, George	1764	Seaman	Naval	Prisoner
Barber, John	1767	Pvt.	Maryland Line	
Barkers, James	1760	Pvt.	Maryland Line	
Barker, William	1759	Pvt.	Maryland Line	
Barnard, William	1759	Pvt.	Militia	
Barnes, Elijah	1755	Pvt.	Militia	Prisoner
Barnes, James	1751	Pvt.	Maryland Line	
Barnes, John	1757	Pvt.	Militia	
Barnes, John	1756	Pvt.	Militia	
Barnes, Nicodemus	1760	Pvt.	Militia	Wounded
Barnes, William	1752	Pvt.	Maryland Line	Indian Wars
Barnet, Daniel	1748	Pvt.	Maryland Line	Prisoner
Barnet, James*	——	Pvt.	Militia	
Barnett, Peter	1760	Pvt.	Militia	
Barns, James	——	Seaman	Naval	
Barret, Isaac*	1759	Pvt.	Militia	
Barret, Jonathan	1761	Pvt.	Militia	
Barret, Richard	1762	Sergt.	Militia	
Barrett, Solomon	1764	Fifer	Maryland Line	
Barrick, Peter	1762	Pvt.		
Bartley, Thomas	1759	Pvt.	Militia	Prisoner
Bateman, George	1755	Pvt.	Maryland Line	
Bateman, Thomas	1758	Pvt.	Maryland Line	
Bateman, William	1757	Pvt.	Continental Line	Prisoner
Battin, John*	1747	Pvt.	Continental Line	Wounded
Baum, John*	1758	Pvt.	Militia	Wounded
Bayley, Mountjoy	——	Capt.	Maryland Line	
Beall, Christopher	1752	Pvt.	Maryland Line	
Beall, Lawson*	1758	Pvt.	Maryland Line	
Beall, Ninian*	1761	Pvt.		Va. Service
Beall, Robert L.	1765	Pvt.	Militia	
Beall, Samuel B.	1763	Pvt.	Maryland Line	
Beall, Thomas	1761	Pvt.	Maryland Line	
Beall, William D.	——	Major	Maryland Line	Invalid
Bean, Conrad	1753	Pvt.	Continental Line	
Bean, Henry	1754	Pvt.	Militia	
Bean, Leonard	1758	Pvt.	Maryland Line	
Bearcroft, John	——	Pvt.	Maryland Line	Prisoner
Beard, Frederick*	1758	Pvt.	Militia	

Beard, William	1765	Drum.	Maryland Line	
Beard, William	1760	Pvt.	Militia	N. C. Service
Beatty, Henry	1760	Pvt.	Militia	
Beaven, Charles	1755	Lieut.	Maryland Line	
Beaver, Martin	1760	Pvt.	Maryland Line	
Bechtel, Philip	1759	Pvt.	Militia	Penn. Service
Beck, Thomas*	1762	Drum.	Militia	
Beckett, Humphrey*	——	Surgeon	Maryland Line	Invalid
Beckwith, Benjamin	1760	Pvt.	Militia	
Beckwith, George*	1760	Pvt.	Militia	
Beckwith, Nehemiah	1757	Corpl.	Militia	
Beckwith, William	1760	Pvt.	Militia	
Beddo, Thomas*	1761	Pvt.	Militia	
Bell, James	——	Pvt.	Militia	
Bell, John	1756	Pvt.	Maryland Line	
Bell, John*	——	Pvt.	Militia	
Belt, John Sprigg	——	Lieut.	Maryland Line	
Bennett, Daniel	1746	Pvt.	Maryland Line	
Bennett, Jesse	1759	Pvt.	Maryland Line	
Benson, Joseph	1764	Pvt.	Militia	
Benson, Perry	——	Capt.	Militia	Invalid
Berry, Robert*	——	Capt.	Navy	
Berry, William*	——	Sergt.	Continental Line	
Betts, Jacob	1752	Sergt.	Maryland Line	
Bicknell, Esan	1760	Pvt.	Maryland Line	
Biddell, Richard	1756	Pvt.	Maryland Line	
Bingham, Robert*	——	Pvt.		
Birch, Thomas*	1746	Pvt.	Militia	
Biscoe, Josiah	1760	Seaman	Navy	State Militia
Bishop, Jacob*	1765	Pvt.	Continental Line	Germ. Regt.
Black, Hugh	1737	Pvt.	Militia	Wounded
Black, John	1763	Pvt.	Continental Line	Va. Service
Black, Rudolph	1762	Pvt.	Militia	
Black, Samuel	1762	Pvt.	Boat Service	
Blackburn, James	1752	Pvt.	Militia	Va. Service
Blackburn, Samuel	1755	Pvt.	Militia	
Blackmore, George	1760	Pvt.	Continental Line	Tenn. Service
Blade, Eli	1764	Pvt.	Militia	
Blades, John L.*	——	Pvt.	Maryland Line	
Blake, Jacob	——	Pvt.	Maryland Line	

Blandford, Richard	——	Pvt.	Militia	——
Blanford, Joseph*	——	Pvt.	Militia	——
Blewer, John	——	Pvt.	Maryland Line	Invalid
Board, John	1751	Pvt.	Maryland Line	——
Boles, Samuel*	1750	Seaman	Navy	Del. Service
Bolton, James	1748	Pvt.	Militia	N. C. Service
Bomgardner, George	1754	Pvt.	Maryland Line	——
Bomgardner, William	1753	Pvt.	Maryland Line	——
Bond, Benjamin	1756	Sergt.	Militia	——
Bond, James	1758	Pvt.	Maryland Line	——
Bond, John	1762	Sergt.	Maryland Line	——
Bond, Samuel	1754	Pvt.	Militia	——
Boone, Adam	1762	Pvt.	Militia	——
Boone, John	1759	Ensign	Maryland Line	——
Booth, Edward	1753	Pvt.	Maryland Line	——
Boreland, Thomas	1740	Pvt.	Maryland Line	——
Boren, John	1755	Pvt.	Militia	——
Boss, Adam*	1762	Pvt.	Militia	——
Boswell, Jesse*	1755	Pvt.	Maryland Line	——
Bowdy, John*	1755	Pvt.	Maryland Line	——
Bowen, James	——	Sergt.	Maryland Line	——
Bowen, Sabritt*	——	Sergt.	Continental Line	——
Bowen, Stephen	1761	Pvt.	Maryland Line	——
Bower, Jacob*	1749	Pvt.	Maryland Line	——
Bowers, George	1757	Pvt.	Maryland Line	Wounded
Bowers, George	1761	Pvt.	Continental Line	——
Bowers, Leonard*	1760	Pvt.	Maryland Line	Prisoner
Bowers, Sebastian	1760	Pvt.	Militia	——
Bowie, William	1764	Pvt.	Militia	——
Bowling, William	1760	Pvt.	Maryland Line	——
Bowman, Philip	1755	Ensign	Militia	——
Bowman, Sparling	1752	Ensign	Militia	——
Boyd, Benjamin	1761	Surgeon	Continental Line	——
Boyd, James	1759	Pvt.	Maryland Line	Del. Service
Boyd, John	1756	Pvt.	Militia	——
Boyd, William	1754	Pvt.	Militia	——
Boyer, John*	1762	Pvt.	Militia	——
Bradley, Cornelius	1754	Pvt.	Maryland Line	——
Braithwaite, William*	1752	Pvt.	Maryland Line	——

Bramble, William	1761	Pvt.	Maryland Line	Prisoner
Brandenburg, William	1758	Pvt.	Militia	
Branson, John	1756	Pvt.	Maryland Line	
Brashears, Ignatius	1753	Pvt.	Maryland Line	
Brashears, Morris	1756	Pvt.	Maryland Line	
Bratton, William	1755	Seaman	Navy	
Breakbill, Peter*	1760	Pvt.	Militia	Penn. Service
Breeze, John	1755	Pvt.	Militia	Penn. Service
Brewer, Thomas*	1754	Pvt.	Maryland Line	Injured
Brian, Daniel	1754	Pvt.	Maryland Line	
Brierly, George*	1757	Pvt.	Militia	
Bright, James*	1752	Pvt.	Maryland Line	
Briley, John	1750	Pvt.	Maryland Line	
Brimmage, John	1760	Pvt.	———	N. C. Service
Briscoe, Henry	1763	Pvt.	Militia	
Briscoe, Philip	1757	Pvt.	Militia	
Britt, John	1752	Pvt.	Maryland Line	
Brittingham, Solomon*	1765	Pvt.	Maryland Line	
Britton, Joseph	1753	Pvt.	Continental Line	Prisoner
Brookover, John	1760	Pvt.	Militia	Va. Service
Brooks, John	1752	Pvt.	Militia	
Brooks, William	1745	Pvt.	Militia	N. C. Service
Browning, Jeremiah	———	Pvt.	Continental Line	Injured
Bruce, Robert	———	Pvt.	Maryland Line	
Bruce, William	———	Capt.	Maryland Line	
Bruner, Jacob	1759	Pvt.	Maryland Line	Penn. Service
Bruner, Jacob*	1763	Pvt.	Militia	
Brunner, Valentine*	1758	Pvt.	Militia	
Bryan, Charles*	1754	Pvt.	Continental Line	
Bryan, Luke	1759	Sergt.	Militia	
Bryan, Thomas	1741	Pvt.	Militia	
Bryant, James	———	Seaman	Navy	
Bullock, John	1753	Pvt.	Maryland Line	
Bullock, William T.*	1760	Pvt.	Militia	
Burch, Benjamin*	———	Pvt.	Militia	
Burch, Benjamin*	———	Sergt.	Militia	Prisoner
Burch, Francis	1760	Sergt.	Militia	
Burch, John*	1759	Pvt.	Militia	Va. Service

Name	Year	Rank	Service	Notes
Burch, Zachariah*	1757	Pvt.	Maryland Line	
Burgess, Edward	1752	Pvt.	Maryland Line	
Burgess, Josias	1758	Pvt.	Maryland Line	Prisoner
Burgoon, Robert	1749	Pvt.	Militia	
Burk, John*	1758	Pvt.	Maryland Line	Va. Service
Burk, Martin	1752	Pvt.	Maryland Line	Wounded
Burk, Nathan	1754	Pvt.	Maryland Line	
Burk, Richard	1756	Pvt.	Maryland Line	Prisoner
Burns, John	1761	Pvt.	Maryland Line	
Burns, Thomas	1751	Pvt.	Maryland Line	
Burrough, Norman*	—	Pvt.	Continental Line	
Burroughs, Elisha*	—	Pvt.		
Burrows, Jeremiah	1752	Sergt.	Militia	
Burton, Joshua	1746	Pvt.	Continental Line	Penn. Service
Bushnell, Samuel	1747	Pvt.		Invalid
Butler, Noble	1760	Pvt.	Militia	Wounded
Butler, Richard	1750	Pvt.	Maryland Line	
Butler, Richard	—	Q. M.	Militia	
Butler, Zachariah	1754	Sergt.	Militia	N. C. Service
Butt, Archibald	1764	Pvt.	Maryland Line	N. C. Service
Butt, Baruch	1755	Pvt.	Maryland Line	
Butt, Thomas*	—	Music'n	Maryland Line	
Byers, William	1762	Seaman	Naval Service	
Byrnes, James	1755	Pvt.	Continental Line	
Cahill, Elisha	1762	Pvt.	Militia	
Cahill, James	1749	Pvt.	Militia	
Cahoe, Thomas	—	Pvt.	Maryland Line	Wounded
Callahan, Dennis	1748	Pvt.	Maryland Line	
Callender, John	1750	Pvt.	Maryland Line	Prisoner
Campbell, Eneas	—	Lieut.	Militia	
Campbell, John	1761	Pvt.	Militia	
Campbell, Thomas	1741	Pvt.	Continental Line	Wounded
Cane, Hugh	1754	Pvt.	Maryland Line	
Caple, Samuel	1754	Pvt.	Militia	
Carey, Michael	1757	Pvt.	Maryland Line	
Carlin, William*	—	Pvt.	Maryland Line	
Carlisle, Benjamin	1761	Pvt.	Continental Line	
Carney, Thomas	1759	Pvt.	Maryland Line	
Carr, Hezekiah*	1760	Pvt.	Maryland Line	Wounded
Carr, John*	—	Pvt.	Maryland Line	

Carr, John	1756	Lieut.	Maryland Line	
Carrel, George	1751	Pvt.	Maryland Line	
Carrol, John	1754	Pvt.	Militia	
Carrol, John*			Maryland Line	
Carroll, William	1756	Pvt.	Militia	
Carter, James	1758	Pvt.	Militia	Wounded
Cary, Saul	1756	Pvt.	Militia	
Casbury, Peter		Pvt.		Invalid
Caseldine, John	1760	Pvt.	Militia	Indian Wars
Cash, William	1756	Pvt.	Militia	Flying Camp
Cassel, Abraham*	1756	Pvt.	Maryland Line	
Castor, Vincent*		Corpl.		
Cauliflower, Michael	1758	Pvt.	Militia	
Cavender, John*	1760	Pvt.	Militia	Del. Service
Chadd, Samuel	1754	Pvt.	Militia	
Chadwick, William	1743	Pvt.	Maryland Line	
Chalmers, James	1762	Seaman	Naval Service	
Chambers, Edward	1764	Pvt.	Maryland Line	
Chapman, Benjamin	1760	Pvt.	Militia	Va. Service
Chatham, William	1760	Pvt.	Militia	
Chenoweth, John*		Sergt.	Maryland Line	
Chenoweth, Thomas*				
Christman, Frederick	1755	Pvt.	Militia	
City, Jacob*	1760	Pvt.	Militia	Va. Service
Clagett, Samuel*		Surgeon	Continental Line	
Clancy, John		Pvt.	Maryland Line	
Clannahan, Robert		Pvt.	Maryland Line	
Clapper, Valentine	1746	Pvt.	Maryland Line	Wounded
Clark, Anthony	1758	Pvt.	Militia	
Clark, Elijah	1754	Pvt.	Militia	
Clark, Jacob	1755	Sergt.	Maryland Line	Prisoner
Clark, James*			Maryland Line	
Clark, John*	1747		Continental Line	
Clark, John	1756	Pvt.	Continental Line	
Clark, John		Sergt.	Maryland Line	
Clark, John	1740	Pvt.	Maryland Line	
Clark, William	1758	Lieut.	Maryland Line	
Clem, John*		Pvt.	Continental Line	
Clemence, Joseph	1733	Pvt.	Militia	
Clemmons, John	1751	Pvt.	Militia	N. C. Service

Clendeman, James	1763	Pvt.	Militia	Penn. Service
Clevidence, John*	1759	Pvt.	Maryland Line	
Cliffton, Thomas	——	Pvt.	Continental Line	
Cline, William	1746	Pvt.	Maryland Line	
Clinkenbread, Isaac	1758	Pvt.	Militia	Va. Service
Clinton, Thomas	1760	Fifer	Maryland Line	
Close, Charles	1757	Pvt.	Continental Line	
Cloward, Abraham*	1757	Pvt.	Maryland Line	
Clutter, Casper	1745	Pvt.	Maryland Line	
Clutter, Simeon	1764	Pvt.		
Cochran, James*	1763	Pvt.	Militia	
Cockey, Edward	——	Col.	Militia	
Coe, Richard	1754	Pvt.	Maryland Line	
Coe, William	1757	Corpl.	Maryland Line	
Coffman, Jacob*	——	——	Continental Line	Prisoner
Coffroth, Conrad	1762	Fifer	Maryland Line	
Coins, Dominick	1753	Fifer	Maryland Line	
Colbert, John W.	1759	Pvt.	Militia	
Cole, Benjamin*	——	Pvt.	Maryland Line	
Cole, Ezekiel	1748	Pvt.	Militia	
Cole, George	1758	Ensign	Continental Line	
Cole, Job	1744	Pvt.	Militia	N. C. Service
Cole, John	1756	Pvt.	Militia	
Cole, Samuel	1762	Pvt.	Militia	
Colegate, Asaph	1765	Pvt.	Maryland Line	
Collins, John	1762	Sergt.	Militia	
Collins, Joshua	1747	Pvt.	Militia	
Collins, Josiah	1757	Pvt.	Militia	Penn. Service
Collins, Timothy*	——	Corpl.	Maryland Line	
Comegys, Cornelius*	——	Ensign	Militia	
Comins, Alexander	1750	Pvt.	Militia	
Commins, Harmon	——	Pvt.	Continental Line	Va. Service
Compton, Edmund	1759	Lieut.	Maryland Line	
Compton, James*	1753	Pvt.	Maryland Line	
Conaway, Charles	1752	Pvt.	Militia	
Conaway, Samuel	1748	Pvt.	Militia	
Congleton, Daniel	——	Pvt.	Maryland Line	
Conley, John	——	Pvt.	Maryland Line	
Conley, Michael*	1750	Pvt.	Maryland Line	
Conn, William	——	Pvt.	Militia	

Name	Year	Rank	Unit	Notes
Connelly, Hugh	——	Pvt.	Continental Line	——
Connelly, John	1762	Pvt.	Maryland Line	——
Connelly, William*	——	Pvt.	Maryland Line	——
Connolly, Patrick	1757	Pvt.	Maryland Line	Del. Service
Constantine, Edward*	——	——	——	——
Cook, Benjamin	1762	Corpl.	Maryland Line	——
Cook, Henry	1763	Pvt.	Maryland Line	——
Cook, William	1753	Pvt.	Militia	Penn. Service
Cooke, William	1760	Pvt.	Maryland Line	——
Cookendorfer, Michael	1751	Fifer	Militia	——
Cooley, Richard*	1756	Pvt.	Militia	——
Coon, Christian	1751	Pvt.	Continental Line	——
Coop, Horatio	1758	Pvt.	Militia	——
Cooper, William*	——	——	Maryland Line	——
Cope, Barachias	1760	Pvt.	Militia	War of 1812
Corbet, Jacob	1758	Pvt.	Maryland Line	——
Cork, William	1756	Pvt.	Maryland Line	——
Corley, George	1747	Pvt.	Militia	——
Coulter, John	1762	Pvt.	Maryland Line	——
Courtney, Thomas*	1759	Sergt.	Maryland Line	——
Courts, Richard H.*	——	Surgeon	Maryland Line	——
Coward, William*	——	Lieut.	Naval Service	Prisoner
Cox, Isaac	1755	Pvt.	Militia	——
Cox, Joseph	1761	Pvt.	——	——
Cox, Nathaniel	1760	Pvt.	Militia	——
Cox, Thomas	1753	Lieut.	Militia	——
Coy, Christopher*	1761	Pvt.	Maryland Line	——
Coy, William	1756	Pvt.	Militia	——
Craig, John	——	Pvt.	Maryland Line	Invalid
Craig, Thomas*	1753	Sergt.	Maryland Line	Prisoner
Craig, William	1755	Pvt.	Militia	Naval Service
Cramer, Jacob	——	Pvt.	Continental Line	——
Crampton, Thomas	1758	Pvt.	Maryland Line	——
Craven, Andrew	1752	Pvt.	Maryland Line	——
Crawford, James	1758	Pvt.	Maryland Line	——
Crawford, Nehemiah	1760	Pvt.	Continental Line	——
Creamer, Daniel*	1757	Pvt.	Militia	Va. Service
Croft, John*	——	Pvt.	——	——

Crosley, James	1741	Pvt.	Militia	
Crosley, Moses	1764	Drum.	Militia	
Crosley, William*	1761	Pvt.	Militia	
Cross, Joseph	——	Lieut.	Maryland Line	
Cross, Robert*	——	Music'n	——	
Crouch, Robert*	1759	Pvt.	Continental Line	
Crouch, Thomas	1750	Pvt.	Militia	
Crouse, John	1760	Pvt.	Militia	
Crum, Adam*	1750	Pvt.	Continental Line	Wounded
Crum, John	1762	Pvt.	Maryland Line	
Crutchey, Benjamin	1745	Pvt.	Maryland Line	
Crutfield, Joshua	1753	Pvt.	Maryland Line	Va. Penn. Serv.
Crutsinger, Solomon*	——	Pvt.	Continental Line	Wounded
Cummings, John	1760	Pvt.	Continental Line	
Currin, James	1752	Pvt.	Maryland Line	
Curtiss, John	1758	Sergt.	Continental Line	
Curtis, Michael	——	——	Maryland Line	
Cusick, Christopher*	——	——	Maryland Line	
Dale, Campbell	1753	Pvt.	Militia	
Dannor, Daniel	1759	Pvt.	Militia	
Davenport, Adrian	1760	Pvt.	Maryland Line	Va. Service
Davidson, James	1760	Pvt.	Maryland Line	Prisoner
Davidson, John	——	Pvt.	Maryland Line	
Davis, Anthony	1745	Pvt.	Maryland Line	
Davis, Enos	1761	Pvt.	Maryland Line	
Davis, Forrest	1762	Sergt.	Maryland Line	
Davis, Ichabod	1758	Pvt.	Militia	
Davis, Levi	1751	Pvt.	Maryland Line	
Davis, Lodovick	1764	Pvt.	Maryland Line	
Davis, Marmaduke*	1760	Pvt.	Militia	
Davis, Philemon	1759	Pvt.	Continental Line	
Davis, Richard	1753	Sergt.	Maryland Line	
Davis, Samuel	1768	Fifer	Maryland Line	
Davis, Thomas*	1753	Pvt.	Maryland Line	Militia
Davis, William	1757	Pvt.	Militia	
Davis, William	1761	Pvt.		
Davis, William F. R.	1763	Pvt.	Maryland Line	Militia
Dawkins, Charles*	——	Sergt.	Maryland Line	
Dawson, Joseph	——	Pvt.	Maryland Line	Prisoner

Dawson, William	1752	Pvt.	Maryland Line	
Day, Daniel*	1756	Pvt.	Maryland Line	
Day, James*	1762	Pvt.	Militia	
Day, John	——	Pvt.	Maryland Line	Deserted
Deakins, William	1739	Pvt.	Continental Line	Wounded
Deal, George	1758	Pvt.	Militia	
Dean, John	1757	Pvt.	Militia	Sea Service
Dean, Noble	——	Pvt.	Maryland Line	
Dean, Robert	1765	Pvt.	Maryland Line	Wounded
Deaver, Aquilla	1756	Pvt.	Maryland Line	
Deaver, John*	——	Lieut.	Maryland Line	
Deaver, Miscal	1753	Pvt.	Maryland Line	
Deaver, William	1761	Pvt.	Maryland Line	Prisoner
Debruler, John	1751	Pvt.	Maryland Line	
De Ford, Thomas	1736	Pvt.	Militia	
Delaney, John	1740	Pvt.	Maryland Line	
Dennis, Edward	1758	Pvt.	Maryland Line	Prisoner
Dennis, Henry	——	Pvt.	Militia	
Dennis, Josiah	1756	Pvt.	Militia	
Dent, John*	1760	Pvt.	Maryland Line	Wounded
Denune, John	1766	Music'n	Maryland Line	
Deverex, William	1761	Pvt.	Maryland Line	
Devin, William*	1766	Pvt.	Maryland Line	
Devon, James	1752	Pvt.	Maryland Line	
Dewall, Thomas	1748	Pvt.	Maryland Line	
Dewitt, Peter	1753	Pvt.	Militia	Va. Service
Dickenson, Edward	——	Pvt.	Maryland Line	Militia
Dickerson, Solomon	1754	Pvt.	Militia	
Dickinson, George	1758	Pvt.	Militia	
Dickson, Joseph	1757	Pvt.	Maryland Line	Wounded
Diffenderffer, Peter	1758	Lieut.	Maryland Line	Penn. Service
Dixon, Henry*	——	Pvt.	Maryland Line	
Dixon, John	——	Pvt.	Maryland Line	Fraudulent
Dodson, Michael	——	Pvt.	Maryland Line	Militia
Dorch, William	——	Pvt.	Maryland Line	Enlisted in Va.
Dorgin, John	1760	Pvt.	Militia	Naval
Dorsey, Daniel	——	Capt.	Maryland Line	
Dorsey, Leaven	——	Pvt.	Maryland Line	Deserted
Dorsey, Nicholas*	——	——	——	
Douglas, Robert	1749	Lieut.	Militia	

Dove, Richard	1744	Pvt.	Maryland Line	
Dowden, Clementius	1762	Pvt.	Militia	Penn. Service
Dowdle, William	1752	Pvt.	Continental Line	Wounded
Dowell, Richard*	—	Capt.	Militia	Va. N. C. Service
Dowling, James	—	Pvt.	Maryland Line	
Downie, Alexander	1741	Pvt.	Maryland Line	
Downing, Francis*	1746	Pvt.	Militia	
Downing, Samuel	—	Pvt.	Maryland Line	
Downs, Michael*	—	—	—	
Doyle, John	1748	Pvt.	Maryland Line	Wounded
Drake, Joseph	1748	Lieut.	Militia	
Drury, Leonard	1759	Pvt.	Militia	
Dudderow, John*	1758	Music'n	Militia	
Due, James	1758	Pvt.	Maryland Line	Prisoner
Duffee, Thomas*	—	Sergt.	Maryland Line	
Dukes, Isaac	1761	Pvt.	Militia	Naval
Duncan, Joseph	1752	Pvt.	Militia	Va. Service
Duncan, Robert	—	—	Maryland Line	
Dunn, William	1751	Pvt.	Continental Line	
Dunning, Butler	1754	Pvt.	Maryland Line	Prisoner
Dunning, Dennis	—	Fifer	Maryland Line	Enlisted in N.J.
Dunnon, Charles	1766	Pvt.	Continental Line	Prisoner
Durham, William*	—	Pvt.	Maryland Line	Wounded
Durham, William	—	Pvt.	Maryland Line	
Durrington, William*	—	Pvt.	Maryland Line	Wounded
Duval, Benjamin	1753	Sergt.	Maryland Line	Militia
Duval, Joseph	1760	Pvt.	Maryland Line	
Duval, Joseph*	—	Pvt.	Maryland Line	
Duval, Samuel	1758	Pvt.	Maryland Line	
Dwire, Thomas	1760	Drum.	Militia	Prisoner
Dych, Peter	1753	—	Continental Line	Va. Service
Dyer, Jonathan	—	Pvt.	Maryland Line	Invalid
Dyer, Walter	1752	Lieut.	Maryland Line	
Eads, Henry	1756	Pvt.	Militia	
Earp, Josiah	1761	Pvt.	Militia	
Easter, John	1760	Pvt.	Militia	
Easton, Giles	1762	Pvt.	Militia	
Easton, Richard	1752	Pvt.	Militia	Sea Service
Ebb, Emmanuel	1742	Pvt.	Maryland Line	Wounded

Eckle, Philip	1737	Pvt.	Militia	—
Edelen, Clement*	1753	Sergt.	Maryland Line	—
Edelman, Leonard	1761	Pvt.	Maryland Line	—
Edleman, Michael	1755	Pvt.	Maryland Line	—
Edwards, Thomas	1745	Sergt.	Maryland Line	—
Eikelberger, John*	—	Pvt.	Maryland Line	Penn. Service
Eisell, John	1756	Pvt.	Continental Line	—
Elgin, Samuel	1758	Pvt.	Flying Camp	—
Elkins, William	1731	Pvt.	Maryland Line	—
Elliott, John*	1755	Pvt.	Militia	—
Elliott, John	—	Wagon.	Maryland Line	Invalid
Elliott, Robert*	1742	Pvt.	Maryland Line	—
Elliott, Thomas*	1755	Pvt.	Maryland Line	Prisoner
Elliott, Thomas	—	Pvt.	Maryland Line	—
Elliott, Thomas	1759	Pvt.	Maryland Line	—
Ellis, Henry	1751	Pvt.	Militia	—
Ellis, John	1760	Pvt.	Militia	—
Ellis, Michael	1759	Fifer	Maryland Line	Prisoner
Ellis, Nathan	1748	Pvt.	Militia	—
Ellis, Thomas	1749	Pvt.	Maryland Line	—
Ellis, Thomas*	1755	Sergt.	Militia	—
Elsey, Thomas	1760	Pvt.	Militia	Va. Service
Emerson, James	1763	Pvt.	Militia	—
Emmitt, John*	1759	Pvt.	Flying Camp	—
Emory, Gideon*	—	Lieut.	Maryland Line	—
Emory, William	1751	Pvt.	Continental Line	—
Ennis, Leonard*	—	Pvt.	Maryland Line	Prisoner
Eperly, George	1760	Pvt.	Militia	—
Erp, Erasmus	1757	Pvt.	Militia	—
Erwin, James*	1758	Pvt.	Maryland Line	—
Etchberger, Wolfgang	1758	Pvt.	Continental Line	—
Etcheson, William*	—	Pvt.	—	—
Evans, Hooper*	—	Pvt.	Flying Camp	—
Evans, John	1757	Sergt.	Maryland Line	—
Evans, Peregrine	—	Sergt.	Maryland Line	—
Evans, Thomas	1754	Pvt.	Maryland Line	Wounded
Evans, Walter	1763	Pvt.	Maryland Line	—
Evans, Zachariah	1755	Pvt.	Flying Camp	—
Everett, Samuel	1763	Pvt.	Militia	Marines

Everly, John	——	Musican	Militia	——
Fagg, Joel	1755	Pvt.	Maryland Line	——
Fairbrother, Francis*	——	Pvt.	Maryland Line	——
Farence, Henry	1765	Pvt.	German Regiment	——
Farmer, Nathaniel	1757	Sergt.	Maryland Line	——
Farmer, Richard	——	Pvt.	Maryland Line	——
Farquhar, James*	——	Pvt.	Militia	——
Farrell, John	——	Pvt.	Maryland Line	——
Fassett, John	1758	Pvt.	Militia	Naval Service
Fearson, Joseph*	1759	Pvt.	Maryland Line	Prisoner
Felmott, Dorus*	1754	Pvt.	Maryland Line	——
Fennell, Stephen	1748	Pvt.	Maryland Line	——
Fenwick, Richard	1761	Pvt.	Maryland Line	——
Fenwick, William	1757	Capt.	Militia	Privateer
Ferguson, John*	——	Pvt.	Maryland Line	Wounded
Fickle, Benjamin	——	Lieut.	Maryland Line	Invalid
Fields, George	1754	Pvt.	Maryland Line	——
Fields, Joseph	1756	Pvt.	Maryland Line	——
Fifer, Jacob*	1754	Pvt.	German Regiment	Va. and N. C.
Figely, Peter	1758	Pvt.	Flying Camp	——
Filler, Frederick*	——	Pvt.	German Regiment	——
Finch, Joseph	1740	Pvt.	Maryland Line	——
Fine, Peter	1750	Pvt.	Flying Camp	——
Finley, Daniel	1752	Pvt.	Maryland Line	Penn. Service
Finley, William*	——	Pvt.	Militia	Made Cannons
Finn, Peter	1750	Pvt.	Continental Line	N. C. Service
Firor, Henry	1760	Pvt.	Militia	——
Fisher, Henry	——	Pvt.	German Regiment	——
Fisher, James*	1751	Pvt.	Maryland Line	Wounded
Fisher, John	——	Pvt.	Militia	Naval Service
Fisher, Joseph	1748	Pvt.	Maryland Line	Prisoner
Fisher, Philip*	1748	Pvt.	German Regiment	——
Fitzgerald, Benjamin	1753	Sergt.	Maryland Line	——
Fitzgerald, Charles	——	Pvt.	Maryland Line	Wounded
Fitzgerald, James	1749	Pvt.	Maryland Line	——
Fitzgerald, Nicholas	1757	Pvt.	Maryland Line	——
Fitzgerald, William	1758	Pvt.	Maryland Line	——
Fitzpatrick, Nathan	1755	Pvt.	Flying Camp	——
Flanigan, Henry*	——	Pvt.	Maryland Line	——

Fleeharty, Stephen	——	Capt.	Maryland Line	——
Fleming, James*	1744	Lieut.	Militia	Wounded
Fleming, Thomas	——	Pvt.	Maryland Line	——
Fletcher, Philip	1755	Fifer	Maryland Line	——
Flint, John	1756	Pvt.	Militia	
Flyn, Thomas	——	Pvt.	Militia	Del. Service
Foard, Hezekiah	——	Lieut.	Maryland Line	——
Foggett, Richard	1750	Pvt.	Militia	——
Forbes, Thomas*	——	Sergt.	——	——
Ford, Alexander	1754	Pvt.	Militia	——
Ford, Benjamin*	1760	Pvt.	Militia	——
Ford, John	1754	Sergt.	Maryland Line	——
Ford, Joseph	1759	Pvt.	Maryland Line	——
Ford, Loyd	1748	Pvt.	Militia	——
Ford, William	1763	Pvt.	Militia	——
Foreman, Leonard*	1758	Pvt.	Militia	——
Forman, Aaron	1755	Pvt.	Flying Camp	Va. Service
Forman, Thomas Marsh*	1758	Capt.	Continental Line	Penn. Service
Forrest, Uriah*	——	Col.	Maryland Line	——
Fortune, William	1745	Pvt.	Maryland Line	Prisoner
Fortune, William	1746	Pvt.	Militia	Penn. Service
Foster, James	1762	Pvt.	Maryland Line	——
Fowler, Elexis*	——	Pvt.	Militia	——
Fowler, Joshua	1759	Sergt.	Militia	——
Fowler, Sadoc	1762	Pvt.	Militia	——
Fox, Adam	1764	Pvt.	Militia	——
Frazier, James	1760	Seaman	Naval Service	——
Frazier, Levin*	1765	Lieut.	Maryland Line	Sea Service
Frazier, Samuel*	——	Pvt.	Continental Line	——
Frazier, William*	——	Lieut.	Maryland Line	——
Fream, William	1750	Pvt.	Militia	——
Freeland, John	1762	Seaman	Naval Service	——
Friend, Gabriel	1768	——	Militia	——
Fry, Nicholas*	1747	Pvt.	Continental Line	——
Fulton, James B.*	1765	Pvt.	Militia	——
Funk, George	1750	Pvt.	German Regiment	——
Gadd, Thomas	1760	Pvt.	Maryland Line	Wounded
Gadd, Thomas	1760	Pvt.	Militia	——
Gaither, Greenbury	1751	Lieut.	Maryland Line	Flying Camp

Name	Year	Rank	Unit	Notes
Gallegher, John	——	Pvt.	Maryland Line	——
Gallion, Gilbert	1758	Pvt.	Militia	Flying Camp
Galloway, Marshal	1760	Pvt.	Maryland Line	——
Galworth, Gabriel	1757	Pvt.	Maryland Line	Flying Camp
Gamble, Abraham	——	Pvt.		——
Gardner, John	1760	Fifer	Maryland Line	——
Gary, Richard	——	Pvt.	Maryland Line	——
Gassaway, John*	1754	Lieut.	Maryland Line	——
Gassaway, Samuel	——	Pvt.	Militia	——
Gates, William*	——	Pvt.	Maryland Line	——
Gay, Henry	1741	Pvt.	Maryland Line	Prisoner
Geasey, Henry	1756	Pvt.	Militia	——
Gebhart, John*	1760	Drum.	Militia	Wounded
Gee, Joseph*	——	Drum.	Maryland Line	——
Geoghegan, Anthony*	——	Musican	Maryland Line	——
Geoghegan, John	1756	Ensign	Maryland Line	Invalid
Gerock, Samuel	1754	Lieut.	Maryland Line	——
Gerrick, Edward	1753	Pvt.	Maryland Line	Prisoner
Gibhart, Adam*	1758	Pvt.	Maryland Line	——
Gibson, John	1758	Pvt.	Maryland Line	——
Gideon, Peter	1752	Pvt.	Militia	Flying Camp
Gilbert, Michael*	——	Capt.	Militia	——
Giles, Aquila	——	Lt. Col.	Continental Line	——
Gill, Daniel	1756	Pvt.	Maryland Line	N. C. Service
Gill, Hugh*	1758	Pvt.	Maryland Line	——
Gill, Moses	1757	Pvt.	Militia	Va. Service
Gillen, Thomas	1758	Pvt.	Maryland Line	——
Gillen, Thomas	——	Pvt.	Maryland Line	——
Gilman, Joseph	1754	Sergt.	Continental Line	——
Gilpen, Benjamin	1762	Pvt.	Maryland Line	——
Gilpin, William	——	Pvt.	Maryland Line	——
Gladson, William	1749	Pvt.	Maryland Line	——
Glasgow, William*	1763	Pvt.	Maryland Line	——
Glass, Michael	——	Pvt.	Militia	Va. Service
Gobble, Christian*	1755	Pvt.	Militia	Prisoner
Goddard, Edward	1753	Pvt.	Maryland Line	——
Goddard, John	1754	Pvt.	Maryland Line	——
Godman, William	1746	Capt.	Continental Line	——
Golder, Archibald*	——	Capt.	Maryland Line	——

Name	Year	Rank	Unit	Notes
Goldsberry, Charles*	1762	Pvt.	Maryland Line	Indian Wars
Gombare, John				Invalid
Goode, William	1762	Pvt.	Maryland Line	
Gooding, James*		Pvt.	Maryland Line	Wounded
Gordon, Archibald		Bugler	Continental Line	Penn. Service
Gordon, Daniel		Corpl.	Militia	
Gough, John B.	1764	Pvt.	Militia	
Gould, William*			Maryland Line	
Grace, Richard		Capt.	Maryland Line	
Grace, William*	1759	Pvt.	Maryland Line	
Graves, Philip	1762	Pvt.	Militia	
Gray, Elijah	1757	Pvt.	Militia	
Gray, Lynch	1757	Pvt.	Continental Line	
Green, Henry*		Pvt.	Maryland Line	
Green, Henry*		Pvt.	Militia	
Green, John	1760	Pvt.	Maryland Line	
Green, Paul	1763	Pvt.	Maryland Line	
Green, Robert*	1755	Ensign	Maryland Line	
Green, William	1761	Pvt.	Maryland Line	
Greenwell, Bennett	1762	Pvt.	Militia	
Greenwell, Ignatius	1750	Pvt.	Militia	
Greenwell, John	1760	Pvt.	Militia	
Greenwood, Joseph	1755	Pvt.	Militia	Del. Service
Greenwood, Philip	1755	Pvt.	Militia	Flying Camp
Griffen, Charles*	1756	Pvt.	Militia	Flying Camp
Griffin, Moses	1757	Pvt.	Maryland Line	Militia
Griffin, Nathan		Pvt.	Maryland & Continental	
Griffin, William	1759	Fifer	Maryland Line	Wounded
Griffith, Chrisholm	1759	Pvt.	Militia	
Griffith, Elijah*	1754	Pvt.	Maryland Line	
Griffith, Elisha	1757	Pvt.	Militia	Wounded
Griffith, Elisha	1750	Sergt.	Militia	
Griffith, Nathan	1759	Pvt.	Continental Line	Flying Camp
Griffith, Philemon	1757	Lieut.	Continental Line	
Griffith, Samuel*		Capt.	Maryland Line	Flying Camp
Griffith, Zadock	1755	Pvt.	Militia	Flying Camp
Grosh, Michael		Pvt.	Continental Line	Germ. Regt.
Grove, David	1756	Pvt.	Militia	Prisoner
Grover, Jonathan	1759	Pvt.	Maryland Line	

Name	Year	Rank	Line	Notes
Groves, William*	1755	Pvt.	Maryland Line	
Gudgeon, William	1762	Pvt.	Maryland Line	
Guest, Richard	1758	Pvt.	Maryland Line	
Guice, John*	1761	Pvt.	Maryland Line	Va. Service
Gunn, John	1760	Pvt.	Maryland Line	
Guthrey, John	1753	Pvt.	Maryland Line	
Gwinn, John*	——	Sergt.	Maryland Line	
Hagan, James	1754	Pvt.	Maryland Line	Wounded
Hagan, Raphael*	1744	Corpl.	Maryland Line	Prisoner
Hahn, George	——	Lieut.	Militia	Wounded
Hahn, Michael*	1748	Pvt.	Maryland Line	Penn. Service
Hahn, Paul	1751	Capt.	Militia	
Haislip, Laban*	——	Pvt.		
Hale, Anon*	1759	Pvt.	Militia	
Hale, Nathan	1757	Pvt.	Militia	
Hale, Richard	1749	Ensign	Militia	
Haley, John	——	Pvt.	Maryland Line	Invalid
Haley, Thomas	1752	Pvt.	Maryland Line	Prisoner
Halkerstone, Robert	1754	Capt.	Maryland Line	Wounded
Hall, Elihu*	——	Lieut.	Maryland Line	Prisoner
Hall, Frederick	1736	Pvt.	Maryland Line	Prisoner
Hall, John	1758	Pvt.	Militia	N. C. Service
Hall, Richard	1749	Pvt.	Maryland Line	
Hall, Sebrut	1762	Pvt.	Militia	
Hamilton, John	1753	Pvt.	Maryland Line	
Hamilton, John*	——	Capt.	Maryland Line	
Hammer, George	1763	Pvt.	Militia	
Hammond, Thomas*	1762	Pvt.	Maryland Line	
Hanck, George	1759	Pvt.	Militia	Flying Camp
Handley, Handly	——	Pvt.	Maryland Line	Wounded
Handy, Levin*	——	Capt.	Maryland Line	
Haney, John	1744	Pvt.	Maryland Line	Wounded
Haney, William*	——	Mattros	Continental Line	
Hanna, Robert	1755	Pvt.	Militia	Flying Camp
Hannon, William	1762	Pvt.	Militia	
Hanson, Samuel*	——	Col.	Continental Line	Militia
Hanspan, John C.	1739	Pvt.	Maryland Line	
Haraman, David	1761	Pvt.	Militia	
Hardin, William	1738	Sergt.	Militia	
Harding, Vachel*	1762	Sergt.	Militia	

Hardy, Arnold	1759	Pvt.	Militia	
Hardy, Elias*	1758	Pvt.	Maryland Line	
Hare, Thomas	1759	Pvt.	Maryland Line	
Hargin, Michael*				Penn. Service
Harman, Lazarus	1758	Pvt.	Maryland Line	
Harper, Samuel A.	1762	Pvt.	Maryland Line	
Harper, William*		Pvt.	Maryland Line	
Harrington, Anthony	1762	Marine	Naval Service	
Harrington, Peter	1755	Pvt.	Militia	
Harris, Richard	1759	Pvt.	Maryland Line	
Harris, Thomas*	1755	Sergt.	Militia	
Harrison, Benjamin	1759	Pvt.	Militia	
Harrison, Joseph	1756	Pvt.	Maryland Line	
Harrison, Kinsey*	1758	Pvt.	Maryland Line	
Harrison, William	1735	Pvt.	Maryland Line	Wounded
Harry, Richard*		Pvt.	Militia	
Hart, Christopher	1753	Pvt.	Militia	Flying Camp
Hart, John	1755	Midship.	Naval Service	
Hartman, Michael*	1760	Pvt.	Maryland Line	
Hartshorn, John*		Lieut.	Maryland Line	
Harvey, Matthew*		Pvt.	Continental Line	
Harvey, Zadock	1733	Pvt.	Maryland Line	Injured
Harvin, Edward	1757	Pvt.	Continental Line	
Harwood, Osborn	1760	Pvt.	Militia	
Hatton, Basil	1760	Sergt.	Continental Line	Militia
Havely, Jacob*		Pvt.	Continental Line	Germ. Regt.
Hawe, William	1761	Pvt.	Maryland Line	
Hawkins, Philip	1756	Pvt.	Maryland Line	Flying Camp
Hawman, Peter*	1754	Pvt.	Maryland Line	
Hayne, Henry		Ensign	Continental Line	Germ. Regt.
Hays, John H.	1759	Pvt.	Maryland Line	Militia
Hays, Samuel		Pvt.	Militia	
Hays, Thomas	1762	Pvt.	Militia	
Hazle, Caleb		Lieut.	Militia	
Head, John	1760	Pvt.	Maryland Line	
Head, William B.	1749	Capt.	Militia	
Heap, Archibald	1758	Pvt.	Militia	
Heap, John	1754	Pvt.	Militia	
Heaton, James*	1746	Pvt.	Continental Line	Germ. Regt.
Heberly, Frederick	1747	Pvt.	Maryland Line	

Heeter, George	1751	Pvt.	Militia	Flying Camp
Heffner, Jacob*	1757	Pvt.	Continental Line	Germ. Regt.
Henderson, Benjamin	1758	Pvt.	Militia	Sea Service
Henderson, James	1760	Pvt.	Militia	
Hendricks, Albert*	1759	Sergt.	Militia	N. C. Service
Hendrickson, Moses	1755	Pvt.	Sea Service	Wounded
Hendrickson, William	1757	Corpl.	Militia	Flying Camp
Hennigar, John	1743	Pvt.	Militia	
Hennis, Benjamin	1760	Pvt.	Maryland Line	
Henwood, Robert*	——	Pvt.	Continental Line	
Herbert, Jeremiah*	1763	Pvt.	Militia	
Herod, John	1757	——	——	Indian Wars
Herrington, Daniel*	1756	Pvt.	Militia	Penn. Service
Hester, Farel	1750	Pvt.	Militia	N. C. Service
Hiatt, Shadrack	1749	Pvt.	Maryland Line	Flying Camp
Hickman, Henry	——	Pvt.	Maryland Line	
Hickmon, Samuel	1761	Pvt.	Continental Line	S. C. Service
Hidgon, Joseph*	1759	Corpl.	Continental Line	Militia
Hill, Frederick*	1751	Pvt.	Continental Line	Flying Camp
Hill, Henry*	——	Capt.	Militia	
Hill, Hermon	1758	Pvt.	Militia	
Hill, James	1764	Pvt.	Militia	
Hill, John	1750	Pvt.	Continental Line	
Hill, Roswell	——	Pvt.	Militia	N. C. Service
Hillary, Ashburn*	1759	Pvt.	Militia	Flying Camp
Hillary, Rignal	——	Lieut.	Maryland Line	
Hillman, William*	1754	Pvt.	Maryland Line	
Hilton, Andrew	1757	Pvt.	Militia	
Hines, Jacob	1752	Pvt.	Militia	
Hissey, William*	1762	Pvt.	Militia	
Hitchcock, Isaac	1763	Pvt.	Sea Service	Prisoner
Hitchcock, Lyman	——	Major	Maryland Line	
Hobbs, James*	1759	Pvt.	Maryland Line	
Hodgkins, Samuel*	1757	Pvt.	Militia	Flying Camp
Hoffman, Henry	1757	Pvt.	Continental Line	Germ. Regt.
Hogg, James	1755	Pvt.	Maryland Line	
Hohne, Christopher	——	Pvt.	Militia	
Holden, Kemp	——	Pvt.	Maryland Line	
Holland, Charles*	——	Pvt.	Militia	

Holland, Edward*	——	Pvt.	Maryland Line	——
Holland, Isaac	1766	Pvt.	Continental Line	——
Holland, John	1761	Sergt.	Continental Line	Prisoner
Holland, Joseph	1754	Pvt.	Continental Line	——
Hollin, William*	1763	Pvt.	Militia	——
Holley, Francis*	——	Pvt.	Militia	N. C. & S. C. Service
Holliday, Robert	1755	Pvt.	Maryland Line	——
Hollidayoke, Daniel*	——	Pvt.	Maryland Line	——
Holloway, Levi	1735	Pvt.	Militia	——
Hommer, Jacob	1753	Pvt.	Militia	——
Hood, Edward	1757	Pvt.	Maryland Line	Wounded
Hood, James*	——	Comm.	Maryland Line	——
Hook, Frederick	——	Ensign	Militia	——
Hook, Joseph*	1756	Corpl.	Continental Line	Germ. Regt.
Hook, Stephen	1756	Pvt.	Militia	——
Hooper, Abraham	1756	Pvt.	Maryland Line	Wounded
Hoops, Adam	——	Capt.	Maryland Line	——
Hopkins, David	1754	Major	Continental Line	——
Hopkins, Thomas	1764	Pvt.	Maryland Line	——
Horbin, Joshua	1755	Pvt.	Militia	N. C. Service
Horrell, Henry	1761	Pvt.	Militia	——
Horrell, John*	1758	Pvt.	Maryland Line	——
Hoshal, Jesse*	1758	Pvt.	Continental Line	Germ. Regt.
Hoskins, Randall	1758	Pvt.	Maryland Line	——
Hoskinson, Charles	1759	Pvt.	Militia	Flying Camp
Hoskinson, Josiah	1755	Sergt.	Maryland Line	——
Housley, John	——	Pvt.	Maryland Line	Wounded
How, John*	1754	Sergt.	Maryland Line	——
Howard, John*	——	Pvt.	Maryland Line	——
Howard, John	1760	Pvt.	Maryland Line	——
Howard, John	1759	Pvt.	Militia	——
Howard, Stephen*	1758	Pvt.	Maryland Line	Prisoner
Howe, Daniel	1764	Pvt.	Maryland Line	——
Howell, Samuel	1760	Q. M.	Maryland Line	Militia
Hubbs, Jacob	1762	Pvt.	Militia	Ky. Service
Hudson, James	1760	Pvt.	Maryland Line	Naval Service
Hudson, Thomas	1755	Pvt.	Militia	——
Huff, Peter	1764	Pvt.	Militia	——
Hughes, James	1756	Pvt.	Continental Line	Germ. Regt.
Hughes, John	1750	Pvt.	Maryland Line	Flying Camp

Hughes, John*	1755	Pvt.	Maryland Line	Flying Camp
Hughes, Joseph	1752	Pvt.	Continental Line	Ky. Service
Hugo, Thomas*	——	Capt.	Maryland Line	
Hukill, Abia	——	Pvt.	Continental Line	
Hukins, Daniel	1761	Pvt.	Maryland Line	Wounded
Humphreys, John	1756	Pvt.	Militia	Flying Camp
Hunt, Jacob	1759	Pvt.	Maryland Line	
Hunt, James	1755	Pvt.	Maryland Line	Prisoner
Hunt, Thomas	1747	Pvt.	Militia	
Hurdle, Lawrence*	1758	Pvt.	Maryland Line	
Hurdle, Robert*	1759	Pvt.	Maryland Line	
Hurley, Salem	1756	Pvt.	Sea Service	Militia
Hurst, Samuel	1764	Pvt.	Maryland Line	
Huston, Philip	——	Drum.	Maryland Line	War of 1812
Hutcheson, Thomas	1757	Pvt.	Militia	
Hutcheson, William	——	Pvt.	Maryland Line	
Hyatt, Asa	1755	Pvt.	Militia	
Iams, Thomas	1754	Pvt.	Militia	
Ijams, John	1765	Pvt.	Maryland Line	
Ijams, Vachel	1759	Pvt.	Militia	N. C. Service
Iles, Samuel	1745	Pvt.	Maryland Line	Militia
Imeson, John	1748	Pvt.	Maryland Line	Flying Camp
Irvington, Jeremiah	1751	Pvt.	Maryland Line	
Itnise, Daniel	1756	Pvt.	Militia	Flying Camp
Jackson, Abednego	1758	Pvt.	Maryland Line	Militia
Jackson, James	1743	Sergt.	Maryland Line	Prisoner
Jackson, William	——	Pvt.	Maryland Line	Penn. Service
Jackson, William*	1759	Pvt.	Militia	
Jacob, Edward	175–	Pvt.	Militia	N. C. Service
Jacob, William*	1755	Sergt.	Militia	Prisoner
James, Thomas	1757	Pvt.	Militia	Prisoner
Jaquet, John*	——	Sergt.	Continental Line	Germ. Regt.
Jarvis, Elisha*	1757	Pvt.	Militia	
Jarvis, John*	——	Pvt.	Maryland Line	
Jarvis, Solomon	1753	Pvt.	Militia	
Jeffers, Jacob*	1761	Pvt.	Maryland Line	
Jefferson, Justinian	1758	Pvt.	Maryland Line	Militia
Jenkins, Philip*	——	Pvt.	Maryland Line	Prisoner
Jenkins, Thomas	1761	Pvt.	Maryland Line	
Job, Daniel	1757	Pvt.	Militia	

Name	Year	Rank	Unit	Notes
John, Thomas	1755	Pvt.	Maryland Line	Wounded
Johnson, Absalom	1757	Lieut.	Militia	Penn. Service
Johnson, Archibald	——	Pvt.	Maryland Line	Forage Master
Johnson, Barney	——	Fifer	Maryland Line	Prisoner
Johnson, Benjamin*	1756	Pvt.	Maryland Line	——
Johnson, Charles	1750	Pvt.	Maryland Line	Wounded
Johnson, Edward	——	Pvt.	Militia	——
Johnson, John*	——	Pvt.	Maryland Line	——
Johnson, Joseph	——	Pvt.	Maryland Line	——
Johnson, Nicholas	1759	Pvt.	Maryland Line	——
Johnson, Richard	1734	Pvt.	Militia	Navy
Johnson, Thomas	1760	Pvt.	Militia	Flying Camp
Johnson, Thomas*	——	Corpl.	Maryland Line	Flying Camp
Johnson, William	1758	Pvt.	Continental Line	Germ. Regt.
Johnston, Benjamin	1756	Pvt.	Militia	——
Jones, Aaron	1760	Pvt.	Maryland Line	——
Jones, Cotter	1758	Pvt.	Maryland Line	——
Jones, David	1765	Pvt.	Militia	——
Jones, Dennis*	1758	Pvt.	Maryland Line	——
Jones, James	1760	Drum.	Maryland Line	Prisoner
Jones, Jason*	1757	Pvt.	Militia	——
Jones, John	1755	Sergt.	Militia	Flying Camp
Jones, John C.*	——	Major	Maryland Line	——
Jones, Joshua	1759	Pvt.	Maryland Line	——
Jones, Neals	——	Corpl.	Maryland Line	Invalid
Jones, Nicholas	1751	Pvt.	Militia	——
Jones, Philip	1758	Matross	Continental Line	——
Jones, Richard*	——	Pvt.	Maryland Line	Militia
Jones, Solomon*	——	Matross	Continental Line	——
Jones, Thomas*	——	Pvt.	Maryland Line	——
Jones, Thomas	1752	Pvt.	Militia	N. C. Service
Jones, Thomas	1752	——	Maryland Line	——
Jones, Thomas	1755	Pvt.	Maryland Line	——
Jones, Thomas*	——	Pvt.	Maryland Line	——
Jones, Thomas	1756	Pvt.	Militia	Flying Camp
Jones, Thomas	——	Pvt.	Maryland Line	——
Jones, Thomas	1754	Pvt.	Maryland Line	——
Jones, William	——	Pvt.	Maryland Line	Deserted
Jones, William*	1762	Pvt.	Maryland Line	——
Jones, William*	——	Pvt.	Maryland Line	Wounded

Jones, William	1760	Sergt.	Militia	
Jones, William	1756	Pvt.	Militia	
Jordan, Hugh	1757	Pvt.	Militia	
Jordan, John*	——	Coronet	Continental Line	
Jordon, John	——	Pvt.	Maryland Line	Wounded
Joseph, William	——	Pvt.	Maryland Line	
Kain, Edward	——	Pvt.	Maryland Line	Invalid
Kaufman, John	1757	Pvt.	Militia	Va. Service
Keates, Thomas	1756	Sergt.	Maryland Line	Wounded
Keech, John	1760	Pvt.	Maryland Line	
Keelan, James	——	Pvt.	Maryland Line	Wounded
Keever, John*	——	Pvt.	——	——
Keiphart, George	1753	Pvt.	Continental Line	Flying Camp
Kelley, Joshua	1751	Ensign	Militia	
Kelley, Moses	1753	Pvt.	Continental Line	Militia
Kelly Samuel	1756	Pvt.	Continental Line	Militia
Kelley, William*	——	Capt.	Militia	
Kelsimere, Francis	1744	Pvt.	Maryland Line	Militia
Kelso, Thomas*	1764	Pvt.	Militia	
Kendall, Aaron	1757	Pvt.	Militia	
Kennedy, James	——	Sergt.	Maryland Line	Wounded
Kent, Isaac	1759	Pvt.	Militia	
Kent, Thomas	1748	Pvt.	Militia	Flying Camp
Kephart, Martin	1758	Pvt.	Maryland Line	Wounded
Kernall, William	1761	Pvt.	Maryland Line	Prisoner
Kerrick, Benjamin	——	Musican	Maryland Line	
Keyser, Jacob*	1750	Pvt.	Continental Line	Germ. Regt.
Keyt, John	1755	Pvt.	Militia	N. J. Service
Kibler, John*	1760	Pvt.	Continental Line	Germ. Regt.
Kidwell, Matthew	1752	Pvt.	Militia	
Kilby, John	——	Seaman	Navy	Prisoner
Kibly, Joseph	1763	Pvt.	Militia	
Kilty, James	1747	Pvt.	Maryland Line	Prisoner
Kilty, John*	——	Capt.	Continental Line	
King, Francis*	——	Corpl.	Maryland Line	
King, George*	——	Pvt.	Maryland Line	
King, Henry	——	——	——	——
King, Isaac	——	Pvt.	Maryland Line	
King, Jeremiah	1759	Pvt.	Maryland Line	
King, John	——	Pvt.	Maryland Line	

Name	Year	Rank	Unit	Notes
King, Thomas	1752	Pvt.	Maryland Line	
Kinsey, David	1742	Pvt.	Maryland Line	
Kirk, John	1754	Pvt.	Militia	Prisoner
Kirk, Thomas	1759	Pvt.	Militia	Flying Camp
Kirk, William*	1762	Pvt.	Militia	Prisoner
Kirkwood, David*	1740	Pvt.	Maryland Line	
Kirshner, Michael	1752	Pvt.	Maryland Line	
Kisby, Richard		Pvt.	Maryland Line	Wounded
Kittle, Abraham	1762	Pvt.	Continental Line	Germ. Regt.
Knick, William*		Pvt.	Maryland Line	
Knight, Jacob	1752	Pvt.	Maryland Line	Militia
Knott, Ignatius	1747	Pvt.	Militia	
Kreis, Peter*		Pvt.	Continental Line	Germ. Regt.
Kugel, John	1757	Pvt.	Militia	
Kyzer, Frederick	1761	Pvt.	Militia	Va. & Ky. Service
Lallen, Michael	1761	Pvt.	Maryland Line	
Lamar, William		Capt.	Maryland Line	
Lamb, Jacob	1766	Pvt.	Militia	
Lamb, Joshua*		Sergt.	Maryland Line	
Lambert, Christopher	1753	Pvt.	Maryland Line	Invalid
Lane, Owen	1755	Pvt.	Militia	
Lang, Francis*	1761	Pvt.	Maryland Line	
Lanham, John		Pvt.	Maryland Line	Invalid
Lanham, Thomas	1757	Pvt.	Maryland Line	
Lankford, Elijah	1752	Pvt.	Maryland Line	
Lansdale, Thomas*		Major	Maryland Line	
Larkin, James*		Sergt.	Continental Line	
Lashley, George	1754	Pvt.	Maryland Line	
Lashley, George	1739	Pvt.	Militia	
Latimore, Richard	1763	Pvt.	Militia	Indian Wars
Lavely, Jacob	1756	Pvt.	Maryland Line	
Law, William	1759	Pvt.	Maryland Line	
Lawrence, Isaac	1762	Pvt.	Maryland Line	S. C. Service
Lawrence, William		Pvt.	Maryland Line	
Lawrence, William*	1750	Pvt.	Maryland Line	
Lawrentz, Wendel*	1759	Pvt.	Continental Line	Germ. Regt.
Layman, William	1750	Ensign	Maryland Line	
Layton, William H.	1755	Pvt.	Maryland Line	Del. Service
Lazenby, Joshua	1759	Pvt.	Militia	

Lazenby, Samuel	1761	Pvt.	Militia	
Lazer, John	1755	Pvt.	Continental Line	
Leach, Joshua*	1756	Sergt.	Militia	
Lee, John*	——	Pvt.	Maryland Line	Militia
Lee, Parker H.*	——	Lieut.	Maryland Line	
Lee, William C.	——	Pvt.	Maryland Line	
Leeke, Henry	——	Sergt.	Maryland Line	
Leips, Philip	1742	Sergt.	——	——
Lemaster, Hugh*	1750	Pvt.	Militia	
Lemon, Jacob*	1763	Sergt.	Maryland Line	Va. Service
Lemon, John	1745	Pvt.	Militia	Penn. Service
Lemmon, Moses	1759	Sergt.	Militia	
Lenox, James	1754	Pvt.	Maryland Line	Flying Camp
Leonard, James	1753	Pvt.	Maryland Line	Del. Service
Leonard, Joseph*	——	Pvt.	Maryland Line	Prisoner
LeVacher de Vaubrun, Jno.*	——	Lieut.	Maryland Line	Lost at Sea
Lewis, Daniel	1755	Pvt.	Militia	N. C. Service
Lewis, George	1767	Pvt.	Militia	
Lewis, John	1757	Pvt.	——	
Lewis, William*	——	Pvt.	Continental Line	Germ. Regt.
Lindsey, John	1759	Sergt.	Militia	Penn. Service
Lingan, Thomas	1758	Lieut.	Maryland Line	Flying Camp
Lingenfelter, Michael	1762	Pvt.	Militia	
Lingrell, Nehemiah	——	Pvt.	Maryland Line	
Linton, Isaac	1764	Pvt.	Militia	
Lipp, John	1746	Pvt.	Militia	
Lister, William	1760	Pvt.	Militia	
Little, Michael	——	Pvt.	Continental Line	
Litzinger, Henry	1735	Pvt.	Continental Line	
Livingston, David*	——	——		
Livingston, Robert	1752	Pvt.	Continental Line	
Lloyd, Thomas*	1756	Pvt.	Maryland Line	Wounded
Loar, Henry	1758	Pvt.	Maryland Line	Prisoner
Logsden, Edward	1752	Sergt.	Militia	
Logue, Richard	——	Pvt.	Militia	
Logue, William*	1760	Pvt.	Sea Service	
Lohr, Peter	1751	Pvt.	Militia	Flying Camp
Lokey, William	1766	Seaman	Sea Service	
Lomass, John*	——	Pvt.	Continental Line	Germ. Regt.

Name	Year	Rank	Service	Notes
Lomax, John	1754	Pvt.	Maryland Line	
Long, John*		Pvt.	Maryland Line	
Long, Jonathan*	1758	Pvt.	Militia	Penn. Service
Long, Joseph*		Pvt.	Maryland Line	
Longstreth, Philip*				
Longwell, William*		Pvt.	Militia	Penn. Service
Lord, Andrew	1756	Pvt.	Maryland Line	
Lord, Henry*		Pvt.	Maryland Line	
Lore, Michael	1755	Pvt.	Militia	
Lorentz, Ferdinand*		Pvt.	Continental Line	Germ. Regt.
Love, David*		Sergt.	Maryland Line	
Low, Henry*	1752	Pvt.	Maryland Line	
Lowe, Basil*	1759	Corpl.	Continental Line	
Lowe, Dennis		Pvt.	Continental Line	
Lowe, John	1760	Sergt.	Maryland Line	
Lowe, John T.*		Lieut.	Maryland Line	
Lowry, Jacob	1758	Pvt.	Militia	Penn. Service
Lowry, Michael	1760	Pvt.	Militia	Penn. Service
Lucas, Basil		Pvt.	Maryland Line	
Lucas, John	1756	Pvt.	Maryland Line	Wounded
Lucas, John		Sergt.	Maryland Line	
Lucas, William*	1754	Pvt.	Militia	Va. Service
Luckett, Samuel	1756	Lieut.	Maryland Line	Militia
Lush, William	1744	Seaman	Sea Service	Prisoner
Lusher, John	1750	Pvt.	Maryland Line	
Luther, George*	1754	Pvt.	Militia	
Luther, Jacob	1757	Pvt.	Militia	
Luther, Michael*	1751	Pvt.	Militia	
Lutz, Henry*		Pvt.	Maryland Line	
Lyles, Richard	1757	Surgeon	Militia	
Lyles, Thomas	1754	Lieut.	Militia	
Lynch, Hugh	1745	Pvt.	Maryland Line	Flying Camp
Lynch, Patrick*		Pvt.	Militia	
Lynch, Thomas	1759	Pvt.	Maryland Line	
Lynch, William*		Pvt.	Maryland Line	Wounded
Lynn, David*		Capt.	Maryland Line	
McAdon, Andrew	1761	Pvt.	Militia	
McAdow, John	1745	Sergt.	Maryland Line	
McAtee, Samuel	1754	Pvt.	Maryland Line	
McCalla, John*		Pvt.	Continental Line	

Name	Year	Rank	Unit	Notes
McCallister, James	1742	Pvt.	Maryland Line	
McCallister, William*	1762	Pvt.	Militia	
McCann, Michael	1728	Pvt.	Maryland Line	
McChan, John	1750	Pvt.	Continental Line	
McClain, William	1754	Pvt.	Militia	Penn. Service
McClung, Samuel	1763	Pvt.	Wagon Service	
McComas, Aaron	1760	Pvt.	Militia	
McConkey, David	——	Pvt.	Militia	Wounded
McConnell, Samuel	——	Pvt.	Maryland Line	
McCormick, John	1750	Pvt.	Militia	Penn. Service
McCoy, John	——	Lieut.	Maryland Line	
McCracken, Joseph*	1748	Pvt.	Maryland Line	
McCullough, William	1753	Pvt.	Maryland Line	
McDaniel, Walter	1747	Pvt.	Militia	
McDaniel, William	1754	Pvt.	Militia	Flying Camp
McDonald, John	1753	Fifer	Maryland Line	N. C. Service
McDonald, William	——	Drum.	Maryland Line	R. I. Service
McDougle, Alexander	1759	Pvt.	Militia	
McDowell, John*	1758	Pvt.	Maryland Line	N. C. Service
McDowell, Thomas*	1758	Pvt.	Maryland Line	
McFadden, John	——	Pvt.	Maryland Line	Flying Camp
McFadden, John	1760	Pvt.	Maryland Line	Militia
McFee, Malcom*	——	Pvt.	——	Wounded
McGee, Charles	1758	Pvt.	Maryland Line	
McGee, William	1755	Pvt.	Maryland Line	
McGraw, Christopher	——	Sergt.	Maryland Line	Wounded
Mackall, Benjamin*	1763	Pvt.	Maryland Line	
McKay, James	1752	Pvt.	Militia	Flying Camp
McKay, John	1764	Pvt.	Maryland Line	
McKeel, Thomas	1749	Ensign	Militia	Prisoner
McKenzie, Moses*	1760	Drum.	Continental Line	Germ. Regt.
Mackey, Thomas	1745	Pvt.	Maryland Line	Prisoner
McKim, Alexander	1748	Pvt.	Militia	
McKinzey, Jesse*	1762	Pvt.	Continental Line	
McKnight, John	1758	Fifer	Maryland Line	
McKoy, Robert	1755	Pvt.	Sea Service	Militia
McLain, Joshua*	——	Pvt.	Militia	
McLean, Arthur	1752	Sergt.	Maryland Line	

Name	Year	Rank	Unit	Notes
McLeod, Robert	——	Pvt.	Maryland Line	——
McMillen, Daniel*	1757	Sergt.	Maryland Line	Injured
McMillan, Samuel*	1753	Pvt.	Militia	Mass. Service
McMillan, William	1756	Sergt.	Militia	Mass. Service
McMinn, Robert	1764	Pvt.	Militia	——
McMullen, Alexander	1747	Pvt.	Continental Line	——
McNabb, Charles	1757	Sergt.	Maryland Line	——
McPherson, Mark*	——	Sergt.	Maryland Line	——
McQuinny, Thomas	1741	Pvt.	Maryland Line	——
Maddin, Joseph	1758	Lieut.	Militia	——
Magin, Charles	——	Pvt.	Maryland Line	Wounded
Magruder, Nathaniel	1758	Lieut.	Maryland Line	Prisoner
Magruder, Norman*	——	Pvt.	Militia	——
Maher, Patrick	1753	Pvt.	Maryland Line	——
Mahony, Edward	——	Pvt.	Maryland Line	——
Mahony, Michael	——	Pvt.	——	Prisoner
Main, Henry	1752	Pvt.	Maryland Line	Prisoner
Mains, Samuel	1760	Pvt.	——	Prisoner
Major, Alexander	1756	Pvt.	Militia	——
Majors, John	——	Pvt.	Maryland Line	——
Malcome, Hugh	1758	Pvt.	Maryland Line	——
Males, John	1744	Pvt.	Maryland Line	Wounded
Malone, Hugh	1756	Pvt.	Maryland Line	——
Malone, Thomas	——	Pvt.	Maryland Line	Wounded
Malott, Dory	1755	Pvt.	Militia	——
Malott, John*	1757	Pvt.	Militia	——
Malott, Thomas	1753	Pvt.	Militia	——
Mankins, William	1760	Pvt.	Militia	——
Manley, John*	——	Pvt.	Continental Line	——
Manly, Jesse	1752	Pvt.	Militia	——
Manning, Henry	1748	Pvt.	Maryland Line	Prisoner
Mansfield, Samuel*	1740	Pvt.	Maryland Line	——
Mansfield, Thomas*	1750	Lieut.	Militia	Naval Service
Mansfield, William*	——	Pvt.	Continental Line	——
Mantz, Peter*	1752	Major	Militia	Flying Camp
Marbury, Leonard*	——	Col.	Continental Line	——
March, Charles	1743	Pvt.	Continental Line	——
Marks, John	1753	Pvt.	Maryland Line	——
Marle, James	1763	Fifer	Militia	——

Maroney, Philip*	——	Capt.	Militia	Flying Camp
Marr, William*	1753	Pvt.	Militia	——
Marsh, John	1756	Pvt.	Militia	Va. Service
Marsh, Joshua*	——	Capt.	Militia	——
Marshall, Hezekiah*	1763	Pvt.	Militia	Wounded
Marshall, Robert*	1761	Pvt.	Maryland Line	Penn. Service
Marshall, Thomas	1758	Ensign	Militia	——
Martin, Jacob	1759	Pvt.	Militia	Flying Camp
Martin, John*	——	Pvt.	Continental Line	Germ. Regt.
Martin, John	1755	Pvt.	Continental Line	——
Martin, Philip	——	Pvt.	Maryland Line	——
Martin, Robert*	——	Pvt.	Continental Line	——
Martin, Samuel	1760	Pvt.	Militia	——
Martindale, John	——	——	——	Invalid
Mason, Arthur	——	Pvt.	Maryland Line	——
Mason, Calvert	——	Pvt.	Maryland Line	——
Mason, Michael	1753	Pvt.	Militia	——
Mason, Peter	1757	Pvt.	Militia	——
Massey, Henry*	1751	Capt.	Sea Service	Militia
Mathias, James	1750	Pvt.	Maryland Line	——
Matkins, John	1762	Pvt.	Militia	Wounded
Matthews, Francis	1758	Pvt.	Maryland Line	Wounded
Matthews, John	——	Corpl.	Maryland Line	Invalid
Maxwell, John	1741	Pvt.	Maryland Line	Penn. Service
Mayer, John	——	Pvt.	Continental Line	Germ. Regt.
Mayhugh, Jonathan	1756	Pvt.	Maryland Line	——
Maynadier, Henry	1757	Surgeon	Maryland Line	——
Mead, James*	——	Drum.	Maryland Line	——
Mead, Samuel	1760	Pvt.	Maryland Line	——
Medlar, Boston	——	Drum.	Maryland Line	——
Medley, William	1763	Pvt.	Maryland Line	——
Meek, John	——	——	——	Invalid
Mefford, Jacob*	1764	Pvt.	Maryland Line	——
Mefford, William	1760	Pvt.	Sea Service	——
Melone, Andrew*	——	Corpl.	Maryland Line	——
Merrick, William	1759	Pvt.	Militia	Sea Service
Merryman, Luke*	——	——	——	——
Middleton, Theodore	1758	Capt.	Maryland Line	——
Mikesell, Jacob	1756	Pvt.	Militia	Flying Camp
Milburn, Nicholas	——	Pvt.	Maryland Line	——

Name	Year	Rank	Service	Notes
Miles, Edward	1762	Pvt.	Militia	
Miles, John	1733	Corpl.	Maryland Line	
Miles, John	1755	Pvt.	Militia	
Miles, Joshua*	——	Capt.	Maryland Line	
Miles, William	1757	Pvt.	Maryland Line	
Miller, George	1752	Pvt.	Maryland Line	Penn. & N. Y. Service
Miller, George	1751	Pvt.	Militia	Penn. Service
Miller, George*	1756	Pvt.	Continental Line	Penn. Service
Miller, John*	——	Pvt.	Maryland Line	
Miller, John*	——	Sergt.	Continental Line	Germ. Regt.
Miller, John*	1762	Pvt.	Militia	
Miller, John*	1765	Pvt.	Militia	
Miller, Josias	1757	Pvt.	Maryland Line	
Miller, Martin	1754	Pvt.	Militia	
Miller, Samuel	1755	Pvt.	Militia	
Mills, Elijah	1757	Capt.	Militia	Penn. Service
Mills, William	1756	Pvt.	Militia	
Mills, Zachariah	1759	Pvt.	Maryland Line	
Millson, James	1754	Pvt.	Maryland Line	
Milstead, John*	——	Sergt.	Maryland Line	
Mitchell, Abel	1750	Pvt.	Sea Service	Prisoner
Mitchell, Charles	1756	Pvt.	Militia	Flying Camp
Mitchell, Solomon	1761	Pvt.	Militia	N. C. Service
Mittag, Frederick	1728	Pvt.	Continental Line	Germ. Regt.
Moler, Joseph	1749	Pvt.	Militia	Ga. Service
Mondy, John*	1757	Pvt.	Militia	
Montgomery, Alexander*	——	Sergt.	Maryland Line	Penn. Service
Montgomery, Hugh	——	Pvt.	——	Penn. Service
Montgomery, John	1760	Midship.	Naval Service	Va. Service
Moore, Abraham	1756	Pvt.	Militia	Va. Service
Moore, Alexander	1754	Pvt.	Militia	
Moore, Asa*	1764	Pvt.	Maryland Line	
Moore, Enoch	1758	Pvt.	Militia	Indian Wars
Moore, George	1749	Pvt.	Continental Line	Militia
Moore, John*	——	Sergt.	Maryland Line	Wounded
Moore, Nicholas*	——	Capt.	Militia	
Moore, Reuben	1754	Pvt.	Maryland Line	
Moore, Thomas L.	1764	Pvt.	Militia	

Revolutionary Pensioners

Name	Year	Rank	Line	Notes
Moore, Zachariah	——	Pvt.	Maryland Line	——
Moreland, Philip	1751	Pvt.	Militia	——
Moreland, Vincent*	——	Pvt.	Militia	——
Moreman, Thomas*	1746	Sergt.	Continental Line	——
Morgan, John	1761	Pvt.	Militia	——
Morgan, John	1767	Pvt.	Maryland Line	——
Morgan, Robert	——	Lieut.	Militia	——
Morgan, Thomas	1761	Pvt.	Maryland Line	——
Morris, Cornelius	——	Pvt.	Maryland Line	——
Morris, James	——	Pvt.	Maryland Line	——
Morris, John	1749	Pvt.	Continental Line	——
Morris, Jonathan	1752	Capt.	Maryland Line	Flying Camp
Morris, Joseph	1761	Pvt.	Militia	——
Morris, William	1744	Pvt.	Militia	——
Morton, Archibald	——	Pvt.	Maryland Line	——
Morton, Samuel	——	Sergt.	Militia	——
Moser, Jacob*	——	Pvt.	Continental Line	Germ. Regt.
Moser, Michael*	——	Pvt.	Continental Line	Penn. Service
Mosier, Francis*	1763	Pvt.	Militia	N. C. Service
Mowland, Richard*	1748	Pvt.	Maryland Line	——
Moyer, John	1755	Pvt.	Continental Line	——
Mudd, Bennett*	1760	Sergt.	Maryland Line	——
Mudd, Jeremiah*	——	Sergt.	Maryland Line	Wounded
Mudd, Richard*	——	Pvt.	Maryland Line	——
Muir, Thomas	1754	Pvt.	Maryland Line	——
Mullikin, Lewis*	1755	Pvt.	Militia	Flying Camp
Mummy, John	1753	Pvt.	Maryland Line	——
Mundle, George	1759	Pvt.	Maryland Line	——
Munn, James*	——	Capt.	Militia	Wounded
Munrow, Briant	1742	Pvt.	Maryland Line	——
Murdock, Benjamin	1759	Capt.	Maryland Line	——
Murdock, William*	——	Coronet	Continental Line	——
Murphy, Hezekiah*	1764	Pvt.	Militia	——
Murray, Matthew	1753	Pvt.	Continental Line	——
Musgrave, John	1760	Pvt.	Militia	——
Mushler, Adam*	——	Pvt.	Continental Line	Germ. Regt.
Muterspaw, Philip	1744	Pvt.	Militia	Penn. Service
Myers, Christopher	1759	Pvt.	Militia	——
Myers, John	1756	Pvt.	Maryland Line	——
Myers, John	——	Pvt.	Militia	Penn. Service

Name	Year	Rank	Unit	Notes
Myers, Philip	1759	Pvt.	Militia	—
Myres, William	1756	Pvt.	Sea Service	Militia
Nagle, Richard	1747	Pvt.	Maryland Line	Flying Camp
Nailor, Isaac	1748	Pvt.	Maryland Line	—
Nailor, Joshua*	1751	Corpl.	Maryland Line	—
Neale, John*	1757	Pvt.	Maryland Line	—
Needham, William A.	—	Sergt.	Maryland Line	Invalid
Neese, Peter	1752	Pvt.	Militia	Penn. Service
Nelson, John*	—	Surgeon	Maryland Line	—
Nelson, Roger*	—	Lieut.	Maryland Line	—
Neves, William	1764	Pvt.	—	Va. Service
Nevitt, John	1758	Pvt.	Maryland Line	—
Nevitt, Joseph	1753	Pvt.	Militia	—
Newman, John	1740	Pvt.	Maryland Line	Flying Camp
Newman, John	1754	Sergt.	Continental Line	Flying Camp
Newman, Joshua	1756	Pvt.	Militia	—
Newton, Basil*	—	Sergt.	Maryland Line	—
Newton, John	1758	Pvt.	Maryland Line	—
Newton, John	1756	Pvt.	Maryland Line	Wounded
Niblet, William	1749	Pvt.	Maryland Line	—
Nichol, John	1740	—	—	—
Nolin, John	1753	Pvt.	Continental Line	Flying Camp
Norman, Basil*	1761	Pvt	Maryland Line	—
Norris, Arnold*	1761	Pvt.	Militia	—
Northcraft, Edward	1757	Sergt.	Maryland Line	Flying Camp
Norton, George	1748	Pvt.	Maryland Line	—
Nowell, James	—	Fifer	Maryland Line	Wounded
Oakes, John*	—	Pvt.	Militia	Mass. & Pa. Service
Oard, William	1754	Pvt.	Militia	Va. Service
O'Brian, Daniel*	—	Pvt.	Maryland Line	Wounded
O'Brian, Dennis	1757	Pvt.	Maryland Line	Flying Camp
O'Conner, Michael	1748	Pvt.	Continental Line	Flying Camp
O'Conner, Thomas	1746	Pvt.	Maryland Line	Flying Camp
O'Daniel, John*	1757	Pvt.	Militia	Va. Service
O'Hara, John*	—	Pvt.	Maryland Line	Wounded
Oldham, Jacob	1759	Pvt.	Militia	Flying Camp
Oldham, John*	—	Capt.	Maryland Line	—
Oliver, William	1756	Pvt.	Militia	Sea Service
Oneal, John	1740	Pvt.	Maryland Line	Penn. Service
Oram, Cooper*	1759	Pvt.	Maryland Line	Penn. Service

Name	Year	Rank	Unit	Notes
Orem, Spedden	1760	Pvt.	Sea Service	
Orendorf, Christian	—	Capt.	Maryland Line	Flying Camp
Orme, Charles	1760	Pvt.	Maryland Line	
Orme, Moses	1756	Lieut.	Militia	
Ormond, William	—	Pvt.	Maryland Line	Invalid
Orr, John*	1762	Pvt.	Militia	Penn. Service
Osman, John	1757	Pvt.	Maryland Line	
Outhouse, Peter	—	Pvt.	Maryland Line	
Outterbridge, Stephen	1761	Pvt.	Militia	
Ovelman, George	—	Pvt.	Militia	Flying Camp
Owens, Joseph	1755	Pvt.	Continental Line	
Owens, Stephen*	—	Pvt.	Maryland Line	
Owings, George	1749	Pvt.	Maryland Line	Indian Wars
Pack, William*	1758	Pvt.	Militia	Flying Camp
Paine, William	1736	Pvt.	Maryland Line	Invalid
Painter, Henry*	1748	Pvt.	Continental Line	Germ. Regt.
Painter, Melcher*	1739	Pvt.	Continental Line	Germ. Regt.
Painter, Michael	1755	Pvt.	Militia	Wounded
Palmer, George*	—	Pvt.	Maryland Line	Prisoner
Palmer, Thomas*	—	Pvt.		
Pamphillon, Thomas	1758	Pvt.	Sea Service	Prisoner
Parkinson, Thomas*	1762	Pvt.	Militia	Flying Camp
Parmor, Charles*	—	Pvt.	Maryland Line	
Parnell, Stephen	1762	Pvt.	Maryland Line	Wounded
Parrish, Edward*	1757	Sergt.	Maryland Line	Wounded
Parrot, Christopher*	1755	Sergt.	Maryland Line	
Patterson, William*	1761	Pvt.	Militia	
Patton, Matthew	1750	Sergt.	Militia	
Patton, Samuel	—	Sergt.	Militia	
Patton, William	1755	Pvt.	Maryland Line	
Paul, Thomas*	—	Sergt.	Maryland Line	
Peace, John	1755	Sergt.	Maryland Line	S. C. Service
Peacock, Neal	1752	Pvt.	Maryland Line	Wounded
Peak, Nathan	1752	Lieut.	Maryland Line	Prisoner
Peale, James	1749	Lieut.	Maryland Line	
Pearce, George	1760	Pvt.	Maryland Line	Wounded
Pearce, John*	—	Pvt.	Maryland Line	Wounded
Pearce, Joshua	—	Pvt.	Maryland Line	
Pearre, Joshua*	1757	Corpl.	Militia	Flying Camp

Name	Year	Rank	Unit	Notes
Pender, Thomas*	1757	Pvt.	Maryland Line	
Pendergast, William*	—	Lieut.	Maryland Line	
Penefill, Thomas*	1760	Pvt.	Maryland Line	Sea Service
Penn, Benjamin*	1753	Pvt.	Militia	
Penn, Shadrach*	—	Major	—	Wounded
Penns, Stephen*	—	Pvt.	Militia	
Perry, Samuel	1757	Pvt.	Maryland Line	Prisoner
Perry, Simon*	1756	Pvt.	Maryland Line	
Perry, Thomas*	1765	Pvt.	Maryland Line	
Pettit, Thomas*	1764	Pvt.	Maryland Line	
Phebus, George	1762	Pvt.	Militia	
Philips, Jacob	—	Pvt.	Militia	Prisoner
Philips, John	1750	Pvt.	Maryland Line	Flying Camp
Philips, William	1766	Pvt.	Militia	
Philpot, Bryan*	—	Ensign	Maryland Line	
Philpott, Charles	1753	Sergt.	Maryland Line	Militia
Pickett, Daniel	—	—	—	—
Pierce, Hugh	—	Lieut.	Militia	
Pierce, John	1754	Pvt.	Continental Line	
Pierce, William	1759	Pvt.	Maryland Line	Prisoner
Pierceall, Richard	1744	Pvt.	Maryland Line	
Pierson, John*	1762	Pvt.	Continental Line	Wounded
Pindell, Richard	—	Surgeon	Maryland Line	
Pippin, Robert*	1752	Pvt.	Militia	
Pitts, Richard*	1749	Pvt.	Maryland Line	Conn. Service
Plain, Jacob*	—	Pvt.	Continental Line	
Plant, John*	—	Corpl.	Maryland Line	
Plummer, Samuel	1754	Pvt.	Militia	
Poe, David*	—	Q. M.	Continental Line	
Pollock, David*	1755	Pvt.	Militia	Penn. Service
Pollock, Elias	1755	Pvt.	Maryland Line	
Pope, John	1753	Pvt.	Maryland Line	
Popham, Benjamin	1763	Pvt.	Maryland Line	
Popp, John	—	—	Continental Line	
Porter, Charles	1760	Pvt.	Militia	Flying Camp
Porter, Ephraim	1761	Pvt.	Militia	
Porter, Nathan	1755	Pvt.	Militia	Sea Service
Posey, Belain*	—	Col.	Militia	Flying Camp
Posey, Benjamin	1760	Pvt.	Maryland Line	
Potterf, Casper	1759	Pvt.	Militia	Va. Service

Potts, Thomas	——	Pvt.	Maryland Line	——
Powell, John	1745	Pvt.	Maryland Line	——
Power, Benjamin	1753	Pvt.	Continental Line	Penn. Service
Power, James	1755	Pvt.	Militia	Flying Camp
Power, Jesse	1761	Pvt.	Maryland Line	——
Price, Nathaniel	1751	Sergt.	Maryland Line	——
Price, Stephen	——	Sergt.	Maryland Line	——
Prigg, William*	——	Ensign	——	——
Proctor, Joseph	1762	Pvt.	Militia	——
Proctor, William	1749	Pvt.	Militia	——
Pry, Jesse	1767	Pvt.	Militia	——
Purnell, Samuel*	——	Pvt.	Maryland Line	——
Purtle, Robert*	——	Pvt.	Maryland Line	——
Puterbaugh, Joseph	1761	Pvt.	Militia	——
Queen, Marsham	1752	Pvt.	Maryland Line	——
Queener, John	1761	Pvt.	Militia	——
Quickle, Adam	——	Pvt.	Militia	——
Rainsburg, John	1759	Pvt.	Militia	——
Ramsay, James	——	Ensign	Continental Line	Flying Camp
Randall, James*	1761	Pvt.	Militia	——
Randall, John*	——	Q. M.	Maryland Line	——
Rankins, Daniel*	1752	Pvt.	Maryland Line	——
Rawlings, Solomon	——	Pvt.	Maryland Line	——
Ray, Benjamin	——	Pvt.	Militia	——
Ray, John*	1756	Pvt.	Militia	Ky. Service
Ray Jonathan	1759	Pvt.	Militia	——
Ray, Joseph	1758	Pvt.	Maryland Line	——
Reardon, James	1751	Pvt.	Militia	——
Reed, Alexander	1753	Pvt.	Militia	——
Reed, George	1749	Pvt.	Maryland Line	——
Reed, John*	1758	Pvt.	Militia	——
Reed, John	1743	Pvt.	Militia	——
Reed, Philip	——	Capt.	Maryland Line	——
Reed, William	——	Pvt.	Maryland Line	——
Reeder, Benjamin	1760	Pvt.	Militia	——
Reese, Jacob	——	Pvt.	Militia	War of 1812
Reiley, Bennett*	——	Pvt.	Continental Line	——
Reily, William*	——	Capt.	Maryland Line	Militia
Rewark, James*	1744	Pvt.	Maryland Line	——
Reynolds, Benedict	——	Pvt.	Maryland Line	Flying Camp

Reynolds, John*	1753	Pvt.	Maryland Line	
Reynolds, Robert	—	Pvt.	Maryland Line	Invalid
Reynolds, Thomas*	—	Pvt.	Maryland Line	Prisoner
Reynolds, Tobias	1761	Pvt.	Maryland Line	
Reynolds, William	—	Pvt.	Maryland Line	
Rhoades, Nicholas	—	Pvt.	Continental Line	Lee's Legion
Rhodes, Zachariah	1756	Pvt.	Militia	
Richards, Paul	1756	Pvt.	Maryland Line	Flying Camp
Richardson, Charles*	1748	Pvt.	Maryland Line	
Richardson, Daniel	1747	Pvt.	Maryland Line	Flying Camp
Richardson, David	1756	Pvt.	Militia	Indian Wars
Richardson, John	—	Pvt.	Continental Line	Invalid
Richardson, Jonathan*	—	Pvt.	Militia	
Richardson, Samuel	1753	Pvt.	Maryland Line	
Richardson, Thomas*	—	Seaman	Navy	
Rickey, Joseph	1748	Pvt.	Militia	Penn. Service
Ridenour, Jacob	—	Pvt.	Maryland Line	Invalid
Ridley, Samuel	1753	Pvt.	Maryland Line	Prisoner
Rigby, William*	1753	Q. M.	Maryland Line	
Rigdon, James*	1762	Pvt.	Militia	
Riggs, Charles	1756	Corpl.	Maryland Line	
Riley, Stephen*	1759	Pvt.	Militia	
Rinehart, Thomas	1741	Pvt.	Militia	Flying Camp
Ringer, Matthias	—	Pvt.	Militia	
Riston, Zadock	1756	Pvt.	Maryland Line	
Ritmeyer, Conrad	1764	Pvt.	Militia	
Ritter, Thomas	1755	Pvt.	Militia	
Roaff, Peter	1760	Pvt.	Maryland Line	Flying Camp
Roberts, Archibald*	1763	Pvt.	Militia	
Roberts, James	1755	Pvt.	Maryland Line	
Roberts, Patrick*	1758	Pvt.	Continental Line	
Roberts, William	1751	Pvt.	Maryland Line	
Roberts, Zachariah	—	Pvt.	Maryland Line	
Roberson, Charles	1760	Pvt.	Maryland Line	Flying Camp
Robertson, Edward	—	Pvt.	Continental Line	Prisoner
Robertson, Mitchell	1754	Sergt.	Maryland Line	
Robertson, Zachariah	1762	Pvt.	Maryland Line	
Robey, Richard	1760	Pvt.	Militia	
Robins, John	1762	Pvt.	Maryland Line	

REVOLUTIONARY PENSIONERS 45

Robinson, Charles*	1756	Pvt.	Militia	
Robinson, James	1748	Pvt.	Militia	Penn. & N. J. Service
Robinson, James	——	Pvt.	Continental Line	Marine
Robinson, John	——	Pvt.	Maryland Line	
Robinson, John*	——	Pvt.	Maryland Line	Died in Service
Robinson, Lambert	1751	Pvt.	Maryland Line	
Robosson, Charles*	1758	Lieut.	Militia	Flying Camp
Roby, Aquilla	1760	Pvt.	Militia	
Rock, Andrew	1762	Pvt.	Maryland Line	Wounded
Rock, William	1760	Pvt.	Maryland Line	
Rockhold, Thomas	1758	Pvt.	Militia	
Rohr, John	1761	Pvt.	Militia	
Rohr, Philip	——	Pvt.	Militia	
Rolle, Robert	——	Lieut.	Sea Service	Prisoner
Rollens, Hannahiah*	1762	Pvt.	Militia	N. J. Service
Rolls, James	1760	Pvt.	Continental Line	
Rose, Isaac*	1747	Sergt.	Maryland Line	
Ross, Horatio	1757	Capt.	Continental Line	
Ross, Reuben	1755	Pvt.	Sea Service	Militia
Ross, Reuben	1758	Pvt.	Maryland Line	
Ross, Robinson*	1759	Pvt.	Maryland Line	
Ross, William	——	Sergt.	Militia	
Rowles, William	1759	Pvt.	Maryland Line	Prisoner
Rowse, Thomas	——	Ensign	Maryland Line	Prisoner
Royse, Solomon*	1763	Pvt.	Militia	Indian War
Ruggles, James	——	Pvt.	Maryland Line	
Rumbley, John	1753	Pvt.	Militia	
Rumfelt, Henry*	1761	Pvt.	Continental Line	Germ. Regt.
Runyan, Henry	1763	Pvt.	Maryland Line	N. J. Service
Rutledge, Joshua*	1758	Lieut.	Maryland Line	Prisoner
Rutledge, Peter	1760	Pvt.	Militia	
Ryan, James*	——	Pvt.	Maryland Line	
Ryan, Peter	1758	Pvt.	Maryland Line	
Saffell, Charles	1750	Drum.	Maryland Line	Flying Camp
Safley, Henry	1759	Pvt.	Militia	Va. Service
Sanders, George	1756	Pvt.	Maryland Line	
Sands, Alexander	1760	Pvt.	Militia	
Sappington, Richard*	——	Surgeon	Continental Line	
Sargeant, William	1760	Pvt.	Militia	

Name	Year	Rank	Unit	Notes
Satterfield, William*	——	Sergt.	Maryland Line	——
Saunders, William	1751	Pvt.	Maryland Line	Wounded
Saylor, George*	——	Pvt.	Militia	Penn. Service
Schimmel, Valentine	1752	Pvt.	Militia	Sea Service
Schneider, John	1750	Pvt.	Continental Line	——
Schrack, Andrew	1756	Mattross	Continental Line	——
Schrader, Jacob	——	Pvt.		
Scott, Abraham	1753	Sergt.	Militia	Penn. Service
Scott, Alexander	1760	Pvt.	Maryland Line	——
Scott, Benjamin*	——	Pvt.	Maryland Line	——
Scott, Isaac	1756	Capt.	Militia	Wounded
Scott, Samuel	——	Pvt.	Maryland Line	——
Scroggin, Thomas	1764	Pvt.	Militia	——
Seager, Nathaniel	1759	Capt.	Militia	——
Sergeant, Elijah	——			
Seward, William*	1760	Pvt.	Sea Service	Militia
Sewell, Charles	1761	Lieut.	Maryland Line	——
Sewall, Clement	1758	Ensign	Maryland Line	Wounded
Sewall, James	1758	Pvt.	Maryland Line	Invalid
Sewell, John	1745	Pvt.	Maryland Line	——
Sewell, Thomas*	——	Pvt.	Sea Service	——
Sewell, William*	——	Pvt.	Maryland Line	——
Shade, Jacob	1767	Pvt.	Continental Line	Va. Service
Shafer, Andrew	1751	Pvt.	Maryland Line	Wounded
Shall, George	1756	Pvt.	Militia	Penn. Service
Shank, Christian	1751	Pvt.	Militia	N. J. Service
Shank, John*	——	Pvt.	Continental Line	Germ. Regt.
Shanks, John	——	Pvt.	Maryland Line	Invalid
Sharp, William*	——	Pvt.	Militia	——
Shaw, Basil	1761	Sergt.	Maryland Line	Indian War
Shaw, Basil	1748	Pvt.	Militia	——
Shaw, Henry	1759	Pvt.	Maryland Line	Va. Service
Shaw, John	——	Sergt.	Maryland Line	——
Shaw, John	——			
Shaw, Victor	1746	Pvt.	Militia	——
Shawn, Frederick	1760	Pvt.	Continental Line	——
Shears, Peter*	1749	Pvt.	Continental Line	Germ. Regt.
Sheets, Jacob*	——	Pvt.	Continental Line	Germ. Regt.
Shellman, John	——	Lieut.	Militia	Flying Camp
Shelor, Daniel	1750	Capt.	Militia	——

Sheppard, Jonathan	——	Pvt.	Continental Line	Prisoner
Shipley, Adam	1759	Pvt.	Militia	——
Shipley, Henry*	——	Pvt.	Militia	Flying Camp
Shipley, Samuel	——	Pvt.	Maryland Line	——
Shirley, Bennet*	——	Pvt.	Maryland Line	——
Shlife, John	1757	Pvt.	Continental Line	Germ. Regt.
Shober, John*	1759	Pvt.	Militia	——
Shockley, John	1756	Pvt.	Maryland Line	——
Shots, John*	1756	Pvt.	Continental Line	Germ. Regt.
Shriner, John	1753	Pvt.	Militia	Penn. Service
Shrupp, Henry	1756	Ensign	Continental Line	Penn. Service
Shryock, John	1752	Pvt.	Continental Line	Germ. Regt.
Shumaker, John	1761	Pvt.	Militia	N. C. Service
Silk, James	1750	Pvt.	Maryland Line	——
Sillaven, William	1758	Pvt.	Militia	——
Silver, George*	——	Pvt.	Continental Line	Flying Camp
Simmonds, Robert	1757	Sergt.	Militia	Flying Camp
Simmons, Aaron*	——	Pvt.	Continental Line	——
Simmons, William	1752	Pvt.	Militia	Prisoner
Simmons, William*	1762	Pvt.	Militia	Flying Camp
Simmons, William	1764	Pvt.	Maryland Line	——
Simons, Frederick	1762	Pvt.	Militia	——
Simpkins, Charles	1750	Pvt.	Maryland Line	——
Simpson, Lawrence*	1763	Pvt.	Maryland Line	——
Simpson, Rezin	1758	Pvt.	Continental Line	——
Simpson, Thomas	1756	Pvt.	Maryland Line	——
Sims, Patrick	——	Col.	Maryland Line	——
Sipes, Daniel	1761	Pvt.	Militia	——
Sisler, Philip*	1742	Pvt.	Continental Line	——
Six, Henry	1753	Sergt.	Militia	——
Skinner, Walter	1760	Pvt.	——	Fraudulent
Slack, John*	1757	Pvt.	Continental Line	——
Slick, William	1754	Pvt.	Militia	Flying Camp
Slusher, John	1754	Pvt.	Continental Line	——
Sluts, John*	——	Pvt.	Militia	Prisoner
Slye, William	1758	Corpl.	Maryland Line	Prisoner
Smith, Adam	1753	Lieut.	Continental Line	Germ. Regt.
Smith, Alexander*	——	Capt.	Militia	——
Smith, Aquilla*	1760	Pvt.	Maryland Line	Wounded
Smith, Benjamin	——	Pvt.	Maryland Line	——

Smith, Charles	1763	Pvt.	Sea Service	——
Smith, Charles*	——	Capt.	Maryland Line	——
Smith, Christian	1752	Pvt.	Continental Line	Germ. Regt.
Smith, Conrad*	1742	Pvt.	Maryland Line	Wounded
Smith, Daniel	1756	Capt.	Militia	——
Smith, Drew	——	Pvt.	——	——
Smith, Edward	1757	Pvt.	Maryland Line	Flying Camp
Smith, Edward	1758	Pvt.	Continental Line	——
Smith, Edward*	——	Lieut.	Maryland Line	——
Smith, Elijah*	——	Pvt.	Maryland Line	——
Smith, Elijah*	1752	Pvt.	Maryland Line	——
Smith, Elwiley	1764	Pvt.	Militia	——
Smith, Henry	1759	Pvt.	Militia	Flying Camp
Smith, Henry	1750	Pvt.	Continental Line	Germ. Regt.
Smith, Jacob*	1758	Pvt.	Militia	——
Smith, James*	1755	Sergt.	Militia	——
Smith, John*	1760	Pvt.	Continental Line	Va. Service
Smith, John	1758	Pvt.	Sea Service	Militia
Smith, John*	1753	Pvt.	Militia	Flying Camp
Smith, John*	——	Pvt.	Continental Line	Militia
Smith, John	——	Pvt.	Militia	Sea Service
Smith, John	1760	Pvt.	Militia	——
Smith, John	1751	Pvt.	Maryland Line	——
Smith, John	——	Corpl.	Maryland Line	——
Smith, John*	1752	Pvt.	Continental Line	——
Smith, Joseph	1753	Pvt.	Militia	——
Smith, Leonard*	1760	Pvt.	Maryland Line	——
Smith, Michael*	1752	Pvt.	Continental Line	Flying Camp
Smith, Michael*	——	Drum.	Continental Line	Germ. Regt.
Smith, Nathan*	1754	Surgeon	Maryland Line	Va. Service
Smith, Philip	1759	Pvt.	Continental Line	Indian Wars
Smith, Richard*	1755	Pvt.	Continental Line	——
Smith, Samuel*	1752	Col.	Maryland Line	——
Smith, Thomas	1760	Pvt.	Maryland Line	——
Smith, Thomas*	1758	Pvt.	Maryland Line	——
Smith, William*	——	——	——	——
Smith, William	——	——	——	——
Smith, William	1751	Pvt.	Militia	——
Smith, William	1752	Pvt.	Maryland Line	——
Smith, William	1744	Pvt.	Maryland Line	——

Smith, William	1755	Sergt.	Maryland Line	British Deserter
Smyth, Daniel	——	Pvt.	Maryland Line	
Smyth, Thomas*	——	Major	Maryland Line	
Snider, Frederick*	——	Pvt.		
Snyder, George	1754	Pvt.	Militia	
Snider, John	——	Pvt.	Maryland Line	Invalid
Snyder, John*	——	Fifer	Maryland Line	Marine
Snyder, Peter	1759	Pvt.	Militia	Penn. Service
Solladay, Philip*	——	Teams'r.		
Sommers, Solomon	1750	Pvt.	Maryland Line	Wounded
Souther, Vallentine	1760	Pvt.	Maryland Line	Va. & N. C. Service
Soward, William				
Sowers, Michael	——	Pvt.	Maryland Line	
Spalding, Daniel	1758	Pvt.	Sea Service	Marine
Spalding, George*	1758	Pvt.	Maryland Line	
Spalding, Henry	1756	Pvt.	Maryland Line	
Spaulding, Aaron	1752	Pvt.	Maryland Line	
Speake, George	1758	Pvt.	Continental Line	Va. Service
Speake, Hezekiah*	1757	Pvt.	Militia	Flying Camp
Spedden, Edward*	——	Lieut.	Sea Service	
Spicer, Samuel	1737	Pvt.	Militia	Penn. Service
Spicket, Daniel	1749	Music'n	Continental Line	Prisoner
Spires, John*	1761	Pvt.	Maryland Line	
Spong, Jacob*	——	Pvt.	Maryland Line	
Spry, William	1756	Pvt.	Militia	Flying Camp
Spyers, Richard*	1753	Pvt.	Maryland Line	
Stafford, John*	1767	Pvt.	Militia	
Stamm, George	——	Music'n	Maryland Line	
Stanley, Christopher	1758	Pvt.	Continental Line	Flying Camp
Stansbury, Luke	——	Pvt.	Militia	N. C. Service
Stansbury, Solomon*	1755	Pvt.	Militia	N. C. Service
Stansbury, Tobias	1757	Capt.	Militia	Sea Service
Staples, John	1754	Sergt.	Continental Line	
Staunton, John	1752	Pvt.	Continental Line	Germ. Regt.
Stephenson, James	1758	Pvt.	Sea Service	Prisoner
Sterling, Henry	1763	Pvt.	Militia	
Sterritt, Stewart	1762	Pvt.	Militia	
Stevens, Benjamin*	1751	Pvt.	Maryland Line	
Stevens, John	1758	Pvt.	Maryland Line	

Stevens, Levi*	1753	Pvt.	Maryland Line	
Stevens, William	—	Lieut.	Militia	Va. Service
Stevenson, James	1745	Pvt.	—	Penn. & S. C. Service
Stewart, Caleb	1756	Pvt.	Maryland Line	
Stewart, Charles	1753	Sergt.	Continental Line	
Stewart, Isaac	1754	Pvt.	Militia	Flying Camp
Stewart, John	1755	Sergt.	Militia	Penn. Service
Stewart, Robert	1747	Pvt.	Maryland Line	
Stewart, William	1739	Pvt.	Maryland Line	Flying Camp
Stilling, Benjamin	1759	Pvt.	Militia	
Stillings, Thomas	1755	Pvt.	Militia	
Stinchcomb, Aquilla*	—	—	Militia	
Stinchcomb, Christopher*	—	Sergt.	—	Del. Service
Stinson, John	1755	Lieut.	Militia	
Stone, Cudbeth*	1758	Pvt.	Maryland Line	Wounded
Stoner, Abraham	1760	Pvt.	Militia	
Stoner, John*	—	Pvt.	Maryland Line	Penn. Service
Stoope, Andrew*	1757	Pvt.	Maryland Line	
Storts, Jacob*	1763	Pvt.	Militia	
Stotler, Henry*	—	Pvt.	Continental Line	Germ. Regt.
Stottlemeyer, George	1759	Pvt.	Continental Line	Germ. Regt.
Studer, Philip	1752	Pvt.	Continental Line	Germ. Regt.
Suit, Edward*	—	Corpl.	Maryland Line	Died in Service
Sullivan, Daniel*	1748	Pvt.	Continental Line	Penn. Service
Sullivan, James	1759	Pvt.	Maryland Line	N. Y. Service
Sullivan, Solomon*	—	Pvt.	Militia	
Summers, Hezekiah*	1750	Pvt.	Militia	
Summers, Horsey	1762	Pvt.	Militia	
Summers, John*	—	Capt.	Militia	
Summers, Peter	1754	Pvt.	Militia	
Summers, Richard*	—	Pvt.	Militia	
Sutherland, Alexander*	—	Drum.	Continental Line	Va. Service
Sutherland, John	—	Pvt.	Militia	
Sutherland, Walter*	1749	Pvt.	Militia	
Sutherland, William*	1749	Sergt.	Maryland Line	Wounded
Sutton, Charles	1755	Sergt.	Continental Line	
Sutton, Jacob	1760	Pvt.	Sea Service	
Swearingen, Van*	1754	Lieut.	Maryland Line	Ky. Service

REVOLUTIONARY PENSIONERS 51

Swingle, George	1757	Major	Militia	
Sydars, Solomon	1749	Pvt.	Militia	Va. Service
Sypherd, Mathias	1763	Pvt.	Maryland Line	
Talbot, Charles	1759	Pvt.	Militia	
Talbot, Henry	1751	Pvt.	Militia	
Talbot, James*	——	Pvt.	Militia	
Talbot, Richard	1758	Ensign	Maryland Line	
Tannehil, James	1760	Pvt.	Militia	Flying Camp
Tannehill, Josiah*	1753	Lieut.	Continental Line	
Tarlton, Jeremiah*	——	Corpl.	Maryland Line	
Tasker, Richard	1759	Pvt.	Maryland Line	
Taylor, Bartholomew	1755	Pvt.	Militia	
Taylor, John*	1765	Pvt.	Maryland Line	
Taylor, John	1750	Pvt.	Maryland Line	Prisoner
Taylor, John*	——	Sergt.	Maryland Line	Wounded
Taylor, Richard*	——	Pvt.	Maryland Line	
Taylor, Richard*	1756	Sergt.	Militia	
Taylor, William	1746	Pvt.	Maryland Line	Wounded
Tennant, James	1759	Pvt.	Militia	R. I. Service
Thomas, Ellis*	1755	Pvt.	Maryland Line	Invalid
Thomas, Giles	1764	Pvt.	Maryland Line	
Thomas, James	——	Pvt.	Maryland Line	
Thomas, James*	1755	Pvt.	Continental Line	
Thomas, John*	1761	Pvt.	Maryland Line	
Thomas, John*	——	Capt.	Maryland Line	
Thomas, John	——	Pvt.	Continental Line	Lee's Legion
Thomas, Nathaniel	1758	Pvt.	Maryland Line	
Thomason, Ezekiel	1758	Pvt.	Maryland Line	
Thompson, Bernard	1765	Pvt.	Continental Line	
Thompson, Electius	1755	Pvt.	Maryland Line	
Thompson, James	1759	Pvt.	Militia	N. C. Service
Thompson, Jesse	1756	Pvt.	Maryland Line	
Thompson, John*	——	Pvt.	Maryland Line	
Thompson, Lambert	——	Pvt.	Maryland Line	
Thompson, William	1748	Pvt.	Militia	Flying Camp
Tilghman, Tench*	——	Col.	Continental Line	
Tilley, James	1756	Pvt.	Maryland Line	Prisoner
Timms, Joseph	1751	Pvt.	Maryland Line	
Tipton, Jonathan	1752	Lieut.	Militia	
Tipton, William	——	Pvt.	Militia	

Name	Year	Rank	Service	Notes
Tomar, Christopher	1751	Pvt.	Militia	Wounded
Tomm, Henry	——	Pvt.	Continental Line	Invalid
Tongue, William*	1756	Pvt.	Militia	——
Toole, James	1750	Ensign	Militia	Prisoner
Toomey, John	1748	Pvt.	Maryland Line	——
Toon, Henry	1752	Pvt.	Militia	——
Townsend, Thomas	1757	Pvt.	Sea Service	Marine
Tracey, Philip	1755	Pvt.	Militia	Flying Camp
Tracy, Charles	1759	Pvt.	Militia	Indian War
Travers, Matthias	1755	Pvt.	Militia	——
Travis, Thomas	1737	Pvt.	Militia	——
Tresler, Frederick	1759	Pvt.	Militia	Penn. Service
Trout, Christian*	1753	Pvt.	Militia	——
Trux, John*	——	Sergt.	Continental Line	Germ. Regt.
Tryer, Andrew	1749	Pvt.	Continental Line	Penn. Service
Twiner, John	1758	Pvt.	Maryland Line	——
Tucker, George	1762	Pvt.	Militia	——
Tucker, George	1763	Pvt.	Continental Line	——
Tucker, John	——	Pvt.	Maryland Line	——
Tucker, Thomas	1750	Pvt.	Militia	——
Turner, Andrew	——	Pvt.	Militia	Wagon Service
Turner, Benjamin	1762	Pvt.	Militia	——
Turner, James	1755	Pvt.	Continental Line	Militia
Turner, John	——	Pvt.	Maryland Line	——
Turner, John*	——	Pvt.	Maryland Line	——
Turner, Robert	1761	Pvt.	Militia	Wagon Service
Turner, Solomon*	1760	Pvt.	Maryland Line	——
Tutwiler, Jonathan	——	Pvt.	Maryland Line	——
Uncles, Benjamin*	——	Pvt.	Maryland Line	——
Uselton, George*	1762	Pvt.	Militia	——
Vallentine, George	1752	Pvt.	Militia	Penn. & Va. Service
Van Buskirk, Peter	1762	Sergt.	Militia	N. J., Penn. & N. Y.
Vance, Samuel	1762	——	——	Patriot
Vane, John	1758	Pvt.	Maryland Line	——
Vantresse, Joseph	1750	Pvt.	Militia	——
Vaughan, John*	——	Gunner	Continental Line	——
Vaughan, William	1754	Pvt.	Maryland Line	——
Veatch, Jeremiah*	1759	Pvt.	Militia	Penn. Service
Vermillion, Samuel	1755	Pvt.	Maryland Line	N. C. Service
Vigal, Adam*	——	Pvt.	Maryland Line	——

Revolutionary Pensioners 53

Name	Year	Rank	Line	Notes
Vincent, Aaron*	1761	Pvt.	Maryland Line	——
Waddle, George	1757	Pvt.	Militia	——
Waggoner, Jacob	1754	Pvt.	Continental Line	Germ. Regt.
Wailes, Edward	1758	Capt.	Militia	——
Waldron, Charles	1759	Pvt.	——	N. C. Service
Walker, John*	1755	Pvt.	Maryland Line	Germ. Regt.
Walker, Robert	1757	Pvt.	Maryland Line	——
Wall, John*	——	Pvt.	Militia	Penn. Service
Wall, William*	1732	Pvt.	Maryland Line	Wounded
Walls, George*	——	Sergt.	Militia	Flying Camp
Walsh, John*	1747	Pvt.	Maryland Line	——
Walters, Jacob	——	Pvt.	Sea Service	Wounded
Waltman, Michael*	1754	Pvt.	Maryland Line	Wounded
Ward, Edward	1757	Pvt.	Militia	——
Warden, James	1744	Pvt.	Maryland Line	——
Warfield, Joseph*	1758	Lieut.	Maryland Line	Flying Camp
Waring, Basil*	——	Lieut.	Continental Line	——
Warren, John	1759	Pvt.	Militia	——
Warrick, Charles*	1761	Pvt.	Continental Line	Prisoner
Waters, James	1756	Pvt.	Continental Line	Va. Service
Waters, Richard*	1758	Capt.	Maryland Line	——
Waters, Willson	——	Surgeon	Continental Line	Sea Service
Watkins, Gassaway*	——	Capt.	Maryland Line	Flying Camp
Watkins, John	1758	Pvt.	Militia	——
Watkins, Leonard*	1754	Sergt.	Maryland Line	Flying Camp
Watkins, Stephen*	1755	Pvt.	Maryland Line	——
Watson, Walter	1763	Pvt.	Maryland Line	——
Weaver, Michael	1751	Pvt.	Continental Line	Germ. Regt.
Webb, Barruck	1761	Pvt.	Maryland Line	Militia
Webb, John	1764	Pvt.	Maryland Line	——
Webb, John*	——	Ensign	Militia	——
Weeden, Horatio	——	Pvt.	Militia	Invalid
Weekly, Thomas	1754	Pvt.	Militia	Flying Camp
Weinnand, Philip	1754	Pvt.	Militia	Flying Camp
Weirick, Michael*	1754	Fifer	Maryland Line	——
Weise, Adam*	1751	Ensign	Militia	——
Weldin, Jesse	1759	Pvt.	Continental Line	Del. Service
Wells, Benjamin*	1755	Marine	Continental Line	Wounded
Wells, Charles	1758	Pvt.	Militia	Va. Service
Wells, Cornelius	1751	Sergt.	Maryland Line	Sea Service

Wells, Duckett	1752	Pvt.	Militia	————
Wells, John	1757	Pvt.	Militia	Flying Camp
Wells, Peter	1759	Pvt.	Militia	War of 1812
Wells, Thomas C.	1765	Sergt.	Militia	————
Welty, John	1744	Pvt.	Maryland Line	Germ. Regt.
Wertz, George	1752	Pvt.	Militia	Penn. Service
Wessinger, Ludwick	——	Pvt.	Continental Line	Germ. Regt.
West, Benjamin	1754	Pvt.	Militia	Sea Service
West, John T.*	——	Pvt.	Maryland Line	Wounded
West, William	1755	Pvt.	Maryland Line	Militia
Wheatley, William*	——	Pvt.	Maryland Line	————
Wheelan, Martin	1751	Pvt.	Maryland Line	Prisoner
Wheeler, Benjamin	1758	Pvt.	Militia	Penn. Service
Wheeler, Charles	1763	Pvt.	Maryland Line	————
Wheeler, Samuel	——	Pvt.	Militia	Va. Service
Whelan, Richard*	1754	Pvt.	Maryland Line	Prisoner
Whetstone, Daniel	1750	Pvt.	Militia	N. C. Service
Whips, Benjamin	1763	Pvt.	Militia	————
Whitacres, William*	——	Pvt.	Maryland Line	————
Whitaker, John*	1753	Pvt.	Militia	————
White, Abraham	1745	Capt.	Militia	————
White, James	1759	Pvt.	Maryland Line	Invalid
White, John*	——	Pvt.	Continental Line	Wounded
White, Joseph	1755	Pvt.	Maryland Line	————
White, Samuel	——	Pvt.	Maryland Line	Invalid
White, Thomas	1759	Pvt.	Maryland Line	————
White, Thomas	1758	Pvt.	Militia	Penn. & Tenn.
Whitemore, Stephen	1749	Pvt.	Maryland Line	————
Whiting, Isaac	——	Pvt.	Militia	————
Whitlack, William	1761	Pvt.	Militia	————
Wilheid, Frederick	1753	Pvt.	Continental Line	Germ. Regt.
Wilkerson, Young	——	Lieut.	Continental Line	————
Wilkins, George	1760	Pvt.	Militia	————
Wilkinson, James	——	Pvt.	Continental Line	————
Willhelm, George	1753	Pvt.	Continental Line	Germ. Regt.
Williams, Abraham	1747	Lieut.	Militia	————
Williams, Alexander	——	Pvt.	Maryland Line	Prisoner
Williams, Benjamin	1762	Pvt.	Maryland Line	————
Williams, Benjamin	——	Pvt.	Maryland Line	Militia
Williams, Charles	——	Pvt.	Maryland Line	————

REVOLUTIONARY PENSIONERS 55

Williams, David	1758	Pvt.	Militia	
Williams, Elisha*	——	Capt.	Maryland Line	Wounded
Williams, Francis	1752	Pvt.	Militia	Flying Camp
Williams, Gabriel*	1756	Pvt.	Maryland Line	Flying Camp
Williams, Gerard*	1759	Sergt.	Militia	Penn. Service
Williams, James	1759	Pvt.	Militia	Penn. Service
Williams, James	1756	Pvt.	Maryland Line	
Williams, Jeremiah*	1759	Pvt.	Maryland Line	
Williams, Jesse	1750	Ensign	Militia	
Williams, John	1755	Pvt.	Maryland Line	
Williams, John	——	Pvt.	Maryland Line	War of 1812
Williams, John*	1755	Pvt.	Maryland Line	
Williams, John*	1754	Sergt.	Militia	Va. Service
Williams, Joseph	——	Pvt.	Militia	Del. Service
Williams, Joseph	——	Pvt.	Continental Line	Germ. Regt.
Williams, Lawrence*	1758	Sergt.	Militia	Penn. Service
Williams, Osborn	——	Lieut.	Maryland Line	
Williams, Robert	1768	Pvt.	Maryland Line	Indian Wars
Williams, William	1761	Pvt.	Militia	Va. Service
Williams, William	1749	Pvt.	Militia	Flying Camp
Williamson, Alexander	1752	Sergt.	Maryland Line	Penn. Service
Willin, Levin	1758	Pvt.	Sea Service	Wounded
Willis, Andrew	1747	Pvt.	Maryland Line	
Willis, Jarvis	1763	Pvt.	Maryland Line	
Wilson, George	1750	Pvt.	Maryland Line	
Wilson, Gilbreath	1742	Pvt.	Maryland Line	
Wilson, James	1763	Pvt.	Maryland Line	
Wilson, Mathew	1741	Pvt.	Militia	
Wilson, Richard	1755	Capt.	Continental Line	
Wilson, William*	——	Pvt.	Maryland Line	
Winchester, James*	1752	Capt.	Maryland Line	War of 1812
Windham, George*	1756	Pvt.	Maryland Line	
Windham, Thomas*	——	Sergt.	Maryland Line	
Wink, Jacob	1755	Pvt.	Continental Line	Germ. Regt.
Winsett, Raphael*	1754	Pvt.	Maryland Line	
Wiseman, Thomas	1750	Pvt.	Maryland Line	Wounded
Wisner, Jacob	1759	Pvt.	Maryland Line	
Wisor, Michael*	1758	Pvt.	Maryland Line	Prisoner
Wolcott, William	1759	Pvt.	Maryland Line	

Name	Year	Rank	Service	Notes
Wolf, David	——	Pvt.	Militia	Va. Service
Wolf, Michael	1751	Sergt.	Maryland Line	Va. Service
Wolford, John	1763	Pvt.	Militia	——
Wood, Aaron*	1757	Pvt.	Militia	N. C. Service
Wood, Benjamin	1763	Pvt.	Militia	——
Wood, John*	1754	Ensign	Militia	——
Wood, John*	1763	Pvt.	Militia	——
Wood, Jonathan	1747	Pvt.	Militia	Flying Camp
Woodburn, Jonathan	1758	Pvt.	Maryland Line	——
Woods, Thomas	——	Pvt.	Maryland Line	——
Woolford, Thomas	1747	Lieut.	Militia	——
Woolheater, Adam	1756	Pvt.	Militia	——
Worley, David	——	Pvt.	Maryland Line	——
Worner, Peter*	——	Pvt.	Militia	——
Worthington, Charles	1760	Surgeon	Sea Service	——
Wright, Absalom*	1762	Pvt.	Maryland Line	——
Wright, Bazzel	1764	Pvt.	Militia	——
Wright, Edward	1738	Pvt.	Maryland Line	Wounded
Wright, Elijah	1756	Pvt.	Militia	Penn. Service
Wright, John	1756	Pvt.	Continental Line	——
Wright, Turbutt*	——	Capt.	Maryland Line	——
Wyckoff, Samuel	1760	Pvt.	Militia	——
Yates, Benjamin*	1745	Pvt.	Militia	——
Yates, Robert	1760	Pvt.	Maryland Line	——
Yeast, Jacob*	——	Pvt.	Maryland Line	——
Yeast, Philip	1743	Pvt.	Militia	Flying Camp
Young, Benjamin	1754	Pvt.	Maryland Line	——
Young, George	——	Pvt.	Continental Line	——
Young, George	——	Pvt.	Continental Line	——
Young, Henry*	——	Pvt.	Maryland Line	——
Young, Jacob	1762	Pvt.	Militia	Sea Service
Young, Matthias*	1760	Pvt.	Militia	——
Young, William*	1757	Pvt.	Maryland Line	——
Younger, Kanard	1760	Pvt.	Militia	Pa. & Va. Service
Yule, James*	1755	Ensign	Continental Line	Mass. Service
Zimmerman, George	1745	Sergt.	Militia	Indian War
Zoll, Jacob	1754	Pvt.	Militia	——

Part II

MARYLAND FEDERAL BOUNTY LAND GRANTS

*Indicates that genealogical data and history of the services are available.

NOTE: Further information on the following names may be obtained for a reasonable fee by addressing the compiler.

Soldier	Rank	Acreage Received	Date of Issue	Warrant Number
Abbot, Levi	Pvt.	100	Aug. 12, 179-	10,930
Adams, John	Pvt.	100	Feb. 9, 1792	10,935
Adams, John	Pvt.	100	Mar. 11, 1791	10,938
Adams, Peter*	Lieut.-Col.	450	————	372
Adams, William*	Lieut.	200	————	373
Ahearn, William	Pvt.	100	Feb. 7, 1790	10,920
Alby, John	Pvt.	100	Feb. 1, 1790	10,933
Allen, Emanuel	Pvt.	100	Aug. 12, 1795	10,926
Allen, James	Pvt.	100	Feb. 7, 1790	10,928
Allen, William*	Pvt.	100	————	1,356
Alvey, Traverse	Pvt.	100	Aug. 14, 1795	10,927
Anderson, Archibald*	Major	300	————	390
Anderson, John	Pvt.	100	Feb. 1, 1790	10,932
Anderson, Michael	Pvt.	100	Apr. 12, 1796	12,711
Andrews, John	Pvt.	100	Nov. 29, 1790	10,934
Appleby, John	Pvt.	100	Aug. 12, 1795	10,919
Armstrong, John	Pvt.	100	Aug. 7, 1794	10,925
Armstrong, John	Pvt.	100	Mar. 11, 1791	10,922
Ashley, James	Pvt.	100	Aug. 14, 1795	10,924
Ashmore, John	Pvt.	100	Aug. 12, 1795	10,931
Askew, Peregrine	Pvt.	100	Feb. 1, 1790	10,937
Austin, Harris	Pvt.	100	Aug. 14, 1795	10,921
Ayers, Frederick	Pvt.	100	Jan. 15, 1793	10,939
Ayers, Thomas*	Pvt.	100	June 9, 1789	10,923
Baber, James	Pvt.	100	Feb. 1, 1790	10,940
Bailey, John	Pvt.	100	June 11, 1790	10,979
Bailey, John	Pvt.	100	Aug. 14, 1795	10,991
Bailey, Thomas	Pvt.	100	Aug. 14, 1795	10,957

Baker, Henry	Lieut.	200	—	239
Baker, Thomas	Pvt.	100	July 18, 1794	10,999
Baldwin, Henry	Lieut.	200	—	245
Baldwin, William J.	Pvt.	100	Jan. 28, 1795	10,953
Baltzell, Charles	Capt.	200	—	238
Banks, Samuel	Pvt.	100	May 4, 1797	10,948
Bantham, John	Pvt.	100	Nov. 14, 1808	434
Bantham, Perry	Pvt.	100	Aug. 14, 1795	10,972
Barret, Joshua	Sergt.	100	Feb. 7, 1790	10,954
Barret, Solomon	Fifer	100	June 28, 1799	14,152
Barton, Joseph	Pvt.	100	Feb. 7, 1790	10,949
Bateman, Nathan*	Pvt.	100	Jan. 27, 1836	2,132
Bautcheby, Joseph	Pvt.	100	Apr. 18, 1797	10,996
Bazil, Daniel	Pvt.	100	Aug. 14, 1795	10,961
Beatty, Thomas	Capt.	300	—	246
Beatty, William*	Capt.	300	Nov. 16, 1815	644
Bennett, Frederick	Pvt.	100	May 6, 1794	10,963
Bennett, John	Pvt.	100	May 11, 1790	11,012
Berry, Edward	Pvt.	100	Sept. 5, 1789	11,011
Berryman, John	Pvt.	100	June 3, 1795	10,941
Bias, James	Pvt.	100	June 11, 1790	10,976
Biddle, Richard	Pvt.	100	Mar. 22, 1797	10,955
Bigges, Benjamin	Pvt.	100	Mar. 25, 1795	14,116
Bigwood, James	Pvt.	100	Mar. 11, 1791	—
Billip, Henry	Pvt.	100	Dec. 22, 1794	11,971
Blackham, George	Pvt.	100	Feb. 7, 1790	10,946
Blake, Jacob	Pvt.	100	Aug. 14, 1795	10,964
Blansford, Richard	Pvt.	100	Aug. 14, 1795	10,945
Blaze, Joseph	Pvt.	100	Aug. 14, 1795	10,947
Body, Robert	Pvt.	100	Jan. 17, 1793	11,019
Boice, George*	Pvt.	100	Oct. 12, 1804	163
Bonham, Malakiah	Lieut.	200	—	240
Boody, John	Pvt.	100	Feb. 1, 1790	10,986
Boss, Christian	Pvt.	100	June 11, 1790	11,013
Boswell, Samuel	Pvt.	100	Feb. 1, 1790	10,959
Bowen, Abraham	Pvt.	100	Aug. 14, 1795	11,973
Bowen, Robert	Pvt.	100	Nov. 29, 1790	10,997
Bowers, George	Pvt.	100	Nov. 5, 1789	10,995
Bowles, Martin*	Pvt.	100	Mar. 13, 1839	2,249
Bowles, Samuel	Pvt.	160-55	—	30,615

FEDERAL BOUNTY LAND GRANTS 59

Bowser, Thomas*	Pvt.	100	Mar. 12, 1846	2,385
Boyd, Benjamin	Pvt.	100	Aug. 14, 1795	10,983
Boyd, Thomas	Lieut.	200	———	248
Boyl, James	Pvt.	100	Jan. 17, 1793	11,021
Bracco, Bennett*	Capt.	300	July 29, 1836	2,167
Brady, John	Pvt.	100	Apr. 18, 1794	10,978
Brady, John	Pvt.	100	Dec. 18, 1794	11,110
Bramble, David	Pvt.	100	Aug. 14, 1795	10,958
Branson, John	Pvt.	100	Aug. 14, 1795	10,942
Brevett, John	Lieut.	200	Oct. 16, 1789	241
Briley, George	Pvt.	100	Dec. 12, 1831	1,790
Brittenham, Solomon	Pvt.	100	July 31, 1797	10,989
Bronnon, Lawrence	Pvt.	100	Apr. 28, 1791	10,981
Brookbank, John	Pvt.	100	Aug. 14, 1795	10,943
Brooks, Benjamin	Major	400	Mar. 11, 1791	228
Brown, Bazil*	Pvt.	100	Sept. 22, 1834	2,068
Brown, George	Pvt.	100	June 3, 1795	14,123
Brown, John	Sergt.	100	Nov. 5, 1789	10,944
Brown, John	Pvt.	100	Aug. 14, 1795	10,956
Brown, Thomas	Pvt.	100	Sept. 6, 1792	11,007
Bruff, James	Capt.	300	Nov. 2, 1791	235
Bruff, William*	Sergt.	100	Aug. 13, 1805	211
Brumigum, Daniel*	Pvt.	100	Oct. 24, 1832	1,886
Buchanan, John*	Pvt.	100	Mar. 31, 1829	1,495
Bucket, Humphrey	Pvt.	100	Mar. 11, 1791	10,984
Buckley, Daniel	Pvt.	100	Jan. 21, 1795	10,998
Buckley, John	Pvt.	100	July 17, 1792	10,966
Buckley, Thomas	Pvt.	100	Dec. 22, 1794	10,994
Bucklip, Charles	Pvt.	100	Feb. 1, 1790	10,968
Bulger, Daniel	Pvt.	100	June 11, 1790	10,985
Bumgardner, George	Pvt.	100	Oct. 6, 1794	10,977
Burgess, Basil*	Lieut.	200	Aug. 2, 1797	234
Burgess, John	Pvt.	100	Aug. 14, 1795	10,987
Burgess, Joshua	Lieut.	200	May 10, 1800	242
Burke, Richard*	Pvt.	100	May 11, 1829	1,507
Burnett, John	Pvt.	100	Aug. 7, 1794	11,905
Burnett, Thomas*	Sergt.	100	Aug. 13, 1805	211
Burton, Isaac	Pvt.	100	Aug. 14, 1795	11,008
Butler, Richard*	Pvt.	100	Jan. 21, 1847	2,407
Butt, Burdick	Pvt.	100	Feb. 3, 1796	10,974

Butt, Edward*	Pvt.	100	Jan.	3, 1824	1,072
Butt, Thomas	Pvt.	100	Feb.	1, 1790	10,982
Butt, Zachariah	Pvt.	100	Jan.	3, 1824	1,073
Button, Levine	Pvt.	100	Feb.	1, 1790	10,992
Buxton, Abijal	Pvt.	100	Mar.	11, 1791	10,956
Buxton, Elijah	Pvt.	100	Mar.	11, 1791	10,951
Caho, Thomas	Pvt.	100	Dec.	18, 1794	11,065
Callahan, John	Pvt.	100	Jan.	8, 1790	11,109
Callahan, Samuel	Pvt.	100	Feb.	7, 1790	11,070
Callihan, Michael	Pvt.	100	Aug.	14, 1795	——
Camile, Clothel	Pvt.	100	Nov.	29, 1790	11,093
Camm, William	Pvt.	100	Nov.	29, 1790	11,001
Campbell, John	Pvt.	100	Feb.	28, 1794	11,052
Camphire, Thomas	Pvt.	100	Jan.	11, 1796	11,086
Cann, Augustine*	Pvt.	100	Aug.	22, 1834	2,059
Carbon, William	Pvt.	100	Sept.	2, 1789	11,044
Cardiff, Thomas	Pvt.	100	Feb.	7, 1790	11,125
Carman, James	Pvt.	100	June	28, 1795	14,094
Carnes, Robert	Pvt.	100	Aug.	14, 1795	11,034
Carney, Thomas	Pvt.	100	Oct.	14, 1795	11,050
Carr, Hezekiah	Drum.	100	July	17, 1810	563
Carrol, John	Pvt.	100	Feb.	1, 1790	11,091
Carson, John	Pvt.	100	Jan.	21, 1794	11,040
Carter, Luke	Pvt.	100	Feb.	7, 1790	11,024
Carter, Samuel	Pvt.	100	Apr.	18, 1797	11,119
Carter, William	Pvt.	100	Feb.	7, 1790	11,027
Carter, William	Pvt.	100	July	8, 1797	11,087
Carty, James	Pvt.	100	Feb.	24, 1795	14,112
Carty, Matthew	Pvt.	100	Dec.	18, 1794	11,103
Cary, John D.	Lieut.	200	Mar.	4, 1800	445
Casey, William	Pvt.	100	Oct.	6, 1794	11,063
Cato, William	Pvt.	100	May	30, 1793	11,042
Cavenah, Thomas	Pvt.	100	Mar.	25, 1795	14,113
Cavenough, Patrick	Pvt.	100	Jan.	8, 1794	11,075
Chamberlin, Josias*	Pvt.	100	Apr.	23, 1807	418
Chambers, George	Pvt.	100	Jan.	8, 1796	11,081
Champlin, Hugh	Pvt.	100	Mar.	16, 1795	11,114
Channon, Thomas	Pvt.	100	May	4, 1797	11,084
Chapman, Henry H.	Lieut.	200	Feb.	11, 1791	444
Chappil, Samuel	Pvt.	100	June	19, 1793	11,089

Chatland, William	Pvt.	100	Apr. 28, 1791	11,071
Childs, George	Corpl.	100	May 11, 1790	11,039
Chittam, Aquilla*	Pvt.	100	Dec. 30, 1839	2,277
Clack, Moses	Pvt.	100	Nov. 26, 1792	12,009
Clagett, Horatio*	Capt.	300	———	———
Clanaham, Robert	Pvt.	100	Jan. 21, 1795	11,069
Clancy, John	Pvt.	100	Feb. 1, 1790	11,028
Clancy, Michael	Fifer	100	Feb. 7, 1790	11,048
Claridge, Levin*	Pvt.	100	Oct. 14, 1831	1,779
Clark, George	Pvt.	100	Mar. 3, 1829	1,357
Clark, George*	Pvt.	100	———	1,484
Clark, John	Pvt.	100	July 10, 1828	1,336
Clark, Michael	Pvt.	100	Aug. 8, 1797	11,095
Clark, Michael	Pvt.	100	Nov. 29, 1790	11,060
Clark, Zachariah	Pvt.	100	June 11, 1790	11,102
Clarke, Thomas	Pvt.	100	Aug. 14, 1795	11,032
Cleary, William	Pvt.	100	Sept. 24, 1792	11,035
Cleaver, Benjamin	Pvt.	100	Aug. 14, 1795	11,029
Clements, Charles	Pvt.	100	Aug. 14, 1795	11,036
Clements, Henry	Lieut.	200	Mar. 10, 1790	441
Clinton, Thomas	Fifer	100	Apr. 5, 1814	632
Coffin, Arthur	Pvt.	100	Mar. 11, 1796	11,038
Coins, Domini	Pvt.	100	Aug. 24, 1793	11,043
Colchetts, Benjamin	Pvt.	100	Mar. 25, 1795	14,115
Cole, Benjamin*	Pvt.	215	———	13,441
Cole, David	Pvt.	100	July 26, 1797	11,111
Cole, John	Pvt.	100	Mar. 22, 1797	11,054
Colegate, Asaph	Pvt.	100	Jan. 16, 1797	11,083
Colin, John	Pvt.	100	June 2, 1797	11,026
Collins, Jacob	Pvt.	100	Aug. 7, 1794	11,100
Collins, James	Pvt.	100	Feb. 24, 1795	14,110
Collins, John	Pvt.	100	Apr. 19, 1797	11,033
Collins, William	Pvt.	100	Aug. 14, 1795	11,031
Conden, Thomas	Pvt.	100	Feb. 1, 1790	11,112
Connelly, Hugh	Pvt.	100	———	827
Conner, David	Pvt.	100	Aug. 14, 1795	11,030
Conner, Michael*	Pvt.	100	Apr. 30, 1806	268
Conner, William*	Pvt.	100	May 8, 1838	2,209
Connolly, Timothy	Pvt.	100	June 14, 1796	11,115
Connolly, William	Pvt.	100	Feb. 1, 1790	11,123

Connor, Patrick	Pvt.	100	Feb. 24, 1795	14,001
Cook, William	Pvt.	100	Feb. 7, 1790	11,055
Cooper, John	Pvt.	100	Aug. 8, 1797	11,056
Cornwell, William	Pvt.	100	Sept. 22, 1795	11,116
Coulter, John	Pvt.	100	May 7, 1806	274
Coulter, William*	Pvt.	100	Sept. 5, 1828	1,357
Coursey, Hampton	Pvt.	100	Mar. 11, 1791	11,053
Cox, William	Pvt.	100	Dec. 22, 1794	11,064
Crady, David	Pvt.	100	Nov. 29, 1790	11,094
Cragan, Dennis	Pvt.	100	Sept. 24, 1794	11,120
Craig, John	Pvt.	100	May 7, 1806	274
Craig, John	Pvt.	100	———	286
Craig, Thomas	Pvt.	100	Aug. 24, 1826	1,187
Craigs, George	Pvt.	100	Nov. 29, 1790	11,099
Crail, William	Pvt.	100	Jan. 11, 1790	11,068
Crane, Henry	Pvt.	100	Jan. 8, 1796	11,074
Crawford, Jacob	Lieut.	200	May 7, 1790	440
Crommy, Andrew	Pvt.	100	Mar. 3, 1792	11,107
Crosier, James	Pvt.	100	Feb. 15, 1796	11,073
Crosier, John	Pvt.	100	Jan. 28, 1793	11,128
Crouch, Joseph	Pvt.	100	Dec. 18, 1794	11,122
Crouch, Robert	Trump.	100	Jan. 18, 1800	11,041
Crowell, Samuel	Pvt.	100	Dec. 18, 1794	11,106
Crowley, Darby	Pvt.	100	Oct. 14, 1795	11,067
Cummins, William*	Pvt.	100	Aug. 14, 1795	11,025
Currin, James*	Pvt.	100	May 5, 1803	2
Curtis, Michael	Pvt.	100	Dec. 22, 1798	11,088
Cusach, Christopher	Pvt.	100	Oct. 6, 1794	11,090
Daley, Matthew	Pvt.	100	Jan. 8, 1796	11,156
Davidson, John	Major	400	———	582
Davis, John	Pvt.	100	Jan. 28, 1795	11,170
Davis, Rezin	Capt.	300	———	586
Davis, Samuel	Pvt.	100	Jan. 22, 1793	11,131
Davis, Samuel	Sergt.	100	Aug. 27, 1789	11,169
Davis, William	Pvt.	100	July 8, 1797	11,164
Dawson, John	Pvt.	100	Jan. 8, 1796	11,133
Day, James*	Pvt.	215	———	———
Deakins, Thomas	Pvt.	100	Dec. 22, 1794	11,154
Deaver, Aquilla	Pvt.	100	Aug. 7, 1794	11,150
Delany, John	Pvt.	100	July 31, 1828	1,343

Denny, Robert	Lieut.	200	————		589
Denoon, John	Pvt.	100	Mar. 11, 1791		11,135
Denson, John	Pvt.	100	Sept. 13, 1799		11,136
Dewett, George	Pvt.	100	Jan. 11, 1796		11,147
Dixon, George	Pvt.	100	Aug. 16, 1797		11,141
Dixon, John	Pvt.	100	Feb. 14, 1797		11,134
Dixon, William	Pvt.	100	June 11, 1790		11,167
Dobson, Henry	Capt.	300	————		592
Dobson, John	Pvt.	100	Jan. 8, 1796		11,165
Donoho, Joseph	Pvt.	100	Mar. 11, 1791		11,160
Doran, Patrick	Sergt.	100	Aug. 4, 1789		11,158
Dorsey, Bazil	Pvt.	100	————		161
Dorsey, Richard	Capt.	300	————		584
Downes, William	Pvt.	100	Aug. 9, 1797		11,137
Downy, John	Pvt.	100	Apr. 28, 1791		11,139
Doyle, James	Pvt.	100	Oct. 14, 1795		11,140
Driskell, Jeremiah	Pvt.	100	Feb. 1, 1790		11,142
Driver, James	Pvt.	100	Dec. 18, 1794		11,161
Dugan, Abraham	Pvt.	100	Nov. 29, 1790		11,162
Duncan, Robert	Pvt.	100	Oct. 14, 1795		11,146
Dunkin, Isaac	Pvt.	100	Jan. 8, 1796		11,138
Dunning, Dennis	Drum.	100	Feb. 1, 1790		11,132
Dunster, Peter	Pvt.	100	Sept. 12, 1792		11,172
Durrington, William*	Pvt.	100	Aug. 2, 1824		1,091
Duval, Edward*	Lieut.	200	————		590
Duval, George	Pvt.	100	Jan. 28, 1795		14,098
Duval, Isaac*	Lieut.	200	————		574
Duval, Richard	Pvt.	100	Aug. 18, 1792		11,148
Dyce, George	Pvt.	100	July 23, 1813		618
Dych, Mathias	Pvt.	100	Oct. 6, 1794		11,145
Dyer, Edward*	Capt.	300	July 27, 1813		620
Dyer, George	Pvt.	100	Jan. 11, 1796		11,153
Dyer, Walter	Lieut.	200	Nov. 14, 1791		587
Dyson, Thomas A.	Lieut.	200	————		588
Eabs, Emanuel	Pvt.	100	Dec. 31, 1791		11,197
Eccleston, John	Major	400	————		671
Edwards, John	Pvt.	100	Aug. 14, 1797		11,195
Elbert, John	Surgeon	150	————		2,157
Elkins, William	Pvt.	100	Aug. 9, 1797		11,186
Elliot, John	Pvt.	100	Nov. 29, 1790		11,189

Elliot, Thomas	Pvt.	100	Nov. 29, 179–	11,191
Elliot, Thomas	Pvt.	100	Apr. 13, 1828	1,300
Ellis, Thomas	Pvt.	100	Dec. 22, 1791	11,183
Ennis, Enock	Pvt.	100	Sept. 5, 1789	11,180
Ennis, John*	Pvt.	100	July 26, 1832	1,867
Ennis, Leonard*	Pvt.	100	Feb. 7, 1790	11,173
Erwin, James	Pvt.	100	Feb. 1, 1790	11,192
Evans, Edward	Pvt.	100	Sept. 12, 1792	11,179
Evans, Edward	Pvt.	100	June 11, 1795	11,190
Evans, Elijah	Capt.	300	———	673
Evans, John	Pvt.	100	Feb. 1, 179–	11,194
Evans, Perry*	Sergt.	100	Apr. 23, 1808	417
Evans, Thomas	Pvt.	100	Feb. 1, 1790	11,176
Faido, Absolom	Pvt.	100	Jan. 11, 1796	11,238
Fairbrother, Francis	Pvt.	100	Feb. 1, 1790	11,210
Fallen, John	Pvt.	100	May 11, 1790	11,198
Farraby, Richard	Pvt.	100	Nov. 29, 1790	11,230
Farrare, Emanuel	Pvt.	100	Feb. 7, 1790	11,233
Fearson, Joseph	Pvt.	100	Dec. 30, 1834	2,089
Felts, Christopher	Pvt.	100	Feb. 7, 1790	11,199
Fennell, Stephen	Pvt.	100	Mar. 11, 1791	11,200
Ferrell, William	Pvt.	100	Feb. 1, 179–	11,226
Fickle, Benjamin	Lieut.	200	———	197
Fields, George	Pvt.	100	Feb. 3, 1792	11,216
Finley, Ebenezer	Lieut.	200	———	2,287
Fisher, Henry	Pvt.	100	Feb. 1, 1790	11,237
Fisher, Samuel	Pvt.	100	Oct. 14, 1795	11,212
Fitzgerald, Benjamin	Sergt.	100	June 20, 1789	11,203
Fitzgerald, Charles*	Pvt.	100	July 19, 1828	1,338
Fitzgerald, John	Pvt.	100	May 1, 1792	11,239
Flannagan, Dennis	Pvt.	100	Nov. 9, 1789	11,232
Flash, Lewis	Pvt.	100	Jan. 11, 1796	11,235
Flora, Jacob	Pvt.	100	Dec. 24, 1791	11,204
Fluhart, Stephen	Sergt.	100	June 11, 1790	11,220
Ford, Benjamin*	Lieut.-Col.	450	———	1,133
Foreman, Leonard*	Pvt.	215	———	———
Foreman, William	Pvt.	100	Feb. 27, 1793	11,219
Forresdale, Stafford	Pvt.	100	May 11, 1790	11,211
Foster, Mark	Pvt.	100	Oct. 10, 1799	11,213
Foster, Moses	Pvt.	100	———	———

Foster, Rigby	Pvt.	100	Apr. 11, 1797	11,222
Foster, William	Pvt.	100	May 1, 1795	14,118
Fowler, Joseph	Pvt.	100	Feb. 1, 1790	11,205
Francis, Alexander	Pvt.	100	June 11, 1790	11,206
Francis, John	Pvt.	100	May 8, 1790	11,214
Franklin, Richard*	Pvt.	100	June 3, 1843	2,322
Frawney, John	Pvt.	100	Aug. 8, 1792	11,202
Frazier, Henry	Pvt.	100	Oct. 14, 179–	11,225
Freeman, Francis	Pvt.	100	Nov. 26, 1792	11,228
Fresh, Stephen	Pvt.	100	June 8, 1797	11,227
Fromley, Thomas	Pvt.	100	Jan. 8, 1796	11,224
Fulham, Charles	Pvt.	100	Mar. 22, 1797	11,208
Fulham, John	Pvt.	100	Jan. 8, 1796	11,223
Furroner, Edward	Pvt.	100	July 9, 1799	11,229
Gadd, Thomas	Pvt.	100	May 1, 1792	11,260
Gainer, Hugh	Pvt.	100	Feb. 7, 1790	11,274
Gaither, Benjamin*	Pvt.	100	Nov. 1, 1849	2,290
Gaither, Henry	Capt.	300	————	854
Gale, John*	Capt.	300	May 22, 1808	422
Gallen, Thomas	Pvt.	100	Feb. 18, 1830	1,597
Gamble, Abraham*	Pvt.	100	Aug. 2, 1844	2,341
Game, Jacob	Pvt.	100	July 9, 1799	11,268
Garnett, Benjamin*	Lieut.	200	————	328
Gassaway, Henry	Lieut.	200	————	859
Gassaway, Nicholas	Lieut.	200	————	862
Gebhart, John*	Pvt.	215	————	96,097
Gee, Richard	Pvt.	100	Nov. 29, 1790	11,276
Geohagan, Anthony	Pvt.	100	Mar. 4, 1828	1,269
George, Southy	Pvt.	100	Nov. 29, 1790	11,278
Gibhart, Adam*	Pvt.	215	————	40,910
Gibson, Jonathan	Capt.	300	————	858
Gilby, Henry	Pvt.	100	Mar. 11, 179–	11,254
Giles, Aquila	Major	400	Sept. 22, 1789	852
Gilham, Thomas	Pvt.	100	Oct. 14, 1795	11,264
Gillen, Thomas*	Pvt.	100	————	1,597
Gilman, Joseph*	Pvt.	100	————	576
Gist, John	Capt.	300	————	857
Gist, Mordecai*	Gen.	580	————	108
Gist, Nathaniel*	Col.	500	————	1,874
Glasgow, William*	Pvt.	215	————	8,178

Glisan, Thomas	Pvt.	100	—	11,284
Glory, William	Pvt.	100	Jan. 8, 1794	11,257
Gold, William	Pvt.	100	May 12, 1797	11,263
Goldsberry, Mark	Pvt.	100	Mar. 16, 1824	1,084
Goldsborough, Charles	Pvt.	100	Jan. 27, 1816	647
Goldsborough, William	Lieut.	200	—	860
Goldsmith, Thomas*	Lieut.	200	June —, 1846	2,399
Goody, Lambert	Pvt.	100	Dec. 22, 1794	11,277
Gordon, John	Pvt.	100	June 11, 1790	11,266
Gorman, John	Pvt.	100	May 11, 179–	11,255
Graham, John	Pvt.	100	Jan. 8, 1796	11,246
Graham, Moses	Pvt.	100	June 11, 1795	11,275
Grant, William	Pvt.	100	Mar. 11, 1791	11,286
Grantham, Henry	Pvt.	100	Feb. 24, 1795	13,123
Gravey, James	Pvt.	100	Apr. 8, 1797	11,250
Gray, Benjamin	Pvt.	100	Jan. 4, 179–	11,252
Gray, James	Capt.	300	—	856
Gray, James*	Pvt.	100	Apr. 26, 1828	1,302
Gray, John	Pvt.	100	Mar. 22, 1797	11,279
Gray, Samuel	Pvt.	100	July 17, 1797	11,249
Green, Amos	Pvt.	100	Oct. 14, 1795	11,269
Green, Clement*	Pvt.	100	—	2,423
Green, Henry*	Pvt.	100	Jan. 8, 1794	11,256
Greenwood, James	Pvt.	100	Dec. 18, 1794	11,243
Greenwood, John	Pvt.	100	Dec. 17, 1799	11,272
Gregory, John	Pvt.	100	June 11, 1790	11,247
Griffith, Charles	Pvt.	100	Dec. 22, 1794	11,285
Grinard, Paul	Pvt.	100	June 7, 1798	11,270
Groves, Isaac	Pvt.	100	Jan. 8, 1796	11,248
Groves, William	Pvt.	100	Apr. 17, 1792	11,253
Grunby, John	Col.	500	—	851
Gwinn, John	Pvt.	100	July 14, 1795	11,262
Gwynn, John*	Pvt.	100	Mar. 28, 1829	1,494
Haden, John	Pvt.	100	July 8, 1796	11,335
Hader, Nehemiah	Pvt.	100	Feb. 1, 1790	11,327
Hagerty, George	Pvt.	100	Nov. 29, 1790	11,365
Halinsdoff, William*	Pvt.	100	—	599
Hall, John	Pvt.	100	Jan. 21, 1795	11,305

Hall, Joseph	Pvt.	100	June	8, 1797	11,292
Hall, Josiah	Col.	500		———	1,044
Hall, Richard	Pvt.	100	Jan.	25, 1832	1,801
Hamilton, Edward	Lieut.	200		———	1,054
Hamilton, George	Pvt.	100	July	18, 1793	11,318
Hamilton, George	Capt.	300		———	1,046
Hamilton, John	Pvt.	100	Mar.	2, 1830	1,613
Hamilton, John*	Capt.	300	May	25, 1789	1,047
Hamilton, John	Lieut.	200		———	1,058
Hamilton, Samuel	Pvt.	100	Nov.	29, 1790	11,344
Hammond, James	Corpl.	100	Sept.	5, 1789	11,359
Hancock, Stephen	Pvt.	100	Oct.	5, 1792	11,332
Handy, George	Capt.	300		———	1,061
Haney, Barney	Pvt.	100	Jan.	11, 1796	11,322
Haney, John	Pvt.	100	Jan.	8, 1796	11,297
Hannon, John	Pvt.	100	Aug.	8, 1797	11,300
Hanson, Samuel	Lieut.	200		———	1,050
Hanson, William	Lieut.	200		———	1,055
Harding, Thomas	Pvt.	100	Oct.	14, 1795	11,309
Hardman, Henry	Major	400		———	1,045
Harman, Edward	Pvt.	100	July	8, 1800	11,311
Harman, Lazarus	Pvt.	100	July	9, 1800	11,353
Harper, Nathan	Pvt.	100	June	13, 1794	11,314
Harper, Samuel	Pvt.	100	Jan.	11, 1796	11,299
Harper, William*	Pvt.	215		———	7,303
Harpham, Robert	Pvt.	100	Mar.	31, 1797	11,339
Harrell, John	Pvt.	100	May	19, 1828	1,316
Harrington, William*	Pvt.	100	Mar.	13, 1835	2,095
Harris, Arthur*	Lieut.	200		———	1,271
Harris, Benton	Pvt.	100	Dec.	22, 1794	11,362
Harris, Henry	Pvt.	100	May	12, 1797	11,364
Harrison, Elisha	Surgeon	300		———	965
Harrison, Thomas	Pvt.	100	Mar.	11, 1791	11,288
Hartman, Michael	Pvt.	100	Jan.	8, 1796	11,349
Harvey, Charles	Pvt.	100	Nov.	1, 1797	11,315
Haslip, Richard	Pvt.	100	Mar.	11, 1791	11,296
Hawke, Michael	Pvt.	100	Feb.	7, 1790	11,354
Hawkins, Henry	Lieut.	200		———	1,057
Hawson, Thomas	Pvt.	100	Jan.	11, 1796	11,291
Hayne, Ezekiel*	Major	400		———	743

Head, John*	Pvt.	100	Oct. 10, 1829	1,384
Head, John	Pvt.	100	July 9, 1800	11,296
Hedge, William	Pvt.	100	June 8, 1797	11,348
Heffner, Jacob*	Pvt.	215	————	67,701
Henwood, Robert	Pvt.	100	————	674
Hewitt, James*	Pvt.	100	Oct. 3, 1835	2,125
Hickens, John	Pvt.	100	Feb. 7, 1790	11,295
Hicks, William	Pvt.	100	Nov. 29, 1790	11,342
Hide, John	Pvt.	100	July 31, 1797	11,319
Higgs, Henry	Pvt.	100	Feb. 1, 1790	11,355
Hillary, Ashburn*	Pvt.	215	————	26,633
Hillary, Rignal*	Lieut.	200	————	1,659
Hillman, William	Pvt.	100	Aug. 27, 1789	11,323
Hogan, Roger	Pvt.	100	Nov. 1, 1797	11,306
Holden, Kemp*	Pvt.	100	Dec. 6, 1839	2,268
Holder, John	Pvt.	100	Feb. 7, 1790	11,336
Holland, Edward*	Mus.	100	Sept. 5, 1789	11,287
Holland, Isaac*	Mus.	100	Feb. 7, 1790	11,289
Holliday, John	Pvt.	100	Nov. 26, 1792	11,369
Holt, Leonard	Pvt.	100	Feb. 7, 1790	11,328
Homes, James	Pvt.	100	Mar. 27, 1794	11,347
Hoops, Adam*	Capt.	300	————	350
Hope, Ralph	Pvt.	100	Jan. 25, 1796	11,345
Hope, William	Pvt.	100	Feb. 1, 1790	11,346
Hopkins, Francis	Pvt.	100	Mar. 11, 1791	11,304
Horney, William	Pvt.	100	Mar. 24, 1797	11,302
Horrell, John*	Pvt.	100	————	1,316
Houseman, Thomas	Pvt.	100	Dec. 28, 1791	11,333
Housley, John	Pvt.	100	Oct. 14, 1793	11,307
Howard, John E.	Col.	500	————	1,043
Hugo, Thomas*	Capt.	300	————	1,049
Hulet, John	Pvt.	100	Apr. 14, 1794	11,313
Hull, John	Pvt.	100	Jan. 8, 1796	11,303
Hunt, James	Pvt.	100	May 4, 1797	11,350
Hurdle, Lawrence*	Pvt.	100	Feb. 1, 1790	11,361
Hutton, James*	Pvt.	100	Oct. 2, 1833	1,974
Hutton, William	Corpl.	100	Feb. 27, 1799	11,360
Ingles, William	Pvt.	100	May 1, 1790	11,381
Ireland, John	Pvt.	100	Feb. 7, 1790	11,403
Irons, John	Pvt.	100	Mar. 11, 1791	11,407

Jackson, James	Pvt.	100	Feb. 7, 1790	11,376
Jackson, John	Pvt.	100	Mar. 11, 1791	11,384
Jackson, Peter*	Pvt.	100	Dec. 17, 1832	1,900
Jackson, William*	—	—	—	—
Jacobs, Henry*	Pvt.	100	Oct. 3, 1835	2,124
Jacobs, Jesse	Pvt.	100	July 22, 1797	11,396
Jameson, Adam	Lieut.	200	May 25, 1789	1,162
Jameson, Adams	Pvt.	100	Oct. 14, 1795	11,389
Jarvins, Daniel	Pvt.	100	Feb. 1, 1790	11,387
Jenifer, Daniel*	Surgeon	—	—	—
Jenkins, Joseph	Pvt.	100	Oct. 14, 1795	11,383
Jenkins, William	Pvt.	100	Dec. 28, 1791	11,390
Jennings, George	Pvt.	100	Dec. 18, 1794	11,399
Johnson, Archibald*	Pvt.	100	Oct. 15, 1828	1,388
Johnson, Benedict	Pvt.	100	Feb. 1, 1790	11,404
Johnson, Benjamin	Pvt.	100	Mar. 11, 1791	11,378
Johnson, Francis*	Pvt.	100	Apr. 27, 1807	346
Johnson, Joseph	Pvt.	100	Feb. 28, 1795	11,377
Johnson, Joseph*	Pvt.	215	—	36,520
Jones, Aaron	Pvt.	100	Feb. 1, 1790	11,391
Jones, Charles	Pvt.	100	Feb. 1, 1790	11,388
Jones, Cotter	Pvt.	100	Mar. 13, 1839	2,250
Jones, James*	Pvt.	100	Nov. 5, 1832	1,894
Jones, John	Pvt.	100	Nov. 29, 1790	11,380
Jones, John*	Capt.	300	Feb. 26, 1794	1,161
Jones, Joseph	Pvt.	100	Dec. 18, 1794	11,395
Jones, Nelsey	Pvt.	100	Jan. 18, 1793	11,379
Jones, Philip*	Pvt.	100	Oct. 12, 1804	165
Jones, Thomas	Pvt.	100	Jan. 21, 1792	11,400
Jones, Thomas	Pvt.	100	Nov. 29, 1790	11,375
Jones, Thomas	Pvt.	100	June 2, 1794	11,374
Jones, William	Pvt.	100	Apr. 14, 1795	14,117
Jones, William	Pvt.	100	Feb. 3, 1792	11,397
Jones, William*	Pvt.	215	—	13,899
Jones, William	Pvt.	100	Sept. 24, 1792	11,372
Jordan, John*	Coronet	150	May 27, 1829	1,510
Joyce, William	Pvt.	100	Jan. 8, 1796	11,392
Kean, Edward*	Pvt.	100	Jan. 31, 1806	225
Kearns, Thomas	Pvt.	100	May 8, 1792	11,413
Keeland, James	Pvt.	100	Jan. 11, 1796	11,410

Keen, Michael	Pvt.	100	Jan. 11, 1796	11,430
Keene, Samuel	Surgeon	300	Sept. 5, 1805	213
Keever, John*	Pvt.	215	——	61,232
Kellow, William*	Sergt.	100	Apr. 24, 1832	1,934
Kelley, David	Pvt.	100	Mar. 22, 1797	11,409
Kelly, James	Pvt.	100	Feb. 1, 1790	11,414
Kelley, Matthew	Pvt.	100	Dec. 23, 1795	11,412
Kelson, George	Pvt.	100	Feb. 1, 1790	11,427
Kennard, John	Pvt.	100	——	464
Kennedy, Thomas*	Pvt.	100	Nov. 6, 1806	294
Kent, Isaac	Pvt.	100	Aug. 4, 1789	11,425
Kephart, Adam	Pvt.	100	Nov. 13, 1840	——
Kerrick, Benjamin	Fifer	100	Sept. 25, 1789	11,429
Kersey, Edward	Pvt.	100	Dec. 13, 1795	11,420
Kettle, Daniel	Pvt.	100	Apr. 19, 1793	11,426
Keys, William	Pvt.	100	Jan. 30, 1792	11,417
Kibler, John*	Pvt.	215	——	30,753
Kidd, John	Pvt.	100	Aug. 3, 1797	11,416
Killegan, James	Pvt.	100	Dec. 22, 1794	11,431
Kilty, John	Capt.	300	Apr. 21, 1796	1,212
Kilty, William	Surgeon	400	Dec. 21, 1792	127
King, George*	Pvt.	215	——	38,515
King, John	Pvt.	100	Apr. 28, 1791	11,423
King, Thomas	Pvt.	100	Sept. 12, 1792	11,411
King, William	Pvt.	100	May 4, 1797	11,418
Kinnard, John	Pvt.	100	June 19, 1809	464
Knight, Jacob	Pvt.	100	Jan. 8, 1796	11,415
Knott, James	Pvt.	100	Feb. 1, 1790	11,419
Knox, John	Pvt.	100	Apr. 6, 1797	11,424
Landis, Roger	Pvt.	100	Mar. 21, 1792	11,432
Lang, Francis*	Pvt.	100	Mar. 11, 1791	11,433
Lansdale, Thomas	Major	400	——	1,227
Lappin, Paul	Pvt.	100	Jan. 8, 1796	11,434
Larkins, William	Pvt.	100	Jan. 8, 1796	11,453
Lawrence, William	Pvt.	100	Sept. 25, 1833	100
Lawrentz, Wendel	Pvt.	215	——	78,517
Laws, Henry	Pvt.	100	Oct. 23, 1828	——
Laws, William	Pvt.	100	Sept. 24, 1799	11,451
Laymore, Thomas	Pvt.	100	Feb. 1, 1790	11,449
Lee, Dudley*	Pvt.	100	May 8, 1850	2,445

Lee, John*	Pvt.	100	June 3, 1795		11,459
Lee, William	Pvt.	100	Dec. 22, 1794		11,446
Lee, William*	Pvt.	100	———		2,450
Leester, Joshua	Pvt.	100	Sept. 5, 1789		11,436
Legg, Edward	Pvt.	100	June 11, 1790		11,469
Lemon, Jacob*	Pvt.	215	———		26,990
Levi, Alexander	Pvt.	100	Nov. 29, 1790		11,460
Lewis, Jonathan	Pvt.	100	Feb. 7, 1790		11,443
Lewis, Richard	Pvt.	100	July 31, 1797		11,468
Lingan, James	Capt.	300	Mar. 19, 1792		1,294
Linton, George	Pvt.	100	Jan. 8, 1796		11,462
Livingston, Robert	Pvt.	100	Sept. 6, 1792		11,437
Lloyd, Michael	Pvt.	100	Feb. 1, 1790		11,455
Loar, Henry*	Pvt.	100	———		1,393
Loffman, Benjamin	Pvt.	100	Jan. 8, 1796		11,456
Logue, William*	Pvt.	215	———		26,057
Loller, Michael	Pvt.	100	Dec. 23, 1793		11,439
Long, John	Pvt.	100	July 17, 1797		11,445
Lord, Levin	Pvt.	100	July 9, 1799		11,438
Love, Charles	Pvt.	100	Apr. 18, 1797		11,435
Love, David	Pvt.	100	May 4, 1797		11,440
Love, John	Pvt.	100	July 18, 1794		11,458
Lowe, Basil*	Pvt.	100	———		2,252
Lowe, Dennis	Pvt.	100	———		2,253
Low, Henry*	Pvt.	215	———		8,454
Lowe, John*	Lieut.	200	Feb. 28, 1795		1,297
Lucas, John	Pvt.	100	Dec. 23, 1795		11,457
Luckett, David*	Lieut.	200	———		1,086
Luckett, Thomas*	Major	400	Apr. 8, 1816		653
Lynch, John	Major	400	———		1,292
Lynch, John	Pvt.	100	Jan. 13, 1792		11,441
Lynch, William	Pvt.	100	May 1, 1797		11,465
Lynn, John	Lieut.	200	———		1,298
McAway, Christopher*	Pvt.	100	Oct. 12, 1804		162
McCann, John	Pvt.	100	Dec. 18, 1794		11,522
McCann, Michael	Pvt.	100	Feb. 1, 1790		11,482
McCay, John	Pvt.	100	Aug. 14, 1797		11,516
McCollon, Daniel	Pvt.	100	Jan. 11, 1796		11,537
McCoy, John	Lieut.	200	Aug. 4, 1789		1,491

McDonald, James	Pvt.	100	Dec. 23, 1795	11,529
McDowell, Hugh	Pvt.	100	July 9, 1794	11,549
McDowell, John*	Pvt.	215	————	38,052
McDowell, Thomas	Pvt.	100	Sept. 26, 1792	11,539
McFadon, James*	Lieut.	200	————	1,079
McGhee, William	Pvt.	100	Sept. 4, 1828	1,355
McGlochlin, William	Pvt.	100	Sept. 24, 1789	11,488
McGuire, Peter	Pvt.	100	Nov. 1, 1797	11,526
McHenry, James	Major	400	————	1,480
McKinley, William	Pvt.	100	Dec. 24, 1794	11,555
McKinsey, Jesse*	Pvt.	100	Apr. 8, 1796	11,512
McKinsey, Joshua	Pvt.	100	Jan. 15, 1793	11,513
McKinsey, Moses	Pvt.	100	Apr. 8, 1796	11,514
McKnight, John	Pvt.	100	Jan. 28, 1795	11,477
McLane, Enock*	Pvt.	100	Sept. 30, 1833	1,970
McMillan, Samuel*	Pvt.	215	————	26,849
McMullen, Hugh	Sergt.	100	Feb. 7, 1790	11,501
McNamara, Darby	Pvt.	100	Sept. 5, 1789	11,498
McNelley, John	Pvt.	100	Dec. 18, 1794	11,527
McPherson, Samuel	Capt.	300	————	1,481
Maddin, William	Pvt.	100	Jan. 11, 1796	11,538
Magraw, Christopher	Drum.	100	Feb. 1, 1790	11,475
Malone, William	Pvt.	100	July 14, 1795	11,556
Manley, John*	Pvt.	100	Dec. 21, 1799	13,525
Manley, William	Pvt.	100	Sept. 24, 1792	11,505
Mann, Daniel	Pvt.	100	Mar. 11, 1791	11,503
Mann, William	Pvt.	100	July 17, 1792	11,481
Mansfield, Henry	Pvt.	100	Dec. 23, 1795	11,530
Mansfield, William*	Pvt.	215	————	88,030
Mantle, George	Pvt.	100	Aug. 8, 1794	11,495
Marbury, Joseph	Capt.	300	Mar. 10, 1790	1,486
Maret, Charles	Pvt.	100	May 11, 1790	11,546
Marsh, Benjamin	Pvt.	100	Feb. 1, 1790	11,474
Marterson, Philip	Pvt.	100	Mar. 11, 1791	11,584
Martin, John*	Pvt.	100	May 2, 1831	1,736
Mason, Caleb	Ensign	150	May 8, 1790	1,494
Mason, Isacher	Pvt.	100	May 8, 1790	11,491
Mason, James	Pvt.	100	May 11, 1790	11,472
Mason, Thomas	Capt.	300	May 24, 1792	1,482
Matterson, Philip	Pvt.	100	Mar. 11, 1791	11,548

Matthews, William	Pvt.	100	Jan. 25, 1790	11,487
Maxwell, James	Pvt.	100	Dec. 13, 1792	11,523
Maxwell, John	Pvt.	100	Feb. 1, 1790	11,519
Mead, James*	Pvt.	100	Jan. 23, 1849	2,434
Meakins, Bennett*	Pvt.	100	May 16, 1838	2,210
Mee, Thomas*	Pvt.	100	Oct. 12, 1804	164
Melvin, Alard	Pvt.	100	Nov. 29, 1790	11,531
Melvin, Peter	Pvt.	100	July 26, 1797	11,532
Milburn, Nicholas	Corpl.	100	Oct. 20, 1789	11,478
Miles, Thomas	Pvt.	100	May 1, 1795	14,119
Miles, Thomas	Pvt.	100	May 1, 1795	11,484
Millford, Jacob	Pvt.	100	Jan. 8, 179–	11,483
Milstead, John	Pvt.	100	Mar. 11, 1791	11,551
Mitchell, Aaron	Pvt.	100	Mar. 11, 1791	11,502
Mitchell, Isaac*	Pvt.	100	May 27, 1839	2,257
Mitchell, Isaac	Pvt.	100	Feb. 11, 1800	11,550
Mitchell, John	Capt.	300	Sept. 25, 1789	1,484
Mitchell, Richard	Pvt.	100	Mar. 11, 1791	11,520
Mitchell, William	Pvt.	100	Feb. 11, 1794	14,063
Modlar, Boston	Pvt.	100	May 12, 1800	11,494
Molohon, Patrick	Pvt.	100	Nov. 29, 1790	11,536
Moore, James	Pvt.	100	June 11, 1790	11,544
Moore, John	Pvt.	100	Feb. 1, 1790	11,493
Moore, John	Pvt.	100	Mar. 16, 1793	11,518
Moore, John	Sergt.	100	Feb. 1, 1790	11,493
Moore, Matthew	Pvt.	100	Feb. 7, 1790	11,489
Moore, William	Pvt.	100	May 11, 1790	11,496
Moore, William	Pvt.	100	Nov. 29, 1790	11,506
Moore, Zachariah	Sergt.	100	July 6, 1810	517
Moore, Zedekiah	Ensign	150	———	1,493
Morgan, David*	Lieut.	200	———	1,191
Morgan, John	Pvt.	100	Jan. 24, 1794	11,542
Morris, Jonathan	Capt.	300	Dec. 11, 1795	1,483
Morris, Neal	Pvt.	100	May 1, 1797	11,528
Mosier, Francis*	Pvt.	215	———	57,649
Muir, Francis*	Capt.	300	———	237
Murphy, Christopher	Pvt.	100	Nov. 29, 1790	11,521
Murphy, Daniel	Pvt.	100	Mar. 24, 1797	11,497
Murphy, Hezekiah*	Pvt.	215	———	26,974
Murphy, James*	Pvt.	100	Dec. 23, 1803	105

Murphy, Thomas	Pvt.	100	Feb. 7, 1790	11,486
Murray, James*	Pvt.	100	Sept. 26, 1843	2,324
Muse, Walker	Capt.	300	Dec. 31, 1789	1,485
Myers, Lawrence*	Lieut.	200	————	1,096
Myers, Christian	Capt.	300	May 25, 1789	1,487
Nabb, Joseph	Pvt.	100	Sept. 13, 1799	11,563
Nailer, William	Pvt.	100	Jan. 8, 1796	11,562
Neagle, Morris	Pvt.	100	Dec. 22, 1794	11,564
Neil, Daniel	Pvt.	100	Mar. 11, 1791	11,571
Nelson, John	Lieut.	200	Jan. 31, 1795	1,592
Nelson, John	Pvt.	100	Dec. 18, 1794	11,568
Nelson, Roger*	Lieut.	200	Dec. 23, 1799	1,600
Nevitt, John*	Pvt.	100	Apr. 10, 1822	1,035
Newman, Thomas	Pvt.	100	Jan. 8, 1796	11,558
Newton, William	Pvt.	100	June 11, 1790	11,559
Niblet, William*	Pvt.	100	Jan. 10, 1789	11,566
Nicholson, Henry	Pvt.	100	Feb. 7, 1790	11,561
Nicholson, John	Pvt.	100	Nov. 29, 1790	11,569
Nicholson, John*	Pvt.	100	July 31, 1845	2,362
Norman, Basil*	Pvt.	100	Jan. 11, 1796	11,565
Norris, Jacob*	Lieut.	200	Feb. 19, 1827	1,236
Nowell, James*	Pvt.	100	Aug. 8, 1815	643
O'Brian, Daniel*	Pvt.	215	————	8,377
O'Brian, Philip	Pvt.	100	Feb. 28, 1791	11,582
Oldham, Edward*	Capt.	300	Feb. 19, 1825	1,110
Onions, John	Pvt.	100	Aug. 27, 1792	11,578
O'Quinn, Daniel	Pvt.	100	Nov. 29, 1790	11,581
Ormes, Charles	Pvt.	100	Apr. 8, 1820	896
Osborn, John	Pvt.	100	June 11, 1795	11,784
Osburn, John	Pvt.	100	June 11, 1795	11,576
Osten, Henry	Pvt.	100	Nov. 29, 1790	11,581
Outhouse, Peter*	Pvt.	100	Dec. 23, 1795	11,573
Owens, Joseph*	Pvt.	100	————	9
Overcreek, Joseph	Pvt.	100	Jan. 8, 1796	11,574
Owens, Stephen*	Pvt.	215	————	————
Owens, Stephen	Pvt.	100	Oct. 6, 1794	11,575
Painter, Henry*	Pvt.	215	————	6,024
Palmer, George*	Pvt.	100	July 20, 1831	1,755
Parkinson, John*	Pvt.	100	Oct. 31, 1831	1,782
Patterson, Thomas*	Pvt.	100	Mar. 17, 1828	1,276

Name	Rank	Acres	Date	Warrant
Peacock, Neal	Pvt.	100	Feb. 7, 1790	11,601
Pearce, Aquilla*	Mus.	100	———	1,919
Pearce, George*	Pvt.	100	———	1,176
Pearce, Joshua	Pvt.	100	Feb. 7, 1790	11,594
Peeker, William	Pvt.	100	Nov. 13, 1797	11,589
Pender, Thomas*	Pvt.	100	July 20, 1831	1,753
Pendergast, William*	Capt.	300	———	1,128
Penefill, Thomas*	Pvt.	215	———	29,741
Pennifield, Thomas*	Pvt.	100	Mar. 11, 1791	11,600
Penny, John	Pvt.	100	Sept. 26, 1791	11,593
Pepper, Elijah	Pvt.	100	Sept. 13, 1799	11,588
Perry, Thomas	Pvt.	100	Mar. 11, 1791	11,612
Perry, Thomas*	Pvt.	215	———	———
Peters, William	Pvt.	100	Aug. 8, 1794	11,596
Petit, Thomas	Pvt.	100	Jan. 25, 1796	1,619
Pherson, William	Pvt.	100	Mar. 22, 1797	11,609
Philips, Lambert	Pvt.	100	Nov. 29, 1790	11,611
Pierce, Aquilla	Mus.	100	Mar. 1, 1833	1,919
Pierce, George	Pvt.	100	Apr. 22, 1820	11,176
Pilkerton, Michael	Pvt.	100	Jan. 8, 1796	11,608
Pindell, Richard*	Surgeon	300	Sept. 25, 1789	1,730
Pippin, Robert*	Pvt.	215	———	26,926
Pocktor, Thomas	Pvt.	100	Jan. 11, 1796	11,615
Pool, James	Pvt.	100	Nov. 29, 1790	11,610
Porter, Thomas	Pvt.	100	Nov. 29, 1790	11,613
Portter, William	Pvt.	100	Mar. 21, 1794	11,590
Potterf, Casper*	Pvt.	215	———	49,468
Powell, William	Pvt.	100	May 12, 1797	11,607
Preston, Stephen	Pvt.	100	Feb. 1, 1790	11,586
Price, Benjamin*	Capt.	300	———	341
Price, Stephen*	Pvt.	100	———	451
Price, Thomas	Lieut.	200	Mar. 21, 1792	1,732
Prout, John	Pvt.	100	Dec. 12, 1792	11,618
Purcell, William	Pvt.	100	Aug. 15, 1795	11,598
Purchase, William	Pvt.	100	Feb. 7, 1790	11,595
Purdy, Joseph	Pvt.	100	Nov. 9, 1792	11,592
Purtle, Robert*	Pvt.	215	———	38,340
Quick, John	Pvt.	100	Dec. 18, 1794	11,624
Quinton, William	Pvt.	100	Jan. 8, 1796	11,623
Raisin, William	Lieut.	200	Oct. 4, 1800	1,844

Ramble, Samuel	Pvt.	100	Jan. 30, 1795	11,637
Ramsey, Henry	Pvt.	100	May 11, 1790	11,629
Ramsey, Nathaniel	Col.	500	Feb. 11, 1791	1,836
Randall, Thomas	Pvt.	100	July 26, 1797	11,667
Rawdon, Daniel	Pvt.	100	June 11, 1790	11,665
Rawlings, Aaron	Pvt.	100	Mar. 11, 1791	11,626
Rawlings, Isaac*	Lieut.	200	———	1,130
Rawlings, William*	Pvt.	100	July 15, 1848	2,429
Raybold, Jacob	Lieut.	200	July 9, 1789	1,845
Redding, Henry	Pvt.	100	Feb. 7, 1790	11,652
Redman, Elisha	Pvt.	100	Mar. 22, 1797	11,663
Redmond, Michael	Pvt.	100	Feb. 7, 1790	11,669
Reed, Philip	Capt.	300	Mar. 31, 1791	1,840
Reese, Henry	Pvt.	100	Jan. 8, 1796	11,632
Reilly, Patrick	Pvt.	100	Sept. 20, 1799	11,649
Reilly, William*	Lieut.	200	July 18, 1789	1,839
Reveley, Francis*	Capt.	300	———	261
Reynolds, James	Pvt.	100	Feb. 1, 1790	11,647
Reynolds, Thomas	Pvt.	100	Aug. 14, 1794	14,134
Rhoades, Nicholas*	Pvt.	100	———	1,169
Richards, Paul	Pvt.	100	Jan. 4, 1796	11,633
Richardson, John*	Pvt.	100	———	1,574
Richardson, Samuel*	Pvt.	100	Aug. 31, 1831	1,764
Richardson, Thomas*	Pvt.	215	———	1,972
Richardson, Thomas	Pvt.	100	Dec. 18, 1794	11,635
Richardson, Thomas	Pvt.	100	Mar. 14, 1793	11,658
Richmond, Christopher	Capt.	300	Sept. 1, 1789	1,841
Ricketts, Nicholas*	Lieut.	200	———	1,124
Rigby, William*	Pvt.	215	———	5,438
Rigdon, James*	Pvt.	215	———	26,913
Riggs, George	Pvt.	100	Jan. 21, 1795	11,668
Riggs, Jacob	Pvt.	100	Jan. 30, 1795	12,503
Riggs, John	Pvt.	100	Feb. 1, 1790	11,627
Riley, Bennet*	Pvt.	100	Oct. 30, 1838	2,236
Riley, Patrick	Pvt.	100	Mar. 11, 1791	11,636
Rivers, Richard	Pvt.	100	Jan. 11, 1796	11,651
Roach, John	Pvt.	100	Dec. 23, 1795	11,644
Roberts, Archibald*	Pvt.	215	———	11,395

Roberts, Edward*	Pvt.	100	Jan. 28, 1833	1,911
Roberts, Joseph	Pvt.	100	May 4, 1797	11,653
Roberts, Patrick	Pvt.	215	———	18,018
Roberts, William	Pvt.	100	Feb. 1, 1790	11,628
Robins, John	Pvt.	100	June 11, 1790	11,638
Robinson, Charles	Pvt.	215	———	6,042
Robinson, William*	Pvt.	100	Dec. 6, 1828	1,424
Robinson, Zachariah*	Pvt.	100	Dec. 12, 1821	1,055
Rommill, John	Pvt.	100	Jan. 11, 1796	11,656
Rone, Paul	Pvt.	100	Feb. 7, 1790	11,645
Roney, Hugh	Pvt.	100	Apr. 26, 1792	11,659
Ross, Alexander	Pvt.	100	Nov. 29, 1790	11,654
Ross, Robinson	Pvt.	100	Sept. 13, 1799	11,648
Rourk, James	Pvt.	100	May 11, 1790	11,634
Rowan, Patrick	Pvt.	100	Dec. 23, 1795	11,642
Rowse, Thomas*	Lieut.	200	———	74
Roxburgh, Alexander	Major	400	June 10, 1789	1,837
Royse, Solomon*	Pvt.	215	———	26,476
Roystan, James	Corpl.	100	Sept. 5, 1789	11,661
Rudolph, Michael*	Capt.	300	———	945
Ryan, James*	Pvt.	100	Apr. 15, 1825	1,120
Ryan, John	Pvt.	100	Dec. 23, 1795	11,631
Saint Clair, William	Pvt.	100	Mar. 22, 1793	11,680
Salmon, John	Pvt.	100	Dec. 23, 1795	11,715
Sanders, George	Pvt.	100	Feb. 7, 1790	11,688
Satterfield, William*	Pvt.	100	May 1, 1795	14,121
Savoy, Philip*	Pvt.	100	Mar. 11, 1791	11,675
Sax, William	Pvt.	100	Jan. 11, 1796	11,676
Scholfield, Joseph*	Pvt.	215	———	31,785
Scoone, George*	Pvt.	100	June 19, 1809	463
Scott, Benjamin*	Pvt.	215	———	88,539
Scott, Charles	Pvt.	100	Nov. 16, 1796	11,692
Scott, James	Pvt.	100	July 17, 1797	11,742
Scott, John	Pvt.	100	Jan. 30, 1795	11,687
Scott, Levi	Pvt.	100	Mar. 11, 1791	11,782
Sears, John	Lieut.	200	June 19, 1789	2,049
Sellman, Jonathan	Major	400	Mar. 31, 1790	2,040

Name	Rank		Date	Ref
Sewall, Clement*	Ensign	150	Dec. 16, 1828	1,444
Sewall, James	Pvt.	100	Mar. 4, 1811	554
Sewell, Thomas*	Pvt.	215	———	84,056
Shanks, John*	Pvt.	100	Apr. 24, 1806	262
Sharpless, Robert	Pvt.	100	Feb. 1, 1790	11,729
Shephard, James	Pvt.	100	Feb. 1, 1790	11,693
Shipley, Henry*	Pvt.	215	———	38,579
Shorter, Rodger	Pvt.	100	Feb. 7, 1790	11,711
Shovell, John	Pvt.	100	Feb. 1, 1790	11,673
Shrink, Abdrew	Pvt.	100	Apr. 7, 1791	11,740
Shurley, Bennet*	Pvt.	100	Mar. 11, 1791	11,706
Sickle, Charles	Pvt.	100	Jan. 11, 1796	11,712
Sidney, Joseph	Pvt.	100	Nov. 29, 1790	11,726
Sikes, William	Pvt.	100	Jan. 11, 1796	11,174
Silvester, Job	Pvt.	100	Nov. 29, 1790	11,721
Silwood, William	Pvt.	100	Dec. 23, 1795	11,698
Sisland, William	Pvt.	100	Dec. 18, 1794	11,473
Skerrett, Clement	Lieut.	200	July 14, 1789	2,047
Slack, Henry*	Pvt.	100	July 16, 1822	1,048
Slack, John	Pvt.	100	Mar. 31, 1797	11,732
Slade, Thomas	Pvt.	100	Jan. 13, 1792	11,716
Slaker, William	Pvt.	100	Dec. 29, 1791	11,735
Sloop, Joseph	Pvt.	100	Oct. 6, 1794	11,689
Smallwood, John	Pvt.	100	Feb. 1, 1790	11,713
Smallwood, William	Maj. Gen	1,100	Apr. 23, 1816	656
Smallwood, William	Pvt.	100	Aug. 14, 1797	11,701
Smith, Alexander	Surgeon	300	Feb. 9, 1790	2,052
Smith, Conrad	Pvt.	100	Jan. 22, 1847	2,408
Smith, Daniel*	Pvt.	100	Apr. 19, 1810	513
Smith, Edward*	Lieut.	200	———	1,180
Smith, Elijah	Pvt.	100	Feb. 7, 1790	11,684
Smith, Jacob*	Pvt.	215	———	39,337
Smith, James	Capt.	300	———	2,046
Smith, James	Pvt.	100	July 8, 1797	11,674
Smith, James	Pvt.	100	Feb. 1, 1790	11,671
Smith, John	Capt.	300	Jan. 26, 1792	2,045
Smith, John	Pvt.	100	Nov. 29, 1790	11,707
Smith, John	Pvt.	100	Sept. 24, 1789	11,678
Smith, John	Pvt.	100	Feb. 7, 1790	11,699
Smith, John*	Pvt.	215	———	43,533

Smith, Joseph*	Coronet	150	May 28, 1789	2,126
Smith, Joseph	Capt.	300	June 19, 1789	2,041
Smith, Joseph	Capt.	300	———	2,043
Smith, Leonard	Pvt.	215	———	57,752
Smith, Michael	Pvt.	100	June 17, 1799	11,679
Smith, Michael	Pvt.	100	Mar. 18, 1795	11,694
Smith, Nathan*	Capt.	300	———	1,069
Smith, Robert	Pvt.	100	Nov. 29, 1790	11,736
Smith, Thomas	Pvt.	100	May 11, 1790	11,738
Smith, Thomas*	Pvt.	215	———	6,280
Smith, William*	Pvt.	100	Apr. 15, 1825	1,119
Smoot, William*	Lieut.	200	Mar. 24, 1827	1,234
Smyth, James	Pvt.	100	June 11, 1790	11,746
Somerville, James	Capt.	300	Feb. 14, 1797	2,044
Sowers, Michael*	Pvt.	100	Jan. 12, 1829	1,461
Spalding, Aaron*	Pvt.	100	Dec. 18, 1794	11,672
Spalding, George	Pvt.	215	———	14,970
Spencer, Humphrey	Pvt.	100	May 9, 1797	11,681
Spires, Richard*	Pvt.	100	Sept. 15, 1830	1,672
Spurrier, Edward	Capt.	300	May 13, 1795	2,042
Stafford, John*	Pvt.	215	———	50,888
Stallions, Abraham	Pvt.	100	May 29, 1795	11,719
Stanton, John	Pvt.	100	May 4, 1797	11,682
Start, Moses	Pvt.	100	Feb. 24, 1795	1,411
Stevens, William*	Lieut.	200	May 19, 1797	2,076
Stevenson, Alexander	Pvt.	100	May 11, 1790	11,717
Stewart, Benjamin	Pvt.	100	Dec. 18, 1794	11,724
Stewart, Charles	Pvt.	100	Apr. 12, 1809	457
Stewart, William	Pvt.	100	Apr. 11, 1797	11,725
Stirling, William	Pvt.	100	Nov. 29, 1790	11,723
Stoddard, William	Lieut.	200	Sept. 25, 1798	200
Stokes, Thomas	Pvt.	100	July 9, 1799	11,747
Stoope, Andrew*	Pvt.	215	———	11,186
Streets, Robert	Pvt.	100	Feb. 1, 1790	11,708
Stringer, Fortunatius	Pvt.	100	Feb. 24, 1795	11,690
Suit, Jesse	Sergt.	100	Sept. 5, 1789	11,695
Sullinger, Daniel	Pvt.	100	Dec. 18, 1794	11,728
Sullivan, Elijah	Pvt.	100	Jan. 11, 1790	11,685
Sullivan, Perry*	Pvt.	100	Aug. 16, 1834	2,058
Sullivan, Philip	Pvt.	100	June 11, 1790	11,745

Sullivan, William*	Pvt.	100	Sept. 24, 1792	11,683
Summers, Hezekiah*	Pvt.	215	———	34,588
Summers, John	Pvt.	100	Nov. 29, 1790	11,718
Summers, Solomon	Pvt.	100	Feb. 7, 1790	11,696
Sutherland, Walter*	Pvt.	215	———	24,998
Swan, John	Major	400	May 11, 1792	2,058
Swanton, Peter	Pvt.	100	Feb. 24, 1795	11,691
Sweeney, Owen	Pvt.	100	Feb. 24, 1795	14,103
Tannehill, Adamson	Capt.	300	June 9, 1789	2,209
Tannehill, Josiah*	Lieut.	200	June 9, 1789	2,219
Tasker, Richard*	Pvt.	100	Feb. 23, 1825	1,113
Taylor, John	Pvt.	100	Aug. 8, 1794	11,776
Taylor, John	Pvt.	100	Oct. 6, 1794	11,767
Taylor, Robert	Pvt.	100	Aug. 8, 1799	11,755
Taylor, Robert	Pvt.	100	Feb. 1, 1790	11,771
Taylor, William	Pvt.	100	July 22, 1797	11,760
Taylor, William	Pvt.	200	Sept. 5, 1789	11,761
Ternan, Dennis	Pvt.	100	Feb. 1, 1790	11,781
Thomas, James*	Pvt.	100	Dec. 6, 1829	1,433
Thomas, John	Pvt.	100	Nov. 29, 1796	11,768
Thomas, John	Pvt.	100	Jan. 21, 1795	11,766
Thomas, Thomas	Pvt.	100	Jan. 11, 1796	11,758
Thompson, Corns	Pvt.	100	May 11, 1790	11,754
Thompson, Jesse*	Sergt.	100	Feb. 1, 1790	11,779
Thompson, John	Pvt.	100	Oct. 8, 1833	1,975
Tilghman, Tench*	Lieut.-Col.	450	———	1,158
Tillard, Edward	Lieut.-Col.	450	Mar. 4, 1800	2,207
Tippet, Notley	Pvt.	100	Feb. 1, 1790	11,770
Topping, Peter*	Pvt.	100	June 26, 1851	2,456
Townley, Henry	Pvt.	100	Jan. 11, 1796	11,757
Towson, William	Lieut.	200	May 25, 1789	2,210
Trout, Christian*	Pvt.	215	———	35,685
Truman, Alexander*	Capt.	300	———	2,156
Trux, John*	Pvt.	215	———	53,666
Tumbleston, Evan	Pvt.	100	Dec. 22, 1794	11,775
Turner, Richard	Pvt.	100	May 1, 1795	14,120
Twiner, John	Pvt.	100	June 11, 1790	11,765
Twiner, John*	Pvt.	100	Jan. 8, 1796	11,764
Uselton, George*	Pvt.	215	———	26,220
Vallow, John	Pvt.	100	June 11, 1795	11,787

Van Buskirk, Peter*	Pvt.	215	—		33,751
Vaughan, John	Sergt.	100	Sept.	5, 1789	11,788
Vigal, Adam*	Pvt.	215	—		533
Wade, Edward	Pvt.	100	Feb.	1, 1790	11,792
Walker, John	Pvt.	100	Feb.	1, 1790	11,791
Walker, John	Pvt.	100	Nov.	1, 1797	11,801
Walker, John	Pvt.	100	Feb.	24, 1795	14,101
Waltman, Michael*	Pvt.	100	Feb.	1, 1790	11,811
Ward, Hugh	Pvt.	100	Jan.	20, 1795	11,793
Ward, Joseph	Pvt.	100	Apr.	6, 1797	11,805
Ware, Francis M.	Lieut.	200	Sept.	21, 1789	2,410
Ware, Hugh	Pvt.	100	May	1, 1797	11,838
Warfield, Walter	Surgeon	400	Mar.	27, 1795	2,405
Warier, Daniel	Pvt.	100	Dec.	18, 1794	11,803
Waring, Basil*	Lieut.	200	—		1,020
Waters, James*	Pvt.	100	Jan.	30, 1795	11,794
Watson, Thomas	Pvt.	100	Jan.	21, 1792	11,810
Watts, William*	Capt.	300	—		2,368
Weaver, Anthony	Pvt.	100	Jan.	8, 1796	11,821
Webb, John*	Pvt.	215	—		530
Webster, Thomas*	Pvt.	100	June	8, 1837	2,180
Wedgbar, William	Pvt.	100	Jan.	30, 1795	11,797
Wedge, Samuel	Pvt.	100	Nov.	29, 1790	11,833
Weise, Adam*	Pvt.	215	—		26,454
Welch, John	Pvt.	100	May	4, 1797	11,823
Welch, John	Pvt.	100	Oct.	10, 1797	11,829
Wells, John	Pvt.	100	Jan.	12, 1792	11,843
West, John	Pvt.	100	July	31, 1789	11,826
Weston, Thomas	Pvt.	100	Jan.	8, 1796	11,847
White, James*	Pvt.	100	July	13, 1825	1,126
White, John*	Pvt.	100	Apr.	22, 1833	1,933
Wiley, John	Pvt.	100	Feb.	7, 1790	11,798
Wilkerson, John	Pvt.	100	Apr.	19, 1797	11,796
Wilkinson, James*	Pvt.	215	—		7,051
Williams, Benjamin	Pvt.	100	Dec.	23, 1834	2,083
Williams, Benjamin	Pvt.	100	Oct.	6, 1794	11,816
Williams, Charles	Pvt.	100	Jan.	30, 1794	11,848
Williams, Jeremiah*	Pvt.	100	May	9, 1820	875
Williams, John*	Pvt.	100	Sept.	5, 1828	1,363
Williams, John	Pvt.	100	May	11, 1790	11,827

Williams, Joseph*	Pvt.	100	May 3, 1832	1,841
Williams, Nathan*	Lieut.	200	————	1,666
Williams, Otho	Brig.-Gen.	850	May 25, 1789	2,401
Williams, Thomas	Pvt.	100	Dec. 24, 1794	11,847
Williams, William	Pvt.	100	Jan. 30, 1795	11,795
Willis, Daniel*	Pvt.	100	Aug. 7, 1849	2,440
Wills, John	Pvt.	100	————	————
Wilmore, John	Pvt.	100	Apr. 24, 1797	11,809
Wilmot, Robert	Lieut.	200	Jan. 28, 1800	2,415
Wilmot, William*	Capt.	300	————	281
Wilson, Barnaby	Pvt.	100	Mar. 11, 1791	11,819
Wilson, Barney*	Pvt.	100	Sept. 22, 1834	2,067
Wilson, David	Pvt.	100	Oct. 6, 1794	11,799
Wilson, James	Pvt.	100	Nov. 29, 1790	11,831
Wilson, John	Pvt.	100	Feb. 1, 1790	11,830
Wimber, Thomas*	Pvt.	100	Dec. 6, 1839	2,267
Winchester, James*	Capt.	300	Dec. 22, 1796	2,407
Winder, Levin	Lieut.-Col.	450	June 2, 1789	2,404
Windows, Henry	Pvt.	100	July 9, 1799	11,828
Wirey, Michael	Pvt.	100	Dec. 22, 1794	11,812
Wisham, John	Pvt.	100	Jan. 19, 1838	2,196
Wood, Aaron*	Pvt.	215	————	10,008
Wood, Gerard*	Surgeon	300	————	2,160
Wood, James	Pvt.	100	July 8, 1797	11,789
Wood, John*	Pvt.	215	————	9,525
Wood, John*	Pvt.	215	————	11,171
Wood, Joseph	Pvt.	100	Oct. 26, 1792	11,854
Wood, Robertson	Pvt.	100	Jan. 11, 1796	11,790
Wood, Thomas	Sergt.	100	Feb. 1, 1790	11,800
Woodham, Robert	Pvt.	100	Sept. 12, 1792	11,852
Woodland, Rhocke	Pvt.	100	Nov. 29, 1790	11,836
Woolford, Michael*	Pvt.	100	Feb. 1, 1816	648
Woolford, Thomas	Col.	500	Feb. 20, 1794	2,402
Worthington, Benjamin	Pvt.	100	Aug. 10, 1790	11,817
Wright, Absalom*	Pvt.	100	Dec. 18, 1794	11,808
Wright, Jesse	Pvt.	100	June 10, 1789	11,806
Wright, Nathan*	Lieut.	200	Feb. 21, 1827	1,220
Wright, Robert	Pvt.	100	Jan. 11, 1796	11,807
Wysham, John*	Pvt.	100	————	2,196

Yates, Benjamin*	Pvt.	214	——	3,134
Young, David	Pvt.	100	Mar. 11, 1791	11,858
Young, Isaac	Pvt.	100	June 8, 1797	11,856
Young, John	Pvt.	100	Dec. 22, 1794	11,855
Young, Samuel	Pvt.	100	June 11, 1793	11,857
Young, William*	Pvt.	215	——	26,901

Part III

List of Maryland soldiers (non-pensioners) established by affidavits and muster rolls found in pension applications. Owing to the fact that services of commissioned officers in the Army are easily proved, the list contains only privates and officers of the Naval or Sea Service.

NOTE: Proof and certification of services of the following men may be secured from the compiler.

Soldier	Establishment
Abbott, Samuel	Q. M., Sea Service
Abel, Henry	Pvt., Maryland Militia
Adams, Alexander	Pvt., Maryland Militia
Adams, George	———, Maryland Militia
Adams, James	Pvt., Flying Camp
Adams, John	Maryland Prisoner of War
Ake, John	Drummer, Maryland Militia
Aldrige, John	Maryland Service
Alfred, Thomas	Maryland Line
Allcock, Martin	Fourth Maryland Regt.
Allison, Luke	Maryland Militia
Ambrose, Malachah	Pvt., Maryland Militia
Anderson, Hugh	Maryland Service
Anderson, Jacob	Pvt., Maryland Service
Arnington, Frederick	Pvt., Maryland Militia
Arnold, John	Maryland Militia
Aulder, James	Maryland Service
Aulpaugh, Philip	Pvt., Flying Camp
Ayers, William	Sergt., Maryland Line
Bagford, William	Maryland Service
Bain, Henry	Maryland Militia
Baker, John	Pvt., Flying Camp
Baker, Joshua	Maryland Service
Baly, James	Pvt., Maryland Militia
Bandy, John	Maryland Service
Banks, James	4th Md. Regt.

Banning, Henry	Maryland Service
Barbers, Jeremiah	Maryland Militia
Barborough, Christian	Pvt., Maryland Militia
Barnes, James	Maryland Militia
Barnes, William	Lieut., Maryland Sea Service
Barnett, Thomas	Maryland Sea Service
Barnett, William	Flying Camp
Barrett, James	Maryland Militia
Baskers, Charles	Maryland Service
Baugh, Michael	Pvt., Flying Camp
Bayley, Josephus	Maryland Service
Bazil, Daniel	Fifer, Maryland Service
Bazill, John	Maryland Militia
Beall, Lloyd	Maryland Service
Beall, Thomas	Maryland Service
Beatty, Henry	Flying Camp
Beatty, William	Flying Camp
Becketh, Nicholas	Pvt., Flying Camp
Bedfield, Zadock	Lieut., Maryland Navy
Belcher, Benjamin	Maryland Service
Bell, Peter	Pvt., Flying Camp
Belt, James	Capt., Maryland Sea Service
Belt, John	Capt., Maryland Sea Service
Belt, Joshua	Cadet
Belt, Thomas	Maryland Service
Bennett, John	Pvt., Flying Camp
Bennett, Joseph	Maryland Militia
Bennett, Luke	Flying Camp
Benson, James	Maryland Service
Benson, Nicholas	Maryland Service
Beringer, Andrew	Maryland Militia
Berrick, Henry	Pvt., Flying Camp
Berry, William	Maryland Militia
Betton, John	Commissary
Beyley, James	Pvt., Flying Camp
Bidlow, William	Capt., Sea Service
Biggs, John	1st Md. Regt.
Biles, Charles	Maryland Service
Billican, Christopher	Maryland Militia
Binghey, William	Pvt., Maryland Line

Binnet, Patrick	Q. M., Continental Line
Biscoe, Mick	Maryland Militia
Black, George	Maryland Militia
Blackstone, John	Sergt., Maryland Line
Bochell, Joseph	Maryland Patriot
Bodfield, Zadock	Maryland Service
Bond, Thomas	Maryland Militia
Booth, Edwin	Maryland Service
Borland, John	Maryland Service
Bose, John	Maryland Militia
Bosman, Rezin	Maryland Line
Boucher, Richard	Maryland Service
Bough, John	Maryland Service
Bowen, Jehu	Maryland Service
Bowman, Jacob	Pvt., Flying Camp
Boyd, John	Maryland Service
Boyer, Abraham	Maryland Militia
Boyer, George	Pvt., Flying Camp
Boyer, Jacob	Pvt., Flying Camp
Boyer, Lambert	Pvt., Flying Camp
Boyes, Arthur	Maryland Militia
Bracken, James	Maryland Service
Bradford, William	Maryland Service
Brewer, Jacob	Maryland Militia
Brice, John	Corpl., Maryland Militia
Bright, Joseph	Maryland Service
Brooks, Ensaw	Maryland Militia
Brooks, John	Maryland Militia
Brooks, Johnson	Pvt., Maryland Militia
Brow, Lawrence	Prisoner of War
Brown, Alexander	Maryland Service
Brown, Jacob	Maryland Service
Brown, Peter	Sergt., Maryland Service
Brown, Richard	Pvt., Maryland Militia
Brown, Zebulon	4th Md. Regt.
Brunwell, George	Maryland Seaman
Buchanan, Andrew	Maryland Patriot
Buchanan, Daniel	Maryland Service
Buchanan, Patrick	Maryland Service
Buchanan, William	Maryland Independent Troop

Buck, George	Maryland Service
Bueher, Abraham	Pvt., Flying Camp
Bull, William	Maryland Service
Bunis, George	Pvt., Maryland Militia
Burns, James	Sergt., Maryland Service
Burns, John	Maryland Militia
Burton, Joseph	Recruiting Officer
Busey, Samuel	Pvt., Flying Camp
Butcher, James	Pvt., Maryland Militia
Butt, Jacob	Maryland Service
Caho, Roger	Flying Camp
Callinberger, Christopher	Pvt., Flying Camp
Campbell, James	Capt., Sea Service
Cannourine, James	Maryland Service
Capel, Abraham	Maryland Service
Carnant, Jacob	Pvt., Flying Camp
Carney, John	Maryland Service
Carrilo, Hamilton	Adj., Maryland Service
Carroll, Daniel	Independent Troop
Carroll, George	Maryland Service
Carsner, John	Maryland Militia
Carter, Ezekiel	Maryland Service
Case, Shadrick	Maryland Service
Cash, William	Flying Camp
Cato, George	Maryland Service
Caughron, Joseph	Maryland Militia
Chalmers, John	Maryland Service
Chambers, Daniel	Pvt., Maryland Line
Chambers, John	Sergt., Maryland Service
Chambers, John	Capt., Sea Service
Chandler, Williamson	Maryland Service
Chapman, Henry	Lieut., Continental Line
Chatley, William	Maryland Militia
Chenoweth, John	Maryland Militia
Chenoweth, Richard	Maryland Service
Cheseltine, William	Sergt., Maryland Militia
Chesley, Robert	Cadet
Chester, Lemuel	Sergt., Maryland Line
Chester, Leonard	Maryland Line
Chester, Samuel	Pvt., Maryland Line

Chitton, John	Maryland Militia
Cillen, John	Maryland Militia
Clapsaddle, Daniel	Maryland Militia
Clarke, Matthias	Maryland Militia
Clements, Benedict	Maryland Militia
Clements, John	Maryland Militia
Clemmons, Samuel	Gunner, Sea Service
Clendennin, John	Maryland Patriot
Clinginsmither, Daniel	Maryland Militia
Clinkscales, William	Maryland Militia
Clinton, Charles	Q. M., Maryland Service
Cocksin, Levin	Sergt., Maryland Service
Cole, Thomas	Sea Service
Colegate, Richard	Maryland Patriot
Coleman, Isaac	Maryland Service
Colston, Henry	Maryland Service
Comegys, Nathaniel	Maryland Militia
Conrad, John	Pvt., Flying Camp
Constable, Samuel	Maryland Line
Cook, James	Maryland Line
Coombs, Richard	Prisoner of War
Cooper, George	Maryland Militia
Copper, James	Pvt., Flying Camp
Corgel, Lawson	Maryland Service
Corgel, William	Maryland Service
Cosden, Jesse	Pvt., Maryland Militia
Cosden, John	Sergt., Maryland Militia
Coursey, Edward	Flying Camp
Covington, Benjamin	Maryland Service
Coxson, John	Maryland Service
Craig, William	Maryland Militia
Cramer, Michael	Pvt., Flying Camp
Crapell, Jacob	Pvt., Flying Camp
Critchell, Benjamin	Pvt., Maryland Line
Cromwell, Stephen	Maryland Patriot
Croysel, Jeremiah	Maryland Service
Cullumber, John	Maryland Service
Cuppenhavis, Thomas	Maryland Service
Curry, Robert	Maryland Service
Dade, Philip M.	Continental Line

Dale, Richard	Sea Service
Darby, Basil	Maryland Militia
Dark, William	Maryland Service
Davenport, Abraham	Maryland Service
Davenport, Arthur	Maryland Militia
David, John	Drummer, Militia
Davie, John	Capt., Sea Service
Davis, James	Maryland Service
Deals, John	Teamster, Maryland
De Long, Francis	Prisoner of War
Dempsey, Patrick	Maryland Service
Denning, George	Pvt., Maryland Militia
Denning, Jonas	Pvt., Maryland Militia
Denning, Nicholas	Pvt., Maryland Militia
Dennis, Henry	Maryland Patriot
Dennis, John	Maryland Patriot
Derrington, William	Pvt., Maryland Line
Derry, William	Capt., Sea Service
Deshaers, Henry	Maryland Service
Deshaers, Thomas	Maryland Service
Dewey, Peter	Maryland Service
Dickey, James	Maryland Service
Doctor, John	Pvt., Maryland Militia
Donovan, Richard	Adj., Flying Camp
Dorgin, John	Sea Service
Dorsey, Cornelius	Maryland Militia
Dowd, Charles	Flying Camp
Dowden, Michael	Maryland Service
Dowling, Thomas	Pvt., Maryland Militia
Drewett, William	Pvt., Maryland Line
Drury, Enoch	Pvt., Maryland Militia
Dugan, Henry	Maryland Service
Dugan, John	Corpl., Maryland Militia
Dunlap, John	Sea Service, 2d mate
Dunn, John	Fifer, Maryland Militia
Dunning, James	Pvt., Maryland Militia
Dunty, James	Pvt., Maryland Militia
Dusterberg, Henry	Maryland Service
Dutterer, John	Pvt., Flying Camp
Duval, Gabriel	Maryland Service

Duval, William	Maryland Service
Dvor (Duval), John	Maryland Service
Dyson, Aquila	Pvt., Maryland Militia
Eader, Samuel	Pvt., Flying Camp
Edelen, John	Pvt., Maryland Militia
Edmonson, George	Q. M., Maryland Line
Edwards, Stouton	Maryland Militia
Eichberger, Woolfgang	Maryland Service
Elgin, Harrison	Lieut., Maryland Militia
Elgin, William	Maryland Militia
Ely, David	Pvt., Flying Camp
Evans, Samuel	Maryland Line
Everett, Thomas	Maryland Service
Ewing, James	Cadet
Fardo, Absolom	Flying Camp, Maryland
Farr, Nicholas	Maryland Line
Faulkner, Abraham	Maryland Militia
Fennel, John	Maryland Line
Ferguson, Alexander	Maryland Service
Ferguson, John	Pvt., Maryland Militia
Fieldings, John	Maryland Service
Fields, Joseph	Maryland Militia
Findley, John	Maryland Militia
Fisher, Abraham	Flying Camp, Maryland
Fisher, Thomas	Maryland Militia
Flach, Philip	Pvt., Flying Camp
Fleming, Arthur	Adj., Maryland Militia
Fleming, William	Maryland Militia
Fletcher, John	Adj., Maryland Militia
Flint, Thomas	Sergt., Maryland Militia
Flowers, Lambert	Corpl., Maryland Militia
Foard, Thomas	Forage Master, Maryland
Ford, Edmund	Corpl., Maryland Militia
Ford, Horatio	Maryland Militia
Ford, John	Paymaster, Maryland
Ford, Mordecai	Maryland Militia
Ford, Thomas	Pvt., Maryland Line
Ford, Thomas	Sergt., Maryland Militia
Forwood, Jacob	Maryland Militia
Foster, John	Pvt., Flying Camp

Foster, John	Maryland Patriot
Foster, Joseph	Independent Troop
Frazier, Solomon	Capt., Maryland Sea Service
Freeman, Abraham	Pvt., Maryland Militia
Freeman, John	Q. M., Maryland Militia
Friend, Augustine	Capt., Maryland Militia
Frost, John	Pvt., Maryland Service
Gardiner, Richard	Maryland Service
Gardner, Elias	Maryland Service
Gaskin, David	Sea Service
Gentry, David	Maryland Service
Gerard, William	Maryland Service
Gesinger, John	Pvt., Flying Camp
Gibson, Jonathan	Maryland Militia
Gill, Stephen	Maryland Patriot
Gist, Joshua	Maryland Service
Godfrey, Barton	Maryland Militia
Goody, Lambert	Pvt., Maryland Line
Gordon, John	Sea Service
Gorman, Abraham	Lieut., Sea Service
Gosnell, Greenbury	Pvt., Maryland Militia
Gossage, Peter	Maryland Service
Gover, Ephraim	Maryland Service
Gover, Robert	Maryland Service
Gover, William	Maryland Service
Gow, William	Corpl., Maryland Line
Graham, Phil	Maryland Line
Grant, Francis	Maryland Service
Grant, John	Maryland Service
Graves, John	Maryland Service
Gray, John	Cadet
Gray, John	Sergt., Maryland Militia
Grayson, George	Sea Service
Grayson, Thomas	Capt., Sea Service
Green, Phil	Sea Service
Green, Richard	Pvt., Maryland Militia
Greenwall, Robert	Maryland Militia
Greenwood, Garner	Pvt., Flying Camp
Greenwood, John	Pvt., Maryland Militia
Griffith, Charles	Flying Camp

NON-PENSIONERS 93

Griffith, Charles	Maryland Militia
Griffith, James	Maryland Militia
Griffith, Nicholas	Maryland Militia
Grinold, Ignatius	Maryland Service
Grisson, Richard	Capt., Sea Service
Grisson, Thomas	Lieut., Sea Service
Grosse, Henry	Pvt., Flying Camp
Guess, Gideon	Drummer, Maryland Militia
Guest, Isaac	Q. M., Maryland Militia
Gwynn, William	Forage Master
Hackenson, Robert	Prisoner of War
Hackner, Daniel	Maryland Militia
Hadaway, Oakley	Maryland Service
Hale, David	Maryland Service
Hale, Nicholas	Ensign, Militia
Haley, John	Pvt., Maryland Militia
Hall, John	Sea Service
Hambleton, Thomas	Maryland Service
Hamilton, George	Maryland Militia
Hamilton, James	Recruiting Officer
Hammond, George	Independent Troop
Hammond, Thomas	Maryland Line
Handy, Joseph	Maryland Service
Hanson, John	Lieut., Sea Service
Hanson, Samuel	Prisoner of War
Hanson, William	Pvt., Flying Camp
Hardin, Edwin	Maryland Militia
Harding, Basil	Pvt., Flying Camp
Harding, Gary	Flying Camp
Harding, Reuben	Pvt., Maryland Militia
Hardington, Abel	Maryland Patriot
Hardman, John	Cadet
Harmon, John	Q. M., Maryland Militia
Harper, David	Maryland Line
Harris, Benjamin	Maryland Service
Harris, Robert	Independent Troop
Harris, Solomon	Maryland Service
Harrman, Jacob	Maryland Patriot
Harry, Martin	Sergt., Flying Camp
Hart, Anthony	Maryland Militia

Harvey, John	Pvt., Maryland Militia
Harvey, William	Maryland Patriot
Harwood, Thomas	Maryland Patriot
Hatton, Joshia	Maryland Service
Hatton, Thomas	Pvt., Maryland Militia
Hawk, George	Pvt., Flying Camp
Hayden, Benjamin	Maryland Service
Hays, Joseph	Maryland Militia
Heard, John	Maryland Service
Heathman, George	Maryland Militia
Heckentown, Martin	Pvt., Flying Camp
Hendrickson, John	Pvt., Flying Camp
Herring, Daniel	Pvt., Maryland Militia
Herring, Nathaniel	Pvt., Maryland Militia
Herrington, Bijah	Maryland Militia
Hester, Frederick	Pvt., Flying Camp
Hewett, Samuel	Wagoner, Militia
Hicks, James	Pvt., Maryland Militia
Hill, Ebenezer	Capt., Sea Service
Hill, William	Pvt., Flying Camp
Hilleary, Osborn	Pvt., Maryland Militia
Hilleary, Migman	Maryland Service
Hilton, William	Flying Camp
Hinds, Daniel	Pvt., Flying Camp
Hinds, Henry	Pvt., Flying Camp
Hines, Henry	Maryland Service
Hines, Martin	Maryland Militia
Hitchcock, Ignatius	Maryland Service
Hofflich, Stephen	Pvt., Maryland Militia
Holland, Francis	Maryland Militia
Holland, William	Maryland Line
Holliday, Daniel	Maryland Line
Hollingsworth, Henry	Maryland Service
Hollingsworth, Jesse	Sea Service
Hollingsworth, Samuel	Independent Troop
Hollingsworth, Thomas	Independent Troop
Holt, Clayborn	Maryland Line
Holts, Jacob	Sergt., Maryland Militia
Hope, John	Maryland Service
Hopkins, Daniel	Independent Troop

Hopkins, Skiplin	Sea Service
Hopkins, William	Maryland Line
Horner, Gustavus B.	Maryland Service
Howard, Benjamin	Maryland Marine
Huffman, Henry	Pvt., Flying Camp
Hull, William	Pvt., Maryland Militia
Hulsman, Henry	Pvt., Flying Camp
Hurley, William	Maryland Line
Hurst, Richard	Pvt., Maryland Militia
Hynes, Thomas	Lieut., Sea Service
Hynson, James	Pvt., Maryland Militia
Irving, George	Maryland Militia
Isaacs, Isaac	Maryland Line
Jackson, George	Maryland Line
Jacobs, William	Flying Camp
Jaffrey, James	Independent Troop
James, Joseph	Maryland Service
James, William	Marine Service
Jarvis, William	Maryland Service
Jeffers, John	Independent Troop
Jenkins, Edward	Pvt., Continental Line
Jenning, Thomas	Maryland Service
Job, Morris	Maryland Patriot
Job, Thomas	Maryland Patriot
Johns, Aquilla	Maryland Service
Johnson, Edward	Pvt., Flying Camp
Johnson, Isaac	Maryland Service
Johnson, James	Pvt., Maryland Militia
Jones, Benjamin	Maryland Service
Jones, George	Maryland Service
Jones, Hezekiah	Pvt., Maryland Militia
Jones, Jacob	Maryland Service
Jones, John	Maryland Militia
Jones, Jonathan	Pvt., Flying Camp
Jones, Thomas	Sergt., Maryland Line
Jones, William	Maryland Service
Jourdan, Richard	Maryland Marine
Kallingberger, Frederick	Pvt., Flying Camp
Keating, William	Pvt., Maryland Militia
Kellar, John	Pvt., Flying Camp

Kelley, Nicholas	Maryland Patriot
Kelly, William	Pvt., Maryland Militia
Kern, Jacob	Pvt., Flying Camp
King, John	Sergt., Maryland Militia
King, Joseph	Q. M., Maryland Service
King, Robert	Maryland Militia
King, William	Independent Troop
Kirk, Thomas	Flying Camp
Kirwin, John	Independent Troop
Kower, George	Pvt., Flying Camp
Lamb, Joshua	Sea Service
Lamdin, Thomas	Sea Service
Langley, James	Maryland Militia
Langley, William	Maryland Patriot
Lantz, Hart	Sergt., Maryland Service
Lawler, Henry	Maryland Service
Lawrence, Richard	Adjt., Maryland Militia
Laws, William	Maryland Militia
Leaf, John	Maryland Service
Lee, Andrew	Pvt., Flying Camp
Lee, Gasham	Maryland Service
Lee, John	Maryland Service
Lemon, George	Maryland Service
Lemon, John	Maryland Line
Lemon, Joseph	Independent Troop
Lemon, William	Sergt., Maryland Militia
Lester, William	Maryland Service
Levie, Nathan	Independent Troop
Lewis, Andrew	Maryland Service
Lewis, William	Maryland Militia
Life, Robert	Pvt., Flying Camp
Lindsey, John	Pvt., Maryland Militia
Lingenfelter, John	Maryland Service
Lingerfelder, George	Maryland Line
Linthicum, Henry	Pvt., Maryland Line
Loar, John	Maryland Line
Loch, John	Pvt., Flying Camp
Lock, John D.	Maryland Service
Long, Patrick	Lieut., Sea Service
Lord, Levin	Pvt., Maryland Line

Lord, William	Maryland Patriot
Lovely, William	Maryland Militia
Lowe, John	Sea Service
Lowe, William	Lieut., Sea Service
Lynch, William	Maryland Service
McAdow, James	Maryland Service
McAllister, John	Maryland Service
McCann, Francis	Pvt., Maryland Militia
McCarter, Jeremiah	Maryland Service
McCim, Alexander	Independent Troop
McClane, Enoch	Sergt., Maryland Line
McClannan, Nathaniel	Pvt., Maryland Militia
McClure, William	Maryland Service
McColester, John	Independent Troop
McComas, Andrew	Maryland Militia
McCrary, John	Flying Camp
McCray, Henry	Maryland Service
McCreecy, Benjamin	Maryland Service
McCullock, Patrick	Maryland Service
Mace, Nicholas	Capt., Sea Service
McGee, Samuel	Pvt., Maryland Line
McGuden, Enoch	Sergt., Continental Line
Mackenheimer, John	Maryland Service
Mackey, James	Teamster, Maryland Service
McLean, Enock	Maryland Service
McLean, Jacob	Pvt., Maryland Militia
Macore, Samuel	Maryland Service
McPherson, Samuel	Maryland Service
McQuire, Michael	Capt., Maryland Militia
Maddox, George	Maryland Militia
Madole, Thomas	Maryland Line
Magers, Charles	Maryland Line
Mahony, Samuel	Pvt., Maryland Service
Maiden, Lawrence	Maryland Service
Mainor, Benjamin	Adjt., Maryland Militia
Malott, David	Maryland Service
Mansfield, George	Sergt., Maryland Militia
Mansfield, Robert	Maryland Militia
Mansfield, Samuel	Maryland Militia
Maroney, Harry	Flying Camp

Marsh, Joshua	Maryland Patriot
Marshall, John	Flying Camp
Marshall, Richard	Maryland Militia
Martin, Hugh	Maryland Militia
Martin, Luther	Independent Troop
Martindale, William	Cadet
Mason, David	Maryland Militia
Mason, James	Maryland Line
Mason, John	Maryland Service
Massey, Henry	Maryland Service
Masterton, John	Maryland Service
Masterton, William	Maryland Service
Matthews, Bennett	Lieut., Sea Service
Maxwell, Robert	Maryland Militia
Maynadier, Henry	Surgeon, Maryland Service
Medcalf, Caleb	Maryland Militia
Mefford, John	Maryland Line
Middleton, Gilbert	Maryland Service
Midlar, Sebastian	Maryland Service
Migiss, Charles	Independent Troop
Miles, Nicholas	Maryland Militia
Miller, George	Maryland Line
Miller, Henry	Maryland Service
Miller, Isaac	Maryland Militia
Miller, Joshua	Sergt., Maryland Militia
Milling, Zachariah	Pvt., Maryland Militia
Mills, Zachariah	Maryland Line
Minn, John	Drum Major, Maryland
Minn, Peter	Adjt., Maryland Militia
Monohan, John	Sergt., Maryland Service
Montgomery, James	Maryland Service
Montle, George	Maryland Line
Moore, John	Sergt., Maryland Militia
Moore, John	Maryland Militia
Moore, William	Maryland Line
Moore, William	Maryland Militia
Morell, Randolph	Pvt., Flying Camp
Morgan, James	Cadet
Moser, Thomas	Continental Line
Mosher, Samuel	Continental Line

Mower, John	Pvt., Flying Camp
Murphy, Hezekiah	Maryland Line
Murray, Edward	Maryland Patriot
Myer, Henry	Pvt., Flying Camp
Nabb, Joseph	Fifer, Maryland Line
Nagle, Isaac	Maryland Militia
Nail, William	Maryland Militia
Naill, David	Pvt., Flying Camp
Neale, William	Maryland Service
Newman, Basil	Maryland Service
Newman, George	Maryland Militia
Newsenger, John	Pvt., Flying Camp
Nichols, John	Maryland Militia
Nichols, Ninian	Pvt., Flying Camp
Nichols, William	Sergt., Maryland Service
Nicholson, James	Maryland Service
Nickle, John	Maryland Line
Ninburne, Nicholas	Maryland Line
North, Jacob	Pvt., Maryland Line
North, William	Pvt., Maryland Militia
Norwood, William	Maryland Militia
Notoley, John	Pvt., Flying Camp
Oden, Benjamin	Maryland Militia
O'Donnell, Dudler	Maryland Service
Offutt, Nathaniel	Sergt., Maryland Militia
Oldham, Edward	Maryland Militia
Orem, Spedden	Sea Service
Osborn, Francis	Pvt., Maryland Service
Osborn, William	Maryland Service
Ott, John	Sergt., Maryland Service
Overfelt, Mathias	Pvt., Flying Camp
Owens, Charles	Maryland Service
Owens, John	Maryland Militia
Ox, John	Sergt., Maryland Militia
Palmer, William	Sea Service
Parker, Aquila	Maryland Militia
Parker, Daniel	Corpl., Maryland Militia
Parkinson, Thomas	Maryland Service
Patten, Mathew	Independent Troop
Pearce, Hugh	Pvt., Maryland Militia

Peirce, John	Maryland Teamster
Pennall, Joseph	Pvt., Flying Camp
Pennington, Henry	Pvt., Maryland Militia
Pentice, William	Sea Service
Peters, Matthew	Maryland Service
Peyton, John	Maryland Service
Philips, James	Maryland Service
Philips, John	Maryland Service
Philips, Levi	Maryland Service
Phillips, Isaac	Sergt., Maryland Militia
Philpott, Bryan	Independent Troop
Pickering, Peter	Sea Service
Platt, Richard	Maryland Service
Plowman, Jonathan	Maryland Militia
Plummer, George	Pvt., Flying Camp
Poland, William	Maryland Service
Porter, James	Pvt., Maryland Militia
Porter, Nathan	Pvt., Maryland Militia
Porter, Nathaniel	Sea Service
Powders, Huel	Maryland Service
Prentice, William	Sea Service
Price, Benjamin	Cadet
Price, Benjamin	Sergt., Flying Camp
Pring, Supering	Maryland Line
Pringle, Mark	Coronet, Cavalry Troop
Proctor, Henry	Maryland Militia
Purdy, Joseph	Drum Major, Maryland
Purdy, William	Maryland Militia
Purnell, Matthew	Maryland Service
Ragan, John	Q. M., Maryland
Rainey, David	Maryland Service
Randall, John	Sergt., Maryland Militia
Randolph, John	Maryland Service
Read, Samuel	Pvt., Maryland Militia
Really, Dennis	Pvt., Flying Camp
Reed, John	Cadet
Reese, David	Independent Troop
Reid, John	Maryland Line
Rensche, Peter	Maryland Militia
Reswick, Joseph	Maryland Militia

NON-PENSIONERS 101

Reveley, Francis	Cadet
Richards, John	Maryland Militia
Richards, Richard	Maryland Militia
Richardson, James	Maryland Line
Richardson, William	Pvt., Flying Camp
Ridenour, John	Maryland Service
Ridley, Mathew	Independent Troop
Riggs, Charles	Maryland Militia
Riley, Nick	Maryland Militia
Ringer, Andrew	Pvt., Flying Camp
Ringstoff, Henry	Maryland Service
Roads, Elisha	Flying Camp
Roads, Jacob	Flying Camp
Roberts, Basil	Maryland Patriot
Roberts, Mathew	Maryland Service
Robey, Charles	Maryland Militia
Robinson, John	Sergt., Maryland Militia
Rockhold, Dawson	Flying Camp
Rollins, John	Maryland Service
Rolliston, Charles	Sergt., Maryland Militia
Ross, Bartholemew	Maryland Line
Rothrock, Benjamin	Armorer, Maryland
Rouce, William	Maryland Service
Rudolph, John	Maryland Service
Rudrick, Matthew	Pvt., Flying Camp
Russell, John	Maryland Service
Russell, Nicholas	Maryland Line
Russell, Thomas	Lieut., Independent Troop
Rutland, Henry	Maryland Line
Rutledge, Joshua	Maryland Service
Rutledge, Thomas	Sergt., Maryland Service
Ryan, James	Independent Troop
Salmon, Edward	Flying Camp
Sanderson, Henry	Maryland Teamster
Sapping, Thomas	Maryland Militia
Sappington, Hartley	Flying Camp
Sappington, James	Maryland Militia
Sappington, John	Maryland Militia
Sappington, Thomas	Maryland Line
Sargeant, Richard	Flying Camp

Sargeant, Thomas	Maryland Line
Sargeant, William	Maryland Militia
Sartain, Robert	Maryland Militia
Sasser, William	Maryland Militia
Scaggs, William	Maryland Service
Schafer, George	Maryland Service
Schnelby, Daniel	Flying Camp
Scholfield, James	Maryland Service
Scoager, George	Maryland Service
Scott, Charles	Maryland Line
Scott, James	Maryland Patriot
Seay, James	Maryland Line
Sevell, Daniel	Pvt., Flying Camp
Shame, Joseph	Pvt., Flying Camp
Shannaham, Elliott	Lieut., Sea Service
Shaw, Daniel	Maryland Patriot
Shaw, John	Maryland Militia
Shaw, Samuel	Maryland Patriot
Shenard, Francis	Maryland Militia
Shenk, John	Pvt., Flying Camp
Sherwood, Phil	Sea Service
Sherwood, William	Maryland Militia
Shinal, Josiah	Maryland Militia
Shultz, David	Maryland Militia
Shyrock, Daniel	Maryland Service
Shyrock, Valentine	Continental Line
Skinner, Mordecai	Maryland Service
Slade, William	Maryland Patriot
Slupe, Joseph	Maryland Line
Slusher, Christopher	Continental Line
Smallwood, Herbert	Maryland Service
Smart, Joseph	Maryland Line
Smith, Charles	Pvt., Flying Camp
Smith, Daniel	Continental Line
Smith, Ebenezar	Maryland Service
Smith, Ephraim	Maryland Militia
Smith, Francis	Maryland Service
Smith, George	Maryland Service
Smith, John	Flying Camp
Smith, John (dyer)	Flying Camp

Smith, Levi	Maryland Line
Smith, Matthew	Pvt., Flying Camp
Smith, Moses	Maryland Line
Smith, Philip	German Regiment
Smith, Thomas	Pvt., Flying Camp
Smith, Thorogood	Independent Troop
Smith, William	Pvt., Flying Camp
Smith, William	Sea Service
Smith, William	Maryland Service
Smith, William	Mate, Sea Service
Smith, Winston	Flying Camp
Smoot, Matthew	Maryland Militia
Snowdinge, Peter	Pvt., Flying Camp
Snyder, John	Flying Camp
Solomon, Edward	Maryland Service
Sparrow, Thomas	Maryland Service
Speak, Andrew	Pvt., Flying Camp
Spear, John	Independent Troop
Spedden, Levin	Maryland Service
Spencer, Richard	Sea Service
Sprigg, Samuel	Flying Camp
Sprigg, William	Flying Camp
Stanely, Christopher	Pvt., Flying Camp
Steene, William	Maryland Militia
Stell, James	Maryland Militia
Stephenson, Nicholas	Maryland Service
Sterling, James	Independent Troop
Sterret, James	Maryland Patriot
Steuart, John	Independent Troop
Stevens, Jacob	Pvt., Flying Camp
Stevenson, John	Maryland Service
Stevenson, Joshua	Maryland Patriot
Stewart, Asa	Pvt., Maryland Militia
Stewart, Charles	Maryland Militia
Stewart, Joseph	Maryland Militia
Stewart, Steven	Maryland Service
Stinchcomb, McLane	Maryland Militia
Stinchcomb, Nathaniel	Maryland Militia
Stinchcomb, William	Maryland Militia
Stockton, George	Maryland Service

Stonebraker, Adam	German Regiment
Stoner, George	Pvt., Flying Camp
Storn, Peter	Maryland Militia
Stouffer, George	Maryland Service
Striser, John	Pvt., Flying Camp
Stuart, Alexander	Maryland Service
Stuart, William	Maryland Service
Sugfried, George	Pvt., Flying Camp
Suit, Jesse	Maryland Service
Summers, George	Maryland Militia
Sutton, Joseph	Maryland Militia
Swallow, Osten	Maryland Militia
Swanton, Peter	Pvt., Flying Camp
Sweary, Richard	Maryland Militia
Swilven, Daniel	Maryland Service
Swilven, Jeremiah	Maryland Service
Swilven, Thomas	Maryland Service
Talbott, Benjamin	Maryland Patriot
Talbott, Henry	Adjt., Maryland Militia
Talbott, John	Maryland Patriot
Tanneyhill, Adamson	Continental Line
Tanneyhill, Cyrus	Continental Line
Taylor, Abbe	Maryland Service
Taylor, Alexander	Maryland Militia
Taylor, James	Maryland Militia
Taylor, William	Independent Troop
Temple, Conrad	German Regiment
Tennally, George	Pvt., Flying Camp
Tennant, Gilbert	Maryland Service
Tenant, Thomas	Sea Service
Teno, Joseph	Flying Camp
Thomas, Basil	Maryland Paymaster
Thomas, George	Maryland Service
Thomas, John	Continental Line
Thompson, John	Maryland Militia
Thornsberry, Francis	Maryland Militia
Tillard, Fragget	Maryland Militia
Tiller, Edward	Maryland Militia
Tiller, Samuel	Maryland Militia
Tillotson, Thomas	Surgeon, Maryland

Tobery, Thomas	Pvt., Flying Camp
Townhill, Sac	Maryland Line
Townsend, Allen	Maryland Service
Townsend, Benjamin	Fifer, Maryland Line
Townsend, Thomas	Sea Service
Townsend, William	Maryland Service
Tracy, Charles	Maryland Militia
Treat, Malachi	Maryland Militia
Trout, John	Maryland Militia
Troutman, John	Maryland Militia
Tucker, John	Maryland Service
Tulley, James	Maryland Militia
Tunex, Henry	Pvt., Flying Camp
Turnbull, George	Independent Troop
Turner, John	Maryland Militia
Tuthaker, Edward	Maryland Militia
Tuttle, William	Maryland Service
Twiner, John	Pvt., Flying Camp
Tyler, William	Maryland Service
Valentine, John	Maryland Militia
Valiant, Benjamin	Maryland Militia
Vanbibber, Abraham	Independent Troop
Van Horn, Gabriel	Q. M., Maryland Service
Van Meter, Jacob	Maryland Service
Vansant, John	Maryland Militia
Vansant, Joshua	Maryland Militia
Viney, Thomas	Maryland Service
Vineyard, John	Fifer, Maryland Line
Wagoner, Peter	Pvt., Flying Camp
Walker, Thomas	Capt., Sea Service
Wallace, Michael	Surgeon, Maryland
Waller, Hezekiah	Sea Service
Wallis, Francis	Maryland Militia
Wallis, Henry	Maryland Militia
Wallis, Hugh	Maryland Militia
Wallis, John	Maryland Militia
Wallis, Samuel	Maryland Militia
Walls, John	Maryland Service
Walters, Isaac	Maryland Militia
Warfield, Ephraim	Maryland Militia

Warmer, Phillip	Maryland Militia
Watson, Abraham	Maryland Service
Watts, Peter	Pvt., Flying Camp
Weaver, Jacob	Maryland Service
Weeden, Henry	Maryland Line
Weedon, Thomas	Maryland Service
Wells, George	Maryland Service
Wells, Thomas	Flying Camp
Welsh, Alexander	Maryland Service
Whaley, Zadock	Sea Service
Wheatley, Francis	Maryland Militia
Wheatley, Silvester	Maryland Militia
Wheeler, John	Maryland Service
Wheeler, William	Maryland Service
Whitcomb, Notley	Maryland Line
White, John	Maryland Line
White, William	Maryland Line
Whitmore, Jonathan	Maryland Service
Wiatt, Henry	Maryland Militia
Wiatt, Samuel	Maryland Militia
Wiatt, William	Maryland Militia
Wilhhier, William	Flying Camp
Wilkins, Henry	Maryland Service
Willet, Benjamin	Maryland Service
Williams, Elie	Maryland Militia
Williams, George	Continental Service
Williams, Joseph	Maryland Militia
Williams, Joseph	Flying Camp
Williams, Phil	Maryland Service
Wilmer, James	Maryland Militia
Willmer, William	Maryland Militia
Wilson, James	Maryland Militia
Wilson, Robert	Maryland Militia
Wilson, William	Q. M., Maryland Line
Winchester, George	Maryland Line
Wingate, Henry	Maryland Service
Winsatt, James	Maryland Militia
Winter, Thomas	Maryland Service
Wolf, Andrew	Pvt., Flying Camp
Wolfe, John	Fifer, Maryland Militia

Wolves, James	Adjt., Maryland Line
Wood, Charles	Maryland Service
Wood, Samuel	Maryland Militia
Wood, Thomas	Maryland Line
Woodall, John	Pvt., Flying Camp
Woodland, John	Maryland Militia
Woodsides, William	Maryland Service
Woodward, Thomas	Maryland Line
Woolford, William	Cadet
Wright, Erza	Maryland Militia
Wright, John	Q. M., Maryland Line
Wright, Joshua	Maryland Service
Yates, Barton	Maryland Line
Yates, Donaldson	Q. M., Maryland Service
Yates, Henry	Maryland Militia
Yates, John	Maryland Line
Yates, Major	Independent Troop
Yaulet, Samuel	Pvt., Flying Camp
Young, Robert	Maryland Militia
Young, Samuel	Maryland Militia

Part IV

MARRIAGES PROVED THROUGH MARYLAND PENSION APPLICATIONS

*Indicates that it is assumed that the marriage occurred in that state.

NOTE: Further information on the contracting parties may be obtained by addressing the compiler.

Maryland County Abbreviations

A. A.—Anne Arundel
Alleg.—Allegany
Balto.—Baltimore
Cal.—Calvert
Carl.—Caroline
Carr.—Carroll
Chas.—Charles
Dorch.—Dorchester
Fred.—Frederick

Harf.—Harford
How.—Howard
Mont.—Montgomery
Pr. Geo.—Prince Georges
Q. A.—Queen Annes
Tal.—Talbot
Som.—Somerset
Wash.—Washington
Wico.—Wicomico

Wor.—Worcester

Groom	Bride	Date	Place
Smallwood Acton	Nancy Cane	Dec. 16, 1823	Clark Co., Ky.
John Adams	Nancy Beatty	Mar. 13, 1790	Hunt. Co., Pa.
John Adams	Sophia Smith	1805	Som. Co., Md.
Littleton Adams	Harriet Smith	Mar. 4, 1793	King Geo. Co., Va.
Mark Adams	Hannah Pettit	Jan. 19, 1784	Phila., Pa.
William Adams	Chaney Dill	ante 1822	Delaware*
Thomas Albert	Catherine Saylor	post 1815	Ohio*
George Alder	Lucy Ann Wynn	Nov. 17, 1778	Maryland*
Allen Alexander	Winifred Tool	Oct. 177–	Mont. Co., Md.
James R. Alexander	Dorcas Garrison	Nov. 26, 1789	York Dist., S.C.
William Alexander	Elizabeth Cruthers	ante 1776	Cecil Co., Md.
Jacob Allen	Elizabeth Wilson, wid.	July 24, 1793	Delaware
John Allen	Mary Grover	Oct. 12, 1791	Balto. Co., Md.
John Allen	Sarah Merriken	ante 1791	Maryland
Robert Allison	Martha McKinley	Feb. 22, 1787	Tennessee*
Joseph Allsop	Mary Freeman	Jan. 10, 1778	Fred. Co., Md.
Clement Alvey	Mary Ann Mudd	circa 1810	Kentucky
Adolphus Ammons	Lucy Edelen	post 1830	Illinois
William Amos	Elizabeth Hugon	circa 1799	Delaware*
William Arasmith	Nancy Potterf, wid.	Dec. 1, 1850	Maryland

James F. Armstrong	Susannah Livingston	Aug. 22, 1782	New Jersey
John Armstrong	Betsy Knick	ante 1800	Virginia*
Matthew Armstrong	Catherine Titman, wid.		
George Arnold	Eve Plum, wid.	June 28, 1831	Millersburg, O.
James Arthur	Elizabeth Gilliam	May 25, 1782	Pr. Geo. Co., Va.
Michael Ashford	Ally Speake		Kentucky
Thomas Ayres	Elizabeth Almony	Jan. 1, 1784	Maryland
Leonard Backenbaugh	Catherine Shroyer	1786	Fred. Co., Md.
David Baggerly	Rebecca Belt	May 19, 1782	Mont. Co., Md.
James Bailey	Christiana Weideman	Jan. 3, 1791	Balto. Co., Md.
James Bailey	Elizabeth Runegan	Mar. 20, 1793	North Carolina
Tomlin Baily	Anne Clagett	post 1800	Virginia
Oliver Barbour	Ann Eliza Foulk		Kentucky*
Elijah Barnes	Catherine Shipley	Aug. 17, 1784	Balto. Co., Md.
James Barnett	Martha Finney	Jan. 1778	York Co., Pa.
John Barnett	Hannah Crouch, wid.	ante 1823	Cecil Co., Md.
Isaac Barret	Lucy Burgess	Aug. 4, 1803	Alexandria, D.C.
John Barret	Sarah Cole	post 1805	Ohio*
Jonathan Barrett	Sophia Beck	Feb. 14, 1828	David. Co., N.C.
Solomon Barrett	Susan Robinson	Mar. 25, 1834	Maryland
John Battin	Mary Heinbecher	July 26, 1787	Phila., Pa.
George S. Baum	Catherine Weirick		Pennsylvania*
John Baum	Mary Forshey	June 1830	Pennsylvania
Lawson Beall	Henrietta Harris	ante 1808	Mont. Co., Md.
Ninian Beall	Christiana Stull	July 25, 1790	Fred. Co., Md.
Conrad Bean	Jane Boston	Nov. 1812	Kentucky
Leonard Bean	Eda Kellow	ante 1820	Kentucky*
John Beaver	Mary Perry	post 1830	Virginia*
James Beckett	Elizabeth Beckett	June 7, 1812	Ohio*
George Beckwith	Ann Clarkson	Oct. 1791	Mont. Co., Md.
Thomas Beddo	Sarah Sullivan	1777	Pr. Geo. Co., Md.
John Bell	Catherine Doyle	Apr. 6, 1773	Balto., Md.
Aaron Berget	Elizabeth Hodgkins	ante 1831	Ohio*
Robert Berry	Lucy Rhodes	Nov. 4, 1773	Middlesex Co., Va.
Robert Bier	Elizabeth Lanham	post 1810	Maryland
Thomas Birch	Mary Gray	1777	Mont. Co., Md.
Jacob Bishop	Mary Powell	Dec. 25, 1781	Pennsylvania
Francis P. Blair	Elizabeth Gist		
Jesse Bledsoe	Sarah Gist		
John Board	Anne Doughty	Nov. 8, 1788	Loudon Co., Va.
Raphael W. Boarman	Mary Smith	post 1800	Maryland
Samuel Boles	Nancy Powell	Feb. 15, 1815	Wor. Co., Md.
James Booker	Priscilla Bracco		Q. A. Co., Md.
Edward Booth	Rachel Reynolds	circa 1780	Cecil Co., Md.
Adam Boss	Harriet Ransdell	Jan. 24, 1822	Pr. Wm. Co., Va.
Jesse Boswell	Mary Kelough	Dec. 24, 1809	York Dist., S.C.
Joseph Boswell	Judith Gist		
William H. Boult	Sarah C. Hughes		Virginia*

John B. Bowen	Barbara Coleman	ante 1852	Indiana
Philip Bowen	Catherine Coleman	ante 1852	Indiana
Sabritt Bowen	Elizabeth Humphrey	Jan. 4, 1792	Balto. Co., Md.
Jacob Bower	Anna Rohrer	Feb. 14, 1782	Wash. Co., Md.
Leonard Bowers	Rebecca Nave	Aug. 2, 1785	Carter Co., Tenn.
Alfred Boyer	Elizabeth Lowman	Dec. 16, 1829	Kentucky*
Alfred Boyer	Zerelda McCoy	Sept. 24, 1834	Kentucky*
John G. Boyer	Mary Zealer	Apr. 10, 1786	Maryland
Jacob Bradenbaugh	Dorcas Ayres	ante 1820	Maryland*
William Braithwaite	Kitty Brookover	May 18, 1786	Fred. Co., Va.
Hackett Bramble	Elizabeth Butler	ante 1790	North Carolina*
William Brannon	Margaret White	——	West. Co., Pa.
James Bratton	Rachel Greathouse	June 11, 1805	Warren Co., Ky.
Thomas Brewer	Susanna Lampley	Aug. 22, 1782	A. A. Co., Md.
George Brierly	Mary Garrison	Mar. 27, 1793	Mason Co., Ky.
Henry Brindle	Susan White	——	Pennsylvania
John Brindle	Eleanor White	——	West. Co., Pa.
Solomon Brittinghan	Leah Brown	Mar. 24, 1783	Fairfield Co., O.
Samuel Brooke	Elizabeth Rutledge, wid.	Apr. 27, 1827	Maryland
John A. Brooks	Drusilla White	——	Pennsylvania
Frederick Brown	Jane Erwin	post 1805	Fred. Co., Md.
John Brown	Mary Lewis	post 1800	Pennsylvania
William Brownfield	Sarah Robinson	——	Pennsylvania
James W. Brudlaw	Maria Winchester	Jan. 30, 1825	Tennessee
Charles Bryan	Catherine Stone	Oct. 6, 1783	Chas. Co., Md.
Zachariah Burch	Mildred Robey	Dec. 22, 1776	Chas. Co., Md.
Thomas Burgess	Ann Bosely	1788	Maryland
John Burke	Mary Stevens	May 2, 1786	Virginia
Elisha Burroughs	Margaret P. Swann	Nov. 30, 1793	Chas. Co., Md.
Richard Butler	Amelia Fischer	May 21, 1786	Fred. Co., Md.
William Butler	Nancy Potterf	post 1848	Ohio
John Butts	Sarah Popham	——	Maryland
Thomas Butt	Mary Taylor	Feb. 6, 1809	——
Joshua Byers	Elizabeth Young	ante 1852	Indiana
Robert Caldwell	Permile Melon	Mar. 22, 1804	——
George Calvert	Emma Hoskinson	post 1830	Ohio
Enos Campbell	Eliza Ann Belt	1791	——
James Campbell	Rachel Lewis	post 1800	Pennsylvania*
John Campbell	Julia Wysham	——	Maryland
Squire C. Carpenter	Elizabeth Smith	post 1810	Kentucky*
Hezekiah Carr	Edith Parsons	Sept. 22, 1790	Amelia Co., Va.
John Carr	Margarett Brownly	July 15, 1779	Harf. Co., Md.
John Carroll	Isabell Bowman	Apr. 20, 1789	Halifax Co., Va.
Robert Carter	Hebe Grayson	ante 1816	——
Pater Casey	Mary Allsop, wid.	Dec. 16, 1794	——
Abraham L. Cash	Kiturah Porter	post 1810	Tennessee
Abraham Cassel	Catherine Lingenfelter	Apr. 24, 1782	Fred. Co., Md.
Joseph Champing	Elizabeth Adams	ante 1820	——

John Chenoweth	Mary Buskirk	Mar. 11, 1793	Shelby Co., Ky.
Jacob City	Betsey Runion	Mar. 1781	
Samuel Clagett	Annie Jane Ramey	Aug. 22, 1786	Fauquier Co., Va.
Zadock Clagett	Jane Murdock, wid.	post 1792	
John Clark	Sarah Louden	Aug. 7, 1794	Berkley Co., Va.
William Clarke	Chaney Dill	ante 1822	Delaware
John Clevidence	Mary Reed	circa 1799	Alleg. Co., Pa.
Abraham Cloward	Ann Harris	June 5, 1781	Somerset Co., N.J.
Simon Cochran	Sarah Clark, wid.	post 1822	Ohio
Edward Cockey	Eleanor Pindell	ante 1795	Balto. Co., Md.
Jacob Coffman	Chloe Richards	Dec. 24, 1826	Casey Co., Ky.
Paul Coffman	Elizabeth Jacob	circa 1810	Hampshire Co., Va.
Benjamin Cole	Elizabeth Long	Nov. 15, 1784	Wash. Co., Md.
Skipworth Cole	Elizabeth Gilbert, wid.	Jan. 22, 1797	Harf. Co., Md.
John B. Coleman	Catherine Young	ante 1852	Indiana
Timothy Collins	Elizabeth McFee	Apr. 21, 1778	Balto. Co., Md.
Cornelius Comegys	Catherine Baker	Oct. 11, 1794	Phila., Pa.
Michael Conley	Rebecca Bradock	Apr. 20, 1825	Brown Co., O.
Michael Connelly	Drusilla Culver	post 1785	Mont. Co., Md.
William Connelly	Priscilla Eshum	Nov. 28, 1788	Dorch. Co., Md.
Christian Cook	Susan Lambert	post 1800	Maryland
Peter Cookerly	Eleanor Price, wid.	1798	Maryland
Richard Cooley	Rachel Lewis	Nov. 6, 1788	Harf. Co., Md.
John Cooper	Elizabeth Durham	post 1800	Balto. Co., Md.
John Corn	Anne Williams	post 1815	Kentucky
John Courts	Priscilla Smallwood	ante 1816	Maryland
Richard Courts	Eleanor Jones	1784	Mont. Co., Md.
James Cowan	Hannah Collins	circa 1800	Pennsylvania
William Coward	Nancy Baker	Oct. 10, 1801	Balto. Co., Md.
Thomas Craig	Elizabeth Fleming	Nov. 9, 1786	West. Co., Pa.
Robert Crain	Mary Wood	ante 1825	Maryland
Robert Crain	Sarah B. Watts		
Daniel Creamer	Sarah Wilson	Dec. 9, 1790	Green Co., Tenn.
John Crider	Rebecca Davis		Ohio
George Cristmore	Lotty Scott, wid.	Mar. 26, 1836	Ohio
Moses Crosely	Rachel Powell	May 1, 1784	Wash. Co., Md.
Robert Crouch	Hannah Cleeves	Nov. 19, 1800	Cecil Co., Md.
William Crouch	Lucinda Rollins	Oct. 17, 1819	Indiana*
Jacob Crumbacker	Catherine Moore	post 1805	Maryland
John Crutcher	Letitia Bean	ante 1833	Kentucky
Solomon Culver	Nancy Arnett	ante 1820	Ohio*
John Cunningham	Catherine Knick	post 1800	Virginia*
John Curtiss	Ealsy Wilkins		Balto., Md.*
Christopher Cusick	Mary Cave	May 10, 1790	Harf. Co., Md.
William Dalrymple	Mary Patterson	ante 1820	Maryland
Aaron Davenport	Elinor King	June 27, 1800	New York*
James Davidson	Mary Howard		A. A. Co., Md.
Marmaduke Davies	Eleanor Wilson	Jan. 30, 1816	Belmont Co., O.

Samuel Davis	Margaret Barrett	*circa* 1808	Kent Co., Md.
Thomas Davis	Johana Whitler	Jan. 2, 1786	Chas. Co., Md.
Thomas Davis	Polly Johnston	*post* 1820	Virginia*
Charles Dawkins	Elizabeth Clare	Dec. 18, 1788	Cal. Co., Md.
George Dawson	Jane Mackall	*post* 1810	Pennsylvania*
James Day	Sarah Mark	Sept. 21, 1823	Mont. Co., Md.
John Deaver	Honor Worth	Aug. 4, 1789	Balto Co., Md.
John Deaver	Sarah Hunt	Jan. 12, 1797	Balto. Co., Md.
John Deaver	Susannah Talbot	Mar. 11, 1777	Balto. Co., Md.
John Dent	Eleanor Cecil	Dec. 19, 1777	Pr. Geo. Co., Md.
William Devin	Mary Harris	Feb. 2, 1799	Mason Co., Ky.
Henry Dixon	Henrietta Varden	June 5, 1783	Chas. Co., Md.
John Dixon	Pamelia Johnson	*ante* 1818	Maryland
Nicholas Dorsey	Rachel Warfield	Dec. 14, 1779	Mont. Co., Md.
Hilleary Dowell	Mical Patterson	*ante* 1828	Maryland
Leven Dowell	Priscilla Patterson	*ante* 1828	Maryland
Richard Dowell	Mary McDaniel	Dec. 13, 1787	Rowan Co., N.C.
Michael Downs	Margaret Lewis	Jan. 17, 1781	Mont. Co., Md.
William Drury	Elizabeth Allison	Jan. 30, 1817	Tennessee*
John Dudderow	Catherine Summers	Aug. 24, 1779	Fred. Co., Md.
Charles Duke	Nancy Elliott	*post* 1797	Georgia*
Williamson Dunn	Mary Flemington	*post* 1790	
William Durham	Anne Tolley	1786	Balto. Co., Md.
William Durrington	Martha Loyal	June 7, 1828	Calloway Co., Ky.
Ephraim Duval	Jemina Hazel, wid.	1794	A. A. Co., Md.
Joseph Duval	Mary Duval	July 1786	Pr. Geo. Co., Md.
Horatio Dyer	Mary Rose Boarman	*post* 1810	Maryland
David Easton	Sarah Jordan	Oct. 1796	Maryland
Clement Edelen	Lucy Aud	Nov. 14, 1827	White Co., Ill.
James Eldridge	Elizabeth Williams	*post* 1800	Kentucky
John Elliott	Sarah Warfield	July 12, 1787	A. A. Co., Md.
Robert Elliott	Martha Creswell	Feb. 23, 1820	Harf. Co., Md.
Joseph W. Elston	Catherine King	*post* 1800	New York
Gideon Emory	Ann Lucretia Hebb	Oct. 1, 1799	Q. A. Co., Md.
Gideon Emory	Elizabeth Clayland	May 17, 1784	Q. A. Co., Md.
Leonard Ennis	Jane Burke	Nov. 1783	A. A. Co., Md.
Isaac Enoch	Nancy Rollins	Aug. 19, 1819	Indiana*
James Erwin	Sarah Harrison	Dec. 20, 1787	Maryland
Samuel Erwin	Eleanor Hollis	Jan. 22, 1837	Maryland*
William Etcheson	Mary Weedin	Feb. 23, 1797	Chas. Co., Md.
Hooper Evans	Fanny Cheshire	May 18, 1791	Dorch. Co., Md.
Francis Fairbrother	Patience Reeves	July 1793	A. A. Co., Md.
Aaron Farden	Mary Lomass, wid.	*post* 1780	Maryland
James Farquhar	Betsy Jack	Feb. 15, 1790	Virginia
John Farrell	Lydia McQuire	Dec. 8, 1778	
Joseph Fearson	Elizabeth Shaw	Apr. 11, 1791	Chas. Co., Md.
Dorus Felmott	Martha Swearengin	Sept. 22, 1794	Lincoln, N.C.
Isaac Ferguson	Lotty Cristmore, wid.	Jan. 21, 1838	Ohio

John Ferguson	Catherine Thomas	1776	Fred. Co., Md.
James C. Ferran	Margaret A. Rogers	ante 1834	————
Jacob Fifer	Katherine Speagle	Feb. 18, 1784	Lincoln Co., N.C.
Frederick Filler	Catherine Border	1782	————
William Finley	Nancy Treadway	Aug. 1789	Tennessee
James Fisher	Nancy Ewins	Feb. 21, 1804	South Carolina
Philip Fisher	Margaret Albrecht	June 27, 1790	Fred. Co., Md.
Henry Flanigan	Lydia Busk	Dec. 1783	Balto. Co., Md.
James Fleming	Polly Whitehair	Feb. 13, 1820	Harrison Co., Va.
Thomas Fleming	Agnes Porter	circa 1777	Fred. Co., Md.
Thomas Forbes	Catherine Seltzer	circa 1785	Wash. Co., Md.
Leonard Foreman	Ann Cavy Adams	post 1800	A. A. Co., Md.
Uriah Forrest	Rebecca Plater	Oct. 11, 1789	St. M. Co., Md.
Thomas D. Foulk	Cassandra Smith	circa 1805	Kentucky*
Daniel Fox	Anna Porter	post 1800	Tennessee
Levin Frazier	Elizabeth Eccleston	Jan. 14, 1781	Dorch. Co., Md.
Samuel Frazier	Penelope Johnson	Dec. 16, 1792	Harf. Co., Md.
William Frazier	Henrietta Johnson	Feb. 11, 1779	Maryland
Nicholas Fry	Margaret Ansel	Mar. 11, 1794	Loudon Co., Va.
Horace Fuller	Mical Patterson	ante 1828	Maryland
D. A. Fulton	Elizabeth Blablock	Jan. 4, 1827	South Carolina*
Horatio S. Fulton	Gilly James	Feb. 21, 1822	South Carolina*
James W. Fulton	Mary Clemmon	Aug. 10, 1837	South Carolina*
Theodore D. Fulton	Elizabeth Parker	1821	South Carolina*
Greenbruy Gaither	Anne Anderson	Apr. 14, 1779	Mont. Co., Md.
Josiah Gaskill	Mary Davis	————	Ohio*
John Gassway	Elizabeth Price	Sept. 27, 1799	A. A. Co., Md.
Samuel Gassaway	Nancy Gassaway	Nov. 10, 1789	Fred. Co., Md.
William Gates	Sarah McDaniel	Nov. 26, 1793	Chas. Co., Md.
John Gebhart	Phoebe Van Sickle	July 1816	Mason Co., Va.
Joseph Gee	Belinda Vernon	Aug. 2, 1781	A. A. Co., Md.
Anthony Geoghegan	Anne Lilly	Dec. 24, 1792	Bourbon Co., Ky.
Adam Gibhart	Sarah Davis	circa 1794	South Carolina*
Amos Gilbert	Sarah Magruder	ante 1814	Kentucky*
Michael Gilbert	Elizabeth Pressbury	Nov. 18, 1782	Harf. Co., Md.
George Gillespie	Sarah Hall	circa 1805	Harf. Co., Md.*
Aaron Gilstrap	Effee Davis	————	Ohio
Christian Gobble	Sarah Grise	1780	Fred. Co., Md.
Charles Goldberry	Anne Goldberry	Oct. 28, 1793	St. M. Co., Md.
Archibald Golder	Sarah Ashmead	Apr. 4, 1782	A. A. Co., Md.
William Gould	Sarah Stanton	May 30, 1789	Dorch. Co., Md.
George Grant	Margaret Young	ante 1852	Wisconsin*
Benjamin Gratz	Maria Gist		
James Gray	Anne Bowen	1792	Maryland
Wesley Grayson	Rebecca Norman	post 1800	Ohio*
William Grayson	Eleanor Smallwood	ante 1800	————
Edward Green	Elizabeth Lynch	post 1810	Pennsylvania*
Henry Green	Elizabeth Boering	June 21, 1778	Balto. Co., Md.

MARRIAGE RECORDS 115

Henry Green	Priscilla Hutton	Dec. 1784	Maryland
Peter Green	Mary Cross, wid.	1799	Q. A. Co., Md.
Robert Green	Elizabeth Reeder	circa 1781	Maryland
Abraham Gregg	Janet Allison	Feb. 25, 1813	Tennessee*
Charles Griffen	Rebecca Kelly	July 31, 1781	Balto. Co., Md.
Lewis Griffith	Mary Patterson	ante 1828	Maryland
Samuel Griffith	Ruth Berry	Apr. 1, 1779	Mont. Co., Md.
George Grimm	Elizabeth Collins	circa 1800	Pennsylvania
William Grover	Sarah Bosly	Nov. 5, 1789	Maryland
William Groves	Mary Spencer	Nov. 20, 1796	Pr. Wm. Co., Va.
John Gwinn	Julia Steel	Sept. 20, 1785	Balto. Co., Md.
Elihu Hall	Gertrude Covenhoven	June 2, 1780	New York*
William Hall	Mary Newton	Dec. 7, 1790	Cal. Co., Md.
John Agnew Hamilton	Margaret Sheperd	Aug. 8, 1735	Balto. Co., Md.
Thomas Hammond	Sarah Boyle	Jan. 23, 1793	Mont. Co., Md.
Levin Handy	Nancy Wilson	Feb. 24, 1785	Wor. Co., Md.
William Haney	Susannah Hay	Oct. 10, 1788	Balto. Co., Md.
Christian Hanker	Catherine Filler, wid.	circa 1806	————
Samuel Hanson	Anne Horner, wid.	Aug. 1774	Chas. Co., Md.
Samuel Hanson	Eleanor Bayley	————	D. C.
Samuel Hanson	Mary Key	Apr. 29, 1777	Phila., Penn.
Vachel Harding	Mary Parker	Mar. 14, 1798	Fred. Co., Md.
Elias Hardy	Cassandra Williams	Mar. 9, 1790	————
William Harper	Bathula Wallace	circa 1793	Dorch. Co., Md.
John Harrell	Martha Davis	Feb. 12, 1789	Fairfax Co., Va.
Thomas Harris	Nancy Woollen	————	Scott Co., Ky.
Kinsey Harrison	Sarah Saffle	1779	Balto. Co., Md.
Richard Harry	Rachel Lingo	ante 1780	Mont. Co., Md.
Nathaniel G. Hart	Anne E. Gist	————	————
John Hartshorn	Agnes Miller	Apr. 17, 1788	Cecil Co., Md.
Ailen Harvey	Margaret Pearce	July 19, 1807	Iredell Co., N.C.
Matthew Harvey	Magdaline Hawkins	Aug. 18, 1788	Botetout Co., Va.
Shelby Harvey	Sarah Davis	————	Ohio
John Hawkins Hays	Teresa Gatton	July 16, 1815	St. M. Co., Md.
Peter Hawman	Elizabeth Hildebrand	Aug. 17, 1781	Fred. Co., Md.
William Haynes	Lydia Souther	————	Ohio*
Joseph Hidgon	Margaret Halbrook	Apr. 5, 1786	North Carolina
Frederick Hill	Elizabeth Defibaugh	Apr. 1, 1779	Bedford Co., Pa.
Henry Hill	Hester Brooke	Apr. 23, 1781	Pr. Geo. Co., Md.
Roswell Hill	Sarah Warren	1782	Pittsylv. Co., Va.
William Hill	Elizabeth Palmer	ante 1831	Ohio
Ashburn Hillary	Eleanor King	May 1, 1791	Maryland
James Heaton	Sarah Castor	————	————
Jacob Heffner	Elizabeth Priest	1828	Kentucky
John Hendrix	Irene Davis	————	Ohio
James Henry	Mary Reed	ante 1799	Pennsylvania
Robert Henwood	Rebecca Miles	Feb. 16, 1785	Loudon Co., Va.
Jeremiah Herbert	Mary Hill	1786	Maryland*

Henry Herring	Elizabeth Poe	*post* 1810	Maryland
Daniel Herrington	Mary McCraig	July 2, 1793	Lycaming Co., Pa.
William Hewit	Susan Burch	*post* 1800	D. C.*
James Hobbs	Rachel Reynolds	*circa* 1780	
Allan Hodges	Sarah Allison	Mar. 30, 1809	Tennessee*
Samuel Hodgkins	Lydia Wright	Mar. 9, 1831	Brown Co., O.
George Hoffman	Mary Young		Maryland
Joseph Hogeland	Anne Hogg		Pennsylvania*
Christopher Hohne	Mary Holland	Jan. 1792	A. A. Co., Md.
Charles Holland	Sarah Gardner	July 20, 1799	A. A. Co., Md.
Edward Holland	Elizabeth Popham		Maryland
Edward Holland	Mary Simpson	Dec. 29, 1793	A. A. Co., Md.
William Holland	Lavina Lewis	Aug. 25, 1789	Guil. Co., N.C.
Francis Holley	Martha Shirell	Feb. 2, 1780	North Carolina
Richard Hollis	Catherine Norris	*ante* 1827	Maryland
John S. Holt	Harriet Toole		Georgia*
George Holtzman	Margaret Deaver		Balto. Co., Md.
James Hood	Kitty Franklin	July 22, 1784	Balto. Co., Md.
Joseph Hook	Anne Channell	Apr. 16, 1821	Balto. Co., Md.
Jesse Hoshal	Mary Hurst	Dec. 22, 1779	Harf. Co., Md.
John How	Rachel Pindell	July 26, 1782	Wash. Co., Pa.
John Howard	Margaret Stattions	1784	Mont. Co., Md.
John Howard	Mary King	1776	A. A. Co., Md.
Stephen Howard	Elizabeth Roy	June 1784	Jamaica, Br. W.I.
Seneca Howland	Agnes King	*post* 1800	New York
Thomas Hudson	Benedicta Coffer	Dec. 24, 1794	Chas. Co., Md.
Aaron Hughes	Adaline Hughes		
Thomas Hugon	Elizabeth Morgan	June 25, 1778	Delaware
Lawrence Hurdle	Nancy Wheeler	1792	Mont. Co., Md.
Robert Hurdle	Susan Riggs	Jan. 29, 1809	D. C.
Nichols Hutchins	Susan Ayres	*ante* 1820	Maryland*
Frederick Ijams	Mary Johnson	*circa* 1789	Wilkes Co., Ga.
Samuel S. Jack	Mary Murray		Chas. Co., Md.
Richard Jackson	Elizabeth Lewis	*post* 1800	Penn.*
William Jackson	Jemina Burnett	Aug. 8, 1814	Carrol Co., Va.
John Jarvis	Anne Richards	Dec. 1779	A. A. Co., Md.
Samuel Jay	Martha Smith, wid.	Feb. 1812	Maryland
Jacob Jeffers	Ann Goldsborough	Dec. 1793	Q. A. Co., Md.
Philip Jenkins	Sarah Knott	1780	Maryland
Ambrose Johnson	Mary Dowell	*post* 1800	North Carolina
Benjamin Johnson	Elizabeth McGraw	Aug. 8, 1829	Kanawaha Co., Va.
John Johnson	Elizabeth Whelan	1785	Wash. Co., Md.
John Johnson	Sophia Norris	*ante* 1827	
Joseph Johnson	Elizabeth Pitt	June 4, 1838	Dist. of Columbia
William Johnson	Elizabeth Luke, wid.		Maryland
Abel Jones	Margaret Lewis	Nov. 23, 1784	Delaware*
Dennis Jones	Eleanor Wilson	Aug. 24, 1785	Frank. Co., Penn.
Jason Jones	Elizabeth Thompson, wid.	Nov. 25, 1799	A. A. Co., Md.

Marriage Records

John Courts Jones	Dorothy Harrison	July 29, 1790	Maryland
Richard Jones	Susannah Culver	Feb. 1778	Mont. Co., Md.
Thomas Jones	Elizabeth Duval	Feb. 4, 1777	Pr. Geo. Co., Md.
Thomas Jones	Elizabeth Jones	ante 1776	Mont. Co., Md.
William Jones	Elizabeth Woolford	Apr. 1792	Maryland
William N. Jones	Mary Sewell	Feb. 27, 1819	Fairfax Co., Va.
John Jordan	Sarah Harrison	Dec. 27, 1787	Maryland
John Keever	Mary Roby	Sept. 2, 1813	Jefferson Co., O.
William Kelley	Martha Loveall	Jan. 1, 1778	Maryland
Thomas Kelso	Penelope Rutledge	Jan. 25, 1789	
Benjamin Kerchevall	Margaret Montgomery	post 1800	Indiana*
Jacob Keyser	Permelia Johnston	Oct. 11, 1785	Loudon Co., Va.
John Kibler	Mary Munford	Apr. 2, 1781	Berkeley Co., Va.
John Kilty	Catherine Quynn	May 9, 1792	A. A. Co., Md.
Alexander King	Rachel Castenl——	post 1800	New York
Charles King	James Ferris	post 1800	New York
Francis King	Mary Jones	Oct. 31, 1780	Somerset Co., N.J.
James B. King	Peggy Cashaday	post 1800	New York
John King	Irene Ely	Oct. 22, 1809	New York*
Moses King	Betsy Brown	post 1800	New York
William King	Mihal Green		Maryland
John G. Kirby	Cecilia Clagett	post 1800	Virginia
William Kirk	Prudence Stevens	Aug. 1785	N. London, Conn.
David Kirkwood	Margaret Leech	May 18, 1795	Camp. Co., Ky.
James Knott	Mary Mudd	circa 1810	Kentucky
Samuel Koffel	Julia Davis		Ohio*
Henry Kriser	Susan Young	ante 1852	Indiana
John Kuhn	Matilda White		Pennsylvania
John George Kuhn	Catherine Smith	circa 1800	Maryland*
Michael Kurchner	Margaret Stoope	circa 1818	Pennsylvania*
Joshua Lamb	Sarah Slicer	ante 1780	A. A. Co., Md.
William Lancaster	Sarah Blades, wid.	Sept. 11, 1813	Kentucky
Francis Lang	Susannah Philips	Sept. 18, 1828	Law. Co., Ind.
Thomas Lansdale	Cornelia V. Howard	Feb. 12, 1782	Maryland
William Lansdale	Elisa C. Moylan	Mar. 10, 1807	Maryland*
James Larkin	Catherine Geilinger	July 3, 1783	Lancaster Co., Pa.
William Lawrence	Margaret Bradley	circa 1778	Delaware
William Lawrence	Rachel Roberts, wid.	July 29, 1828	Guernsey Co., O.
Wendel Lawrentz	Anne Steel	Feb. 28, 1797	Balto. Co., Md.
Benjamin Lawson	Anne Reiley		Maryland*
Joshua Leach	Priscilla Wilkinson	Jan. 6, 1783	Cal. Co., Md.
Charles G. Lee	Maria Hutcheson	post 1800	Indiana*
John Lee	Martha Howlett	Aug. 4, 1779	Harf. Co., Md.
Parker H. Lee	Mary Munnikhuysen	Sept. 19, 1809	Balto. Co., Md.
James Leiper	Elizabeth Smallwood	ante 1800	
Hugh Lemaster	Mary Jupin	Feb. 20, 1792	Wash. Co., Md.
Jacob Lemon	Jane Gilliland	Jan. 3, 1797	Botetout Co., Va.
Joseph Leonard	Mary Ferguson	Feb. 8, 1821	Tal. Co., Md.

William Lindsey	Hannah Lewis	*post* 1800	Pennsylvania*
Thomas Lloyd	Mary Carson	Oct. 2, 1780	Lancaster Co., Pa.
William Logue	Martha Vogan	Nov. 14, 1794	Harf. Co., Md.
Richard Loman	Sarah Connolly	———	Ohio*
John Long	Anne Scott	Feb. 21, 1779	Harf. Co., Md.
Peter Long	Margaret Carr, wid.	Aug. 30, 1791	Balto. Co., Md.
Henry Lord	Amelia Flowers	May 1833	Dorch. Co., Md.
Basil Lowe	Trecy Wood	*circa* 1784	Maryland
Henry Low	Eleanor Kelsoe	July 21, 1836	Wash. Co., Va.
John T. Lowe	Susan Riddle	July 11, 1784	Pr. Geo. Co., Md.
Hiram Loy	Nancy Denune	*post* 1825	Ohio
George Ludwig	Nancy Kline	*circa* 1785	Maryland
John Luke	Elizabeth Riley	———	Maryland*
George Luther	Elizabeth Auman	June 15, 1779	Fred. Co., Md.
Michael Luther	Mary Kindle	Dec. 20, 1789	Fred. Co., Md.
Henry Lutz	Mary Jones	1788	Mont. Co., Md.
Patrick Lynch	Martha Wharley	1783	Bedford Co., Va.
William Lynch	Margaret Robinson	Mar. 1, 1790	Lancaster Co., Pa.
David Lynn	Mary Galloway	Apr. 28, 1795	A. A. Co., Md.
Norman Magruder	Nancy Paugh	1783	Wash. Co., Md.
Thomas Mahoney	Elizabeth Johnson, wid.	Aug. 1827	Maryland
John Manley	Susannah Cox	Apr. 15, 1790	Cecil Co., Md.
Samuel Mansfield	Margaret Boils	Apr. 27, 1780	Sussex Co., N.J.
Thomas Mansfield	Anne Wilkinson	Oct. 11, 1792	Tal. Co., Md.
Peter Mantz	Catherine Hauer	Apr. 23, 1778	Fred. Co., Md.
Leonard Marbury	Ann Somerville	Feb. 2, 1780	Augusta, Ga.
Philip Maroney	Martha Massy	Jan. 3, 1785	Frank. Co., N.C.
William Marr	Arrcy Owings	June 14, 1784	Balto. Co., Md.
Joshua Marsh	Temperance Marsh	Dec. 11, 1785	Balto. Co., Md.
Hezekiah Marshall	Althe Neel	Jan. 18, 1824	Green Co., Pa.
Robert Marshall	Nancy Mardis	Oct. 24, 1797	Kentucky
John Martin	Barbara Funfrock	Feb. 18, 1787	Fred. Co., Md.
Mordecai Martin	Ann Vigal	*post* 1799	Maryland
Robert Martin	Nancy Phoebus	1780	Som. Co., Md.
Henry Massey	Frances Smith	Nov. 2, 1820	Sussex Co., Del.
John McCain	Elizabeth Young	*ante* 1852	Indiana
John McCalla	Margaret McBeath	*circa* 1790	Botetout Co., Va.
John McCaw	Margaret Downs	*post* 1789	Maryland*
Frank McClure	Matilda Bean	*ante* 1820	Kentucky
James McConnell	Amanda Smith	*post* 1815	Kentucky*
Thomas McCormick	Elizabeth Clagett	*post* 1800	Virginia
Dana McCrabb	Sarah Lynch	*post* 1810	Pennsylvania*
Joseph McCracken	Mary Smith	Feb. 26, 1789	Harf. Co., Md.
John McDowell	Sarah Thomas	May 27, 1790	South Carolina
Thomas McDowell	Mary Conner	Aug. 14, 1788	Pennsylvania*
Archibald McKee	Ethel Baggerly	Oct. 7, 1819	North Carolina*
Moses McKenzie	Sarah McKenzie	Dec. 1784	Hampshire Co., Va.
Alexander McKim	Catherine Davey	July 20, 1785	Maryland

MARRIAGE RECORDS 119

Peter McMahan	Barbara Clark, wid.	Nov. 29, 1817	Maryland
Daniel MacMillen	Jane Sconce	Jan. 17, 1811	Cumb. Co., Ky.
William McMillan	Nancy Anderson	1821	Mercer Co., Pa.
Asa McNamara	Jane Howard	1818	Vermont
Mark McPherson	Mary Middleton	circa 1785	Chas. Co., Md.
John McVerley	Nancy Davis	———	Ohio
James Mead	Mary Wilkinson	Mar. 1, 1791	Q.A. Co., Md.
Andrew Meloan	Rachel Ozier	circa 1781	———
Obadiah A. Meloan	E. W. Scruggs	May 8, 1828	———
Luke Merryman	Elizabeth Gorsuch	Jan. 29, 1794	Balto. Co., Md.
Samuel Mickum	Henrietta Dixon, wid.	Nov. 24, 1796	Chas. Co., Md.
Joshua Miles	Jane Glenn	Feb. 6, 1785	Harf. Co., Md.
Thomas H. Miles	Caroline Smith	ante 1844	Maryland
Cornelius J. Miller	Sarah Young	ante 1852	Indiana
George Miller	Judith Wisner	May 1777	Wash. Co., Md.
John Miller	Eleanor Garner	Sept. 7, 1796	Surry Co., N.C.
John Miller	Mary Dotson	July 5, 1787	Shenand. Co., Va.
John Miller	Mary Anne Welch	Dec. 4, 1790	A.A. Co., Md.
John Miller	Rosannah Ulerich	Sept. 1776	Lancaster Co., Pa.
John Milstead	Elizabeth Purnell	Dec. 6, 1798	Staff. Co., Va.
John Milton	Catherine Nelson, wid.	1813	Fred. Co., Va.
John Mitchell	Catherine Derry	Oct. 23, 1777	———
John Mitchell	Elizabeth Weather	Sept. 8, 1836	Pennsylvania
John Mitchell	Lucy Stoddert	ante 1816	———
John Mitchell	Susan Osborn	Oct. 23, 1812	Pennsylvania
Peter Mitchell	Rosannah Bowman	Dec. 15, 1838	Pennsylvania
John Mondy	Rosannah Huffman	Mar. 16, 1788	Wash. Co., Md.
Alexander Montgomery	Lydia Cox	Apr. 27, 1827	Mont. Co., Ind.
Hugh Montgomery	Eve Hartman	1784	Pennsylvania
Asa Moore	Elizabeth Thomas	Mar. 7, 1790	Pr. Geo. Co., Md.
Bernard Moore	Lucy Leiper	ante 1816	———
George Moore	Nancy Ball	Oct. 24, 1780	Maryland
John Moore	Mary Wharton	Dec. 25, 1787	Maryland
Nicholas Moore	Sarah Kelso	Dec. 25, 1793	Balto. Co., Md.
Thomas Morris	Polly Knick	post 1800	Virginia
Daniel Morrison	Anne Reynolds	Mar. 3, 1817	Nova Scotia
Jacob Moser	Elizabeth Onstott	July 1780	North Carolina
Michael Moser	Catherine Color	Feb. 1785	Fred. Co., Md.
Francis Mosier	Polly Scipe	May 27, 1830	Jefferson Co., Tn.
Alfred Mount	Mary Thomas	post 1800	North Carolina
Richard Mowland	Rachel Williams	Mar. 25, 1784	Chester Co., Pa.
James Mudd	Anne Swann	circa 1785	Maryland
Jeremiah Mudd	Barbara Swann	1785	Chas. Co., Md.
Richard Mudd	Mary Berry	Nov. 1793	Mont. Co., Md.
Smith Mudd	Elizabeth Swann	circa 1785	Maryland
Lewis Mullikin	Susannah Jarvis	Nov. 9, 1775	Bute Co., N.C.
James Murden	Mary Portlock, wid.	post 1813	North Carolina
William Murdock	Jane Harrison	May 27, 1783	Mont. Co., Md.

Anthony Murphy	Mary West	Aug. 27, 1787	Pr. Anne Co., Va.
Charles Murphy	Elizabeth Dixon	circa 1807	Chas. Co., Md.
Hezekiah Murphy	Sarah Cotton	Apr. 17, 1794	Nelson Co., Ky.
James Murphy	Mary Craddick	ante 1791	Maryland
Richard Nagle	Catherine Baum	circa 1800	Pennsylvania*
George Nash	Minerva Young	ante 1852	Indiana
John Neale	Margaret Miller	Feb. 27, 1780	Somerset Co., N.J.
John Nelson	Catherine Washington	Nov. 3, 1789	Fred. Co., Va.
Roger Nelson	Elizabeth Harrison	Feb. 2, 1797	Pr. Geo. Co., Md.
Basil Newton	Mary Flatford	Jan. 20, 1785	Cal. Co., Md.
Samuel Nichols	Elizabeth Smyth	Feb. 15, 1801	Maryland
Bazil Norman	Fortune Stephens	Sept. 1782	Mont. Co., Md.
Arnold Norris	Elizabeth Paine	Apr. 10, 1795	Berkeley Co., Va.
Enos Norwell	Elizabeth Langley	Apr. 14, 1828	Pitt. Co., N.C.
Daniel O'Brian	Eleanor Lemon	circa 1780	Maryland
Daniel O'Brian	Martha Gay	Oct. 23, 1795	Chitt. Co., Vt.
James O'Croson	Rosannah White	———	Pennsylvania
John O'Daniel	Sarah Rude	Apr. 10, 1794	Nelson Co., Ky.
John O'Hara	Susan Tayman	July 3, 1790	Pr. Geo. Co., Md.
John Oldham	Anna Albright	Apr. 12, 1795	Balto. Co., Md.
John Oliver	Susan Cole	post 1815	Maryland
John Onion	Juliet Pendergast, wid.	Mar. 26, 1787	A.A. Co., Md.
John Orr	Elizabeth Johns	Dec. 1792	Fayette Co., Pa.
William Osborn	Catherine VanBuskirk	———	New York
Stephen Owen	Mary Ann Gaunce	Nov. 1, 1804	Cecil Co., Md.
William Pack	Margaret O'Neal	Apr. 11, 1782	Mont. Co., Md.
Melchoir Painter	Ann Mary Miller	Dec. 7, 1779	Wash. Co., Md.
Thomas Paris	Barbara Young	ante 1852	Wisconsin*
Samuel Parran	Elizabeth Dalrymple	ante 1828	Maryland
Edward Parrish	Clemency Hughes	May 20, 1782	Balto. Co., Md.
William Parrish	Jane Hollidayoke	post 1790	A.A. Co., Md.
Christopher Parrott	Martha Clark	Jan. 21, 1781	Pr. Geo. Co., Md.
John Pattern	Elizabeth White	———	Pennsylvania
Kanada Patterson	Sarah Grace	Dec. 1802	Rowan Co., N.C.
James Patton	Catherine Neiman (?)	ante 1820	Pennsylvania
Thomas Paul	Catherine De Camp	1781	Phila., Penn.
John Peace	Rebecca Haislip, wid.	Jan. 12, 1819	Tenn.
John Pearce	Martha Crouch	Sept. 22, 1836	Indiana
John Pearce	Sarah Hennis	1780	Virginia
Joshua Pearre	Milly Ann Arnold	Oct. 30, 1828	Will's'n. Co., Tn.
Leon Pecor	Charlotte Sewell, wid.	June 30, 1830	Balto. Co., Md.
William Pendergast	Juliet Marbury	Sept. 15, 1784	A.A. Co., Md.
Benjamin Penn	Rebecca Ryan	ante 1775	Indiana
Stephen Penn	Mary McNay	Feb. 16, 1786	Chas. Co., Md.
Thomas Pennefield	Esther Beane	July 1790	Pr. Geo. Co., Md.
Simon Perry	Elizabeth Fountain	Feb. 12, 1791	King Geo. Co., Va.
Thomas Perry	Mary Blake	July 1, 1817	Greenbrier Co., Va.
Thomas Petet	Sarah Clutter	Nov. 1788	Harrison Co., Va.

Marriage Records

Bryan Philpot	Elizabeth Johnson	Nov. 16, 1796	Balto. Co., Md.
John Pickler	Lydia Grace	———	Indiana*
John Pierson	Elizabeth Warren	Feb. 3, 1794	North Carolina
Robert Pippin	Mica Johnston	June 16, 1820	Wash. Co., Va.
Richard Pitt	Anne Berry	post 1790	Virginia*
Richard Pitts	Sarah Osborn	Dec. 1784	New Haven, Conn.
Jacob Plain	Catherine Folks	Apr. 24, 1788	A.A. Co., Md.
John Plant	Mary Davis	June 14, 1788	Chas. Co., Md.
David Pollock	Anne Rowland	1786	Cecil Co., Md.
Charles Porter	Kiturah Van Vacter	Aug. 23, 1784	Berkeley Co., Va.
William Portlock	Mary Murphy, wid.	May 4, 1807	Virginia
Belain Posey	Margaret Corry	Nov. 5, 1777	Chas. Co., Md.
Casper Potterf	Nancy Longnecker	Aug. 6, 1832	Ohio
William Poythness	Mary Gilliam	May 25, 1782	Pr. Geo. Co., Va.
Benjamin Price	Eleanor Boyd	ante 1774	Fred. Co., Md.
James Price	Elizabeth Johnson, wid.	Apr. 26, 1836	Virginia*
James Price	Terah Zelifrom	Nov. 3, 1800	
William Prigg	Susan Wells	Nov. 1776	Lan. Co., Penn.
Robert Purdle	Catherine Sitler	Aug. 4, 1796	St. M. Co., Md.
Samuel Purnell	Ann Dixon	ante 1775	Fred. Co., Md.
William Rampley	Nancy Ayres	ante 1820	Maryland*
John Randall	Deborah Knapp	Jan. 7, 1783	A.A. Co., Md.
Peyton Randolph	Rhody Pearce	post 1822	North Carolina*
Benjamin F. Raney	Maria Beckett	ante 1830	Ohio*
Daniel Rankins	Eleanor Tongue	Mar. 29, 1792	Loudon Co., Va.
William Rears	Mary Adams	ante 1820	———
John Reed	Marion Ashley	Nov. 30, 1833	Darke Co., O.
Bennett Reiley	Francis Frazier	1792	Fairfax Co., Va.
William Reily	Barbara Hodgkin	Sept. 28, 1791	Balto., Md.
Daniel Reisher	Christiana Croft, wid.	Oct. 28, 1799	Frank. Co., Pa.
James Rewark	Sophia McCauley	circa 1780	Maryland
James Rewark	Susannah Tucker	July 17, 1784	A.A. Co., Md.
John Reynolds	Sarah Weaver	———	South Carolina
Thomas Reynolds	Elizabeth McDonald	1799	Nova Scotia
William Rhodes	Mildred Burch	post 1800	D.C.*
Charles Richardson	Nancy Matthews	Mar. 15, 1788	Som. Co., Md.
Thomas Richardson	Margaret Sands	Jan. 5, 1796	Maryland
Jacob Riddle	Mary Harper	circa 1785	Pr. Geo. Co., Md.
William Rigby	Ara Williamson, wid.	Feb. 25, 1817	Fairfax Co., O.
James Rigdon	Elizabeth Peachy	Aug. 3, 1812	Fleming Co., Ky.
Stephen Riley	Mary Hook	Jan. 2, 1783	Balto. Co., Md.
John Ringer	Anna Saylor	Nov. 1841	Ohio
Solomon Ritchey	Rachel Davis	———	Ohio
Robert Roach	Juliet Clagett	post 1800	Virginia
Archibald Roberts	Mary Ann Bosley	July 24, 1787	Fred. Co., Md.
George Roberts	Patsy Pippin	post 1835	Virginia*
Hazel Roberts	Rachel Gassaway	ante 1828	Ohio*
Patrick Roberts	Catherine Austin	June 20, 1810	Balto Co., Md.

Charles Robinson	Mephyteca Galloway	June 30, 1787	Balto. Co., Md.
John Robinson	Jane Rowland	circa 1778	Bucks Co., Pa.
Charles Robosson	Rebecca Hanson, wid.	Feb. 1786	A.A. Co., Md.
Byrd Rogers	Mary Truman	———	Kentucky
Selah Rollins	Isabella Fuller	Aug. 12, 1831	Indiana*
James Rolls	Margaret Heter	1779	Pennsylvania
Lawrence Ross	Cassandra Lutes	1808	Estell Co., Ky.
Robinson Ross	Sarah Triger	1792	Dorch. Co., Md.
Solomon Royse	Sarah Stotts	Nov. 3, 1796	Green Co., Ky.
Henry Rumfelt	Mary Fite	July 1781	Sussex Co., N.J.
Joshua Rutledge	Elizabeth McComas	Apr. 25, 1820	Harf. Co., Md.
Peter Rutledge	Ruth Robinson	June 1816	Harrison Co., Ky.
Edward Ryan	Polly Young	ante 1852	Indiana
James Ryan	Eleanor Green	Mar. 1774	Balto. Co., Md.
Daniel Sampy	Peggy Hinnys	1785	Wash. Co., Md.
Vincent Sanders	Mary Young, wid.	1818	Maryland
Richard Sappington	Cassandra Durbin	Oct. 8, 1784	A.A. Co., Md.
John Sargeant	Julia Comegys	post 1815	Pennsylvania*
Levi Satterfield	Nancy Simmons	Feb. 15, 1810	North Carolina
William Satterfield	Unicy Clements	1781	Anson Co., N.C.
George N. Saylor	Anna Wilk	Dec. 16, 1794	Franklin Co., Pa.
John Schatz	Elizabeth Leschom	Sept. 18, 1791	———
Christopher Schenck	Juliana Schniten	May 30, 1781	Maryland
Sarah Schick	Sarah Finley	———	———
Michael Schip	Catherine Smith	———	Pennsylvania
Thomas Schip	Mary Smith	———	Pennsylvania
Joseph Scholfield	Mary Russel	Aug. 22, 1812	———
Benjamin Scott	Lotty Anderson	Sept. 23, 1800	Wor. Co., Md.
Nathan Scribner	Sarah Whitacre, wid.	Feb. 1804	Q.A. Co., Md.
John Seiter	Polly King	post 1800	New York
John Sellman	Clarissa Montfort	1794	Georgia
William Seward	Nancy Lee	Dec. 1789	Dorch. Co., Md.
Thomas Sewell	Charlotte Coleman	Nov. 13, 1828	Balto. Co., Md.
William Sewell	Rebecca Disney	Dec. 7, 1790	A.A. Co., Md.
John Shank	Ellen Crow	July 15, 1822	Balto. Co., Md.
William Sharp	Elizabeth James	Sept. 15, 1782	Maryland
Jacob Sheats	Hannah Harple	Mar. 27, 1790	Fred. Co., Md.
James Shelby	Mary Pindell	ante 1830	Kentucky
Orvilla Shelby	Caroline Winchester	Feb. 15, 1825	Tennessee
Joseph Shelton	Priscilla Riggs	post 1800	Kentucky*
William Shepherd	Elizabeth Coleman	ante 1852	Indiana
Henry Shipley	Ruth Howard	Aug. 1782	Balto. Co., Md.
Bennett Shirley	Susannah Peake	May 15, 1793	St. M. Co., Md.
John Shober	Susanna Bowers	Dec. 22, 1785	Virginia*
Peter Shockley	Lucinda Wimbra	ante 1828	Maryland*
George Shryock	Elizabeth Lewis	Jan. 1808	Maryland
George Silver	Nancy Griffith	Apr. 12, 1782	Fred. Co., Md.
Aaron Simmons	Sarah Thompson	Jan. 30, 1783	Chas. Co., Md.

Marriage Records

William Simmons	Sarah Darton	Aug. 9, 1796	Balto. Co., Md.
Thomas Simpson	Sophia Clagett	post 1800	Virginia
Lawrence Simpson	Sarah Carrico	circa 1795	Chas. Co., Md.
James L. Sims	Matilda Mudd	circa 1810	Kentucky
John Slack	Margaret Aurman	Sept. 22, 1789	Fred. Co., Md.
John Sloan	Sarah Patterson	————	Indiana*
John Sluts	Catherine Welsh	June 22, 1790	Fred. Co., Md.
Alexander L. Smith	Martha Griffith	Aug. 1792	Harf. Co., Md.
Aquilla Smith	Catherine Conway	Sept. 6, 1785	Balto. City
Charles Smith	Mary Bowling	Jan. 19, 1782	Chas. Co., Md.
Conrad Smith	Anne Black, wid.	Oct. 17, 1792	York Co., Pa.
Daniel Smith	Sophiah Ashley	July 2, 1789	South Carolina*
Drew Smith	Jane McMelone	circa 1800	South Carolina*
Elijah Smith	Margaret Preston	Aug. 8, 1783	Henry Co., Va.
Elijah Smith	Priscilla Abbott	1785	Dorch. Co., Md.
Jacob Smith	Catherine French	circa 1814	Morgantown, Va.
James Smith	Margaret Truax	Jan. 25, 1783	Loudon Co., Va.
John Smith	Catherine Hohn	Aug. 5, 1786	Fred. Co., Md.
John Smith	Elizabeth Mullikin	Jan. 1, 1791	Mont. Co., Md.
John Smith	Sarah Tydings	Sept. 26, 1785	A.A. Co., Md.
John Smith	Susan Hawn	Oct. 4, 1778	Shenand'h. Co., Va.
Leonard Smith	Mary McManus	Dec. 17, 1796	Rich. Co., Ga.
Michael Smith	Nancy Levite, wid.	Sept. 18, 1797	Mont. Co., Ky.
Michael Smith	Rebecca Ludwig	1784	Maryland
Nathan Smith	Anne Chew	July 3, 1784	Cecil Co., Md.
Richard Smith	Elizabeth Church	Jan. 12, 1785	Pr. Geo. Co., Md.
Samuel Smith	Isabel Carroll, wid.	May 1795	Halifax Co., Va.
Thomas Smith	Anne Boyles	Aug. 13, 1802	Hunt. Co., Pa.
William Smith	Charity Lee	1777/8	North Carolina
Thomas Smyth	Anna Maria Garnet	Dec. 1793	Kent Co., Md.
William Smyth	Isabella Thornburgh	Dec. 30, 1817	————
Frederick Snider	Elizabeth Pennybacker	Jan. 25, 1785	Berkley Co., Va.
John Snyder	Elizabeth Forter	Aug. 27, 1793	Tal. Co., Md.
Philip Solladay	Anna Christiana Flick	circa 1779	Sharpsburg, Md.
George Spalding	Susanna Shutteworth	June 12, 1811	Wash. Co., Ky.
Hezekiah Speake	Eleanor Tucker	1783	Mont. Co., Md.
Edward Spedden	Anne Manning	July 1773	Dorch. Co., Md.
John Spires	Mary Hinton	Aug. 24, 1784	Maryland
Jacob Spong	Elizabeth Miller	May 1775	Cumb. Co., Pa.
Jesse Spradlin	Sally Stone	post 1800	Kentucky*
Samuel Sprigg	Violetta Lansdale	post 1800	Maryland
Richard Spyers	Rebecca Gentle	Feb. 1787	Pr. Geo. Co., Md.
John Stafford	Mary Gilbert	1822	Dixon Co., Tenn.
Samuel Starr	Jane Davis	————	Ohio
Benjamin Stevens	Priscilla Vanderwolf	circa 1790	Maryland
Levi Stevens	Mary Furniss	Aug. 24, 1791	Som. Co., Md.
William Stevens	Nancy City	circa 1800	Virginia
Christopher Stinchcomb	Magdaline Zimmerman	Oct. 16, 1793	Balto. Co., Md.

James Stockman	Nancy Lewis	*post* 1800	Pennsylvania
Walter Stoddert	Margaret Smallwood	*ante* 1800	
William Stoddert	Lucy Smallwood	*ante* 1816	Maryland
Sylvester Stone	Lucy Beckett	Dec. 11, 1817	Ohio*
John Stoner	Mary Jack	Apr. 20, 1815	Nelson Co., Ky.
Andrew Stoope	Sarah Shaw	Dec. 10, 1796	Bristol, Pa.
John Storer	Dorothy Jones, wid.	July 27, 1812	Maryland
Jacob Storts	Polly Notestine	Oct. 17, 1830	Ohio
Alexander Stuart	Elizabeth Thomas, wid.	1804	Maryland
Solomon Sullivan	Sarah McComb	1774	Dorch. Co., Md.
Stephen Sullivan	Mary Sullivan	*circa* 1794	North Carolina*
Hezekiah Summers	Ruth Dawson	Apr. 13, 1831	Monon. Co., Va.
John Summers	Anne Clagett	Dec. 8, 1774	Fred. Co., Md.
Richard Summers	Elizabeth Lewis, wid.	Nov. 21, 1822	Accomac Co., Va.
Alexander Sutherland	Peggy Wallace	July 27, 1784	Bedford Co., Va.
William Sutherland	Katherine Ensminger	Aug. 6, 1789	Rockbr'g. Co., Va.
John Swan	Sarah Boult		
John Swiney	Martha Durrington, wid.	Mar. 7, 1842	Kentucky
Josiah Tanneyhill	Margaret Wilkins	Apr. 27, 1786	Pittsburg
Andrew Tarborne	Elizabeth Arthur	Mar. 29, 1801	Pr. Geo. Co., Va.
Jeremiah Tarlton	Eleanor Medley	Jan. 20, 1782	St. M. Co., Md.
John Taylor	Leggy Crutchley	Oct. 11, 1824	A.A. Co., Md.
John Taylor	Ruth Bailey	Mar. 16, 1780	Mont. Co., Md.
Richard Taylor	Anne Wollow	Dec. 29, 1793	Hamp. Co., Va.
Richard Taylor	Mary Johnson	Nov. 1788	Mont. Co., Md.
Wright Taylor	Cassandra Turner, wid.	Dec. 14, 1829	Kentucky
William Thatcher	Debora Young, wid.	*ante* 1852	Indiana
James Thomas	Rebecca Logsden	Apr. 8, 1793	Kentucky
John Thomas	Elizabeth Gibson	May 9, 1779	Tal. Co., Md.
John Thomas	Elizabeth Perryman	1782/3	Rock. Co., N.C.
Philip Thomas	Cornelia Lansdale	Nov. 8, 1804	Maryland*
Electius Thompson	Martha Holley, wid.	*post* 1807	Alabama*
John Thompson	Elizabeth Connaway	Jan. 3, 1786	A.A. Co., Md.
Tench Tilghman	Anna Maria Tilghman	June 9, 1783	Tal. Co., Md.
James Tillet	Mary Jones, wid.	*post* 1829	Virginia
Luke Tipton	Tersa Cole	*post* 1805	Ohio*
John Titman	Catherine Fite		
Joseph Tolle	Charlotte Bean	*ante* 1833	Kentucky
William Tongue	Elizabeth Thomas	May 1794	Wash. Co., Md.
David Trimel	Polly Zelifrom	Oct. 19, 1802	
Christian Trout	Elizabeth Gerhart	Sept. 15, 1795	Rock. Co., Va.
John Trux	Catherine Flannigan	June 10, 1811	Fred. Co., Md.
John Tucker	Nancy Wofford	1791	South Carolina
Richard Tucker	Elizabeth Johnson	*post* 1785	Maryland*
John Turner	Anne Elizabeth Mariner	Feb. 7, 1788	Harf. Co., Md.
Solomon Turner	Cassandra Harvey	July 22, 1785	Fred. Co., Md.
John Twiner	Judith Peck	Dec. 1, 1789	Sullivan Co., Tn.
Benjamin Uncles	Margaret Plaister	*circa* 1781	Fred. Co., Md.

Marriage Records

Abraham Van Buskirk	Jane Burdette	Nov. 29, 1778	New Jersey
John Van Horn	Eve Finley	—	—
John de Vaubrun	Anne Howard	Sept. 1781	A.A. Co., Md.
John Vaughan	Nancy Callicott	Oct. 16, 1794	Halifax Co., Va.
Adam Vigal	Ann Barnes	circa 1790	Mont. Co., Md.
Aaron Vincent	Rebecca Smith	Aug. 30, 1792	Dorch. Co., Md.
Edward Wailes	Sarah Oden	Mar. 21, 1781	Pr. Geo. Co., Md.
John Walker	Mary Shultz	Oct. 18, 1811	Fred. Co., Md.
John Wall	Elizabeth Scarberry	1771	Rowan Co., N.C.
William Wall	Kitturah Wright, wid.	Sept. 27, 1831	Caroline Co., Md.
Benjamin Walls	Elizabeth Harry	July 30, 1835	Maryland
George Walls	Martha Naylor	Mar. 28, 1784	Pr. Geo. Co., Md.
George Walls	Sarah Club	Jan. 20, 1824	Maryland
Albert Walrath	Catherine Yule	post 1810	Herk. Co., N.Y.
William Wanton	Mary Elizabeth Hughes	—	Virginia*
Edward Ward	Lucy Wilson	Aug. 6, 1779	Maryland
Joseph Ward	Elizabeth Patterson	ante 1828	Maryland
Joseph Warfield	Elizabeth Dorsey	Aug. 6, 1778	Maryland
George Washburn	Eleanor Rankins	post 1834	Ohio
James Waters	Dradin King	—	—
Richard Waters	Elizabeth Boyle	Dec. 20, 1818	Tal. Co., Md.
Gassaway Watkins	Eleanor Clagett	Apr. 22, 1803	Balto. Co., Md.
Leonard Watkins	Mary Higdon	Dec. 1781	Maryland
Stephen Watkins	Sarah Miller	June 26, 1804	Virginia
Christian Waetherman	Martha Runegan	ante 1793	North Carolina*
John Webb	Susannah Duval	June 15, 1775	Fred. Co., Md.
Isaac Webster	Clemency Gilbert	post 1800	Maryland
Michael Weirick	Elizabeth Rimby	Nov. 16, 1784	Pennsylvania
Adam Weise	Catherine Patton	Dec. 10, 1820	Pennsylvania
Benjamin Wells	Mary Altz	Aug. 2, 1805	Kanawaha Co., Va.
Charles Wells	Mary Williamson	—	—
Cornelius Wells	Sarah Hiller	Nov. 8, 1839	D.C.
Duckett Wells	Sarah Leakin	Jan. 20, 1774	Maryland*
Enos West	Jane Robinson	—	Harf. Co., Md.
William Wheatley	Rhoda Tull	1782/3	Dorch. Co., Md.
Birdsey W. Wheeler	Machel Fulton	Dec. 23, 1805	York Dist., S.C.
William Whitacre	Sarah Carman	ante 1786	Q.A. Co., Md.
John White	Eleanor Williams	May 13, 1788	Westmoreland, Pa.
John Whittingham	Sarah Patterson	ante 1828	Maryland
Jacob Wilcox	Catherine Sellman	post 1810	Georgia*
George Wilcoxen	Anne Hoskinson	—	Ohio*
James Wilkinson	Celestine Crudeau	Mar. 5, 1810	New Orleans
Simon Willard	Sarah Patterson	ante 1828	Maryland
Elisha Williams	Harriet Beale	May 6, 1784	Mont. Co., Md.
Gabriel Williams	Margaret Lytton	June 22, 1784	Wash. Co., Md.
Gerard Williams	Ruth Clemens	Feb. 2, 1792	Pittsburg, Pa.
James Williams	Elizabeth Miller	May 26, 1805	Adams Co., O.
Jeremiah Williams	Mary Gaither	Dec. 15, 1784	A.A. Co., Md.

John Williams	Elizabeth Moser, wid.	Sept. 1814	Tennessee
John Williams	Mary Chappell	Feb. 8, 1784/5	Pr. Wm. Co., Va.
Moses W. Williams	Jane Williams	post 1810	Kentucky
Thomas Williams	Agnes Hartshorn	Aug. 20, 1800	Cecil Co., Md.
David Williamson	Ara Lemon	Dec. 12, 1804	
George Wilson	Elizabeth Burch	post 1800	D.C.*
Josiah Wilson	Margaret B. Walls	Jan. 30, 1817	Pr. Geo. Co., Md.
Thomas Wilson	Maria Smyth	June 3, 1806	Maryland
Charles H. Wiltberger	Verlinda Burch	post 1800	D.C.*
Lucitius Winchester	Amanda Bledsoe	Apr. 11, 1830	Tennessee
Valerius Winchester	Samuella Price	Oct. 24, 1833	Tennessee
George Windham	Mary Card	Nov. 1782	St. M. Co., Md.
Thomas Windham	Sarah Lamb, wid.	July 21, 1785	A.A. Co., Md.
Raphael Winsett	Susannah Cissell	1783	St. M. Co., Md.
William Wistel	Catherine Purdle	post 1801	Maryland
George Wolfe	Letitia Hood	post 1810	Maryland
Henry Wolfe	Rachel Hood	post 1805	Maryland
Aaron Wood	Matilda Mayhew	July 22, 1824	York Co., S.C.
John Wood	Catherine City	circa 1799	Virginia
John Wood	Rachel Bratton	Feb. 7, 1824	Edward Co., Ill.
John Woodfield	Mahala Moore	post 1800	
John Woodside	Elinor Montgomery	1772	Delaware
Beale Worthington	Elizabeth Ricketts		Maryland
Turbutt Wright	Anne Wright	Nov. 4, 1792	Q.A. Co., Md.
Alfred Wynne	Alemead Winchester	Feb. 15, 1825	Tennessee
Benjamin Yates	Sarah Robinson	July 16, 1835	Highland Co., O.
Jacob Yeast	Elizabeth Wyle	circa 1774	Fred. Co., Md.
Henry Young	Mary Garrish	circa 1774	Fred. Co., Md.
Henry Young	Nancy Spyres	post 1810	Ohio
Henry Young	Sally Kriser	ante 1852	Indiana
John Young	Sarah Wells, wid.	post 1844	D.C.
Josias Young	Emiline Wood	ante 1825	Maryland
Matthias Young	Hannah Angle	ante 1852	Indiana
Samuel Young	Debora Anne Hevelin	ante 1852	Indiana
William Young	Rebecca Grinage	Sept. 4, 1816	Col. Co., Ga.
James Yule	Margaret Christman	Sept. 12, 1779	New York

Part V

MISCELLANEOUS LIST OF REVOLUTIONARY SERVICES FROM STATES OTHER THAN MARYLAND ESTABLISHED THROUGH PENSION APPLICATIONS.

NOTE: Proof and certification may be secured for a reasonable fee by addressing the compiler.

Soldier	Service
Abbott, Benjamin	Conn., & N. Y.
Abbott, Samuel	Q. M., Sea Service
Abbot, Samuel	New York
Abell, Garrett	New York
Abrams, John	New York
Acher, Albert	New York
Acherson, Abraham	New York
Acker, Benjamin	New York
Acker, Henry	New York
Acker, Jacob	New York
Acker, Jacob	New York
Acker, Jacob	New York
Acker, Peter	New York
Acker, Solomon	New York
Ackerman, William	New York
Ackerson, Cornelius	New York
Ackerson, Derick	New York
Ackerson, John	New York
Ackerson, John	New York
Ackler, John	New York
Ackler, Leonard	New York
Ackley, Jacob	New York
Ackley, Joel	New York
Adair, James	Pennsylvania
Adams, Bartholomew	Delaware
Adams, Ebenezer	N. Y. & Conn.
Adams, Elijah	Conn. & N. Y.

Adams, Elijah	New York
Adams, Emanuel	New York
Adams, Isaac	Capt., Penn. Militia
Adams, James	Lieut., Ky. Service
Adams, James	New York
Adams, John	Pennsylvania
Adams, John	Va. Sea Service
Adams, Levi	New York
Adams, Littleton	Virginia
Adams, Matthew	New York
Adams, Nathan	Capt., Delaware
Adams, William	New York
Adamy, Henry	New York
Adamy, John	New York
Addison, Jacob	Delaware
Adkins, Stephen	Delaware
Adley, Peter	New York
Adner, George	New York
Adriance, Isaac	New York
Agard, Joseph	Conn. & N. Y.
Agard, Noah	Conn. & N. Y.
Agens, James	New York
Ake, William	Delaware
Akeley, Benjamin	New York
Aker, John	New York
Akin, James	Conn. & N. Y.
Akins, Samuel	New York
Akley, Jacob	New York
Albein, John	New York
Aldrich, Jacob	New York
Aldrich, Robert	New York
Aldridge, William	Kentucky
Alexander, James	North Carolina
Alexander, John	Pennsylvania
Alexander, John	Delaware
Alexander, Jonathan	New York
Allen, Amasa	Conn. & N. Y.
Allen, Benjamin	Connecticut
Allen, Charles	Capt., Virginia
Allen, David	Penn. & N. Y.

Miscellaneous List Other States

Allen, Ebenezer	Major, Vermont
Allen, George	New York
Allen, James	New York
Allen, Jesse	New York
Allen, John	Conn. & N. Y.
Allen, John	New York
Allen, John	New York
Allen, Lathrop	Conn. & N. Y.
Allen, Nathan	Vt. & N. Y.
Allen, Patrick	Pennsylvania
Allen, Reuben	Conn. & N. Y.
Allen, Stephen	Connecticut
Allen, Samuel	New York
Allen, Samuel	New York
Allen, William	North Carolina
Allen, William	Connecticut
Allerton, Jonathan	New York
Alliston, Isaac	New York
Alliston, Jeremiah	New York
Alliston, John	New York
Alliston, Joseph	New York
Alliston, Robert	New York
Allworth, Thomas	New York
Alsdorph, Lawrence	New York
Alvord, Thomas	New York
Ambler, James	Conn. & N. Y.
Ambler, John	New York
Ames, Levi	New York
Ames, Peter	R. I. & N. Y.
Amidon, Philip	Capt., Massachusetts
Anderson, Alexander	Virginia
Anderson, Enoch	Capt., Delaware
Anderson, Ezekiel	Pennsylvania
Anderson, Isaac	Pennsylvania
Anderson, John	Capt., North Carolina
Anderson, Robert	Col., South Carolina
Andrews, Timothy	Connecticut
Ankrim, John	Capt., Pennsylvania
Archie, James	Capt., Pennsylvania
Armstrong, Abel	Capt., North Carolina

Armstrong, Alexander	Pennsylvania
Armstrong, James	Col., Pennsylvania
Armstrong, John	Capt., New York
Artman, Andrew	Lieut., Pennsylvania
Ashman, George	Pennsylvania Patriot
Askey, Thomas	Capt., Pennsylvania
Austin, Aaron	Capt., Connecticut
Ayres, John	Delaware
Baker, John	Pennsylvania
Baker, Thomas	Capt., Massachusetts
Baley, Samuel	Paymaster, Virginia
Ball, William	Continental Line
Banks, Samuel	Delaware
Baptist, John	Continental Line
Barham, Benjamin	Continental Line
Barham, Hartwell	Continental Line
Barksdale, Samuel	Virginia
Barnes, Ellis	Capt., New Jersey
Barnett, Hugh	Ensign, North Carolina
Barnett, Thomas	Lieut., North Carolina
Barnes, John	Capt., New York
Barr, Alexander	Major, Pennsylvania
Barr, David	Pennsylvania
Barrett, Cheswell	Coronet, Continental
Barrow, Gresham	Capt., Connecticut
Barry, Andrew	Capt., South Carolina
Barker, John	Capt., New Jersey
Basy, William	Virginia
Baum, Frederick	Pennsylvania
Baxton, John	Capt., Pennsylvania
Bayer, Frederick	Continental Line
Bayley, William	Capt., Pennsylvania
Baylor, George	Col., Continental Line
Beach, Elijah	Capt., Connecticut
Beach, Jabez	Connecticut
Beadles, John	Capt., Virginia
Beall, Ninian	Virginia
Beard, William	North Carolina
Bechtel, Philip	Connecticut
Bedkin, Henry	Adjt., Continental

Beeman, Friend	Connecticut
Beeman, Isaac	Connecticut
Belcher, John	Lieut., Connecticut
Bell, George	Pennsylvania
Bell, William	Capt., North Carolina
Benham, James	Connecticut
Bennett, John	Major, Continental
Bennett, Patrick	Q. M., Continental
Bight, Andrew	Lieut., Pennsylvania
Billups, John	Capt., Virginia
Birge, David	Connecticut
Bishop, Jacob	Capt., Pennsylvania
Black, James	Pennsylvania
Black, John	Virginia
Black, Thomas	North Carolina Patriot
Black, William	Capt., Pennsylvania
Blackburn, Samuel	Virginia
Blackmore, George	Tennessee
Blaine, Ephraim	Col., Pennsylvania
Blaine, William	Capt., New York
Blair, James	Lieut., Pennsylvania
Boiller, Joseph	North Carolina
Boles, John	Sergt., Virginia
Boles, Samuel	Delaware
Boltone, James	North Carolina
Bowyer, William	Col., Virginia
Boyd, James	Delaware
Boyd, Thomas	New York
Boyer, Elias	Delaware
Boyers, John	Col., Virginia
Brackett, Samuel	Massachusetts
Bradley, Philip	Col., Pennsylvania
Bradley, Philip	Capt., Connecticut
Bradley, Thomas	Major, Delaware
Brady, John	Capt., Pennsylvania
Breakhill, Peter	Pennsylvania
Breeze, John	Pennsylvania
Brimmage, John	North Carolina
Briscoe, Parmenias	Capt., Kentucky
Brookover, John	Virginia

Brooks, William	North Carolina
Brown, Jacob	Col., North Carolina
Bruce, John	Sea Service
Bruen, Caleb	Capt., Continental
Bruen, Jeremiah	Capt., Continental
Bruner, Jacob	Pennsylvania
Bryarly, Elisha	North Carolina
Bryarly, Richard	North Carolina
Buchanan, Archibald	Col., Pennsylvania
Buchanan, Arthur	Capt., Pennsylvania
Buchanan, James	Capt., Virginia
Buckley, John	Capt., Virginia
Burch, John	Virginia
Burfoot, Thomas	Lieut., Virginia
Burk, John	Virginia
Burnett, Henry	Capt., Virginia
Burrall, Charles	Col., Connecticut
Burress, Thomas	Delaware
Burton, Benjamin	Capt., Massachusetts
Burton, Joshua	Pennsylvania
Burton, May	Capt., Virginia
Burton, Thomas	Virginia
Bush, Henry	Continental Line
Butler, William	Pennsylvania
Butt, Archibald	North Carolina
Butts, William	Massachusetts
Caldwell, David	Capt., North Carolina
Camp, George	Gunner's Mate, Sea Service
Campbell, Charles	Capt., Virginia
Campbell, Gus	Surgeon's Mate
Campbell, McDonald	N. J. & Penn.
Campbell, Thomas	Virginia
Campbell, William	Capt., Pennsylvania
Campbell, William	Capt., Artillery
Camper, Tilman	Va. & Ky.
Caney, Joseph	North Carolina
Cann, James	German Regiment
Cannon, James	Pennsylvania
Cannon, William	Pennsylvania
Carder, Sanford	Virginia

Carey, John	Sergt., Continental
Carll, John	Massachusetts
Carnall, Patrick	Virginia
Carr, Thomas	Capt., Pennsylvania
Carrance, William	Pennsylvania
Carter, Barnabas	Virginia
Carter, Thomas	Surgeon's Mate
Cartwright, Justinian	Sergt. Major, Artillery
Carvel, Moses	Capt., Tennessee
Casana, Hugh	Pennsylvania
Cave, Bilfield	Lieut., Virginia
Cavender, John	Delaware
Chadwick, Elihu	Lieut., New Jersey
Chadwick, Thomas	Capt., New Jersey
Chaffee, William	Connecticut
Chalfflin, Solomon	Virginia
Chandler, John	Col., Connecticut
Chapman, Benjamin	Virginia
Chapman, Elijah	Connecticut
Chase, Robert	Virginia
Chenoweth, Richard	Capt., Kentucky
Chessman, James	Capt., Pennsylvania
Chester, John	Col., Connecticut
Child, Josiah	Capt., Connecticut
Chinn, Perry	Virginia
Choice, Tully	Ensign, Virginia
Choice, William	Lieut., Virginia
Christ, Adam	Invalid
Christie, James	Virginia
City, Jacob	Virginia
Claggage, Robert	Major, Pennsylvania
Claggage, Thomas	Capt., Pennsylvania
Clark, James	New York
Clark, John	Capt., North Carolina
Clark, Oliver	Connecticut
Clarke, William	Capt., Virginia
Clements, John	Virginia
Clemmons, John	North Carolina
Clendeman, James	Pennsylvania
Cleveland, Benjamin	Col., North Carolina

Cleveland, Stephen	Vermont
Clifton, James	Capt., Sea Service
Clifton, Robert	Mate, Sea Service
Clinkenbread, Isaac	Virginia
Clinton, Charles	Capt., Pennsylvania
Clinton, Thomas	New Jersey
Coates, William	Virginia
Cocke, William	Virginia
Coe, Zacheriah	Capt., Connecticut
Coffman, Christopher	Lieut., Pennsylvania
Cole, Job	North Carolina
Collins, James	Pennsylvania
Collins, Josiah	Pennsylvania
Collins, Stephen	Connecticut
Collyer, John	Va. & N. C.
Commins, Harmon	Virginia
Condran, William	Sea Service
Connally, Thomas	Pennsylvania
Connolly, Patrick	Delaware
Conway, Henry	Capt., Virginia
Conway, John	Capt., New Jersey
Cook, George	Capt., Sea Service
Cook, William	Connecticut
Cook, William	Pennsylvania
Cooke, Michael	Virginia
Coon, Joseph	Connecticut
Cooper, John	Pennsylvania
Corbell, Malachi	Virginia
Cotton, James	Virginia
Couch, Joshua	Connecticut
Covenhoven, John	New Jersey
Cowan, Thomas	Capt., North Carolina
Coxson, John	Continental Line
Craig, Alexander	Capt., Pennsylvania
Craig, John	Pennsylvania
Crandol, Amariah	Connecticut
Crawford, William	Col., Virginia
Crawford, William	Ensign, Pennsylvania
Creamer, Daniel	Virginia
Creekbaum, Peter	German Regiment

Croft, William	German Regiment
Crosby, John	Sea Service
Cross, Samuel	Delaware
Crow, Job	Sea Service
Crow, Henry	Surgeon's Mate
Crubb, Curtis	Col., Pennsylvania
Crutfield, Joshua	Virginia
Crutfield, Joshua	Pennsylvania
Cunningham, Christopher	Capt., North Carolina
Curry, James	Sea Service
Cute, Christian	Continental Line
Cutler, John	Capt., Massachusetts
Dagget, George	North Carolina
Daily, William	Connecticut
Daniel, Moses	Lieut., Pennsylvania
Dark, William	Capt., Virginia
Davenport, Adrian	Virginia
Davenport, William	Capt., Virginia
Davenport, William	North Carolina
Davidson, Ephraim	Capt., North Carolina
Davis, Benjamin	North Carolina
Davis, James	Virginia
Davis, Jesse	Capt., Virginia
Dearman, George	New Jersey
Delap, Thomas	Continental Line
Delong, Solomon	Pennsylvania
De Neal, James	Ensign, Virginia
Denison, George	Connecticut
Dennis, John	Capt., Pennsylvania
Denny, William	Pulaski Legion
Deveny, Aaron	Lieut., North Carolina
Devoe, David	Continental Line
Dewitt, Peter	Virginia
Dickey, John	Capt., Virginia
Dickson, Joseph	Col., North Carolina
Dickson, Thomas	North Carolina
Diffenderffer, Peter	Pennsylvania
Dillard, Thomas	Capt., Virginia
Dixon, John	Capt., Virginia
Dodd, Eli	Delaware

Dodge, John	Massachusetts
Dorman, David	Delaware
Dorsey, Richard	Lieut., Continental
Dowden, Clementius	Pennsylvania
Dowell, David	Pennsylvania
Dowell, Richard	Virginia
Dowell, Richard	North Carolina
Downey, Emmanuel	Capt., Virginia
Drummond, Patrick	Pennsylvania
Ducker, John	Continental Line
Dudley, Thomas	Capt., Virginia
Dulin, John	Capt., New York
Dunbar, John	Lieut., Virginia
Duncan, James	German Regiment
Duncan, Joseph	Virginia
Dunning, Dennis	New Jersey
Durkee, John	Col., Connecticut
Durnin, Hugh	Pennsylvania
Dych, Peter	Virginia
Dyer, Charles	Virginia
Dyer, Thomas	Capt., Continental
Dyre, Christopher	Capt., Rhode Island
Eager, James	Capt., Pennsylvania
Eagles, William	Virginia
Eagleston, Joseph	Capt., Continental
Eaken, Joseph	Surgeon's Mate, Continental
Eatheridge, James	North Carolina
Edgar, David	Capt., Continental
Edwards, Samuel	Connecticut
Edwards, Thomas	Capt., Virginia
Eichholtz, John	Continental Line
Eikelberger, John	Pennsylvania
Elliott, John	Capt., Pennsylvania
Ellis, John	Sea Service
Elsey, Thomas	Virginia
Elwood, Abraham	Connecticut
Elwood, Isaac	Connecticut
Elwood, Stephen	Connecticut
Enos, Roger	Col., Connecticut
Epperson, Richard	Virginia

Erwin, John	Pennsylvania
Fair, John	Continental Line
Farrant, Henry	Pulaski Legion
Ferguson, Robert	Virginia
Fields, William	Capt., Virginia
Fifer, Jacob	Virginia
Fifer, Jacob	North Carolina
Finley, Daniel	Pennsylvania
Finn, Peter	North Carolina
Finney, Edmund	Continental Line
Fisbourne, Benjamin	Capt., Pennsylvania
Fitches, Andrew	Capt., Connecticut
Flathenay, Joshua	Vermont
Flowers, Benjamin	Col., Artillery
Floyd, John	Col., Kentucky
Flyn, Thomas	Delaware
Ford, Elisah	South Carolina
Ford, Thomas	New Jersey
Forman, Aaron	Virginia
Forman, Thomas	Pennsylvania
Forney, Peter	Ensign, North Carolina
Fortune, William	Pennsylvania
Fowler, Amos	Connecticut
Fowler, Samuel	South Carolina
Freeman, Edward	Sea Service
Freeman, Israel	New Jersey
Freeman, Matthew	Capt., New Jersey
French, Samuel	Connecticut
French, Samuel	Connecticut
French, Truman	Connecticut
Friend, Joseph	Capt., Pennsylvania
Fries, George	Lieut., Pennsylvania
Fry, Benjamin	Capt., Virginia
Fry, Gabriel	Virginia
Frymiller, Jacob	German Regiment
Fuller, Elisha	Marine, Massachusetts
Gallup, Amos	Lieut., Connecticut
Gallup, Nehemiah	Sergt., Connecticut
Gardiner, Nathaniel	Surgeon's Mate, Continental
Gardner, William	Connecticut

Garner, George	Lieut., Virginia
Gaston, Robert	Lieut., South Carolina
George, William	Capt., South Carolina
Getselman, John	Continental Line
Gibson, John	North Carolina
Gill, Daniel	North Carolina
Gill, Erasmus	Capt., Continental
Gill, Moses	Virginia
Given, David	Capt., Virginia
Glass, Michael	Virginia
Golson, William	Capt., North Carolina
Goode, Francis	Capt., Virginia
Goodenough, Ithaman	Lieut., Vermont
Goodenough, Levi	Capt., Vermont
Goodwin, Uriah	Capt., South Carolina
Gordon, Archibald	Pennsylvania
Gordon, Peter	Q. M., New Jersey
Graham, Moses	Lieut., Pennsylvania
Graham, William	Virginia
Graham, William	Col., North Carolina
Graff, George	Capt., Pennsylvania
Graiffe, Jared	Capt., Pennsylvania
Graves, John	Capt., North Carolina
Gray, David	Sergt., Virginia
Greacy, John	North Carolina
Green, Richard	New Jersey
Greene, William	Rhode Island
Greenwood, Joseph	Delaware
Gregory, Daniel	Connecticut
Griffith, Joseph	Pennsylvania
Guice, John	Virginia
Hahn, Michael	Pennsylvania
Haires, Jacob	New Jersey
Hait, Samuel	Capt., Connecticut
Hall, David	Col., Delaware
Hall, Isaac	North Carolina
Hall, John	North Carolina
Hall, John	New York
Hambright, Henry	Capt., Pennsylvania
Hammon, Abraham	Virginia

Hampton, Andrew	Col., North Carolina
Hancox, Edward	Connecticut
Hanks, Richard	Continental
Harding, Seth	Sea Service
Hardy, John	Virginia
Hardy, Robert	Capt., Sea Service
Hargin, Michael	Pennsylvania
Hargus, John	Virginia
Harper, Andrew	Surgeon's Mate, Continental
Harrington, Ephraim	Massachusetts
Harris, Benjamin	Capt., Virginia
Harris, Henry	Virginia
Harris, William	Virginia
Harrison, Peyton	Capt., Virginia
Harrison, William	Ensign, Continental
Harvey, Robert	Virginia
Harwood, Robert	Continental Line
Hase, Daniel	Capt., Pennsylvania
Heard, James	Continental Line
Helen, Leonard	Capt., Virginia
Helphenstine, Philip	Continental Line
Henderson, John	Capt., Virginia
Henderson, Thomas	New Jersey
Hendricks, Albert	North Carolina
Hendrickson, Daniel	Col., New Jersey
Herd, John	Capt., Continental
Herndon, Benjamin	Capt., North Carolina
Herrick, Samuel	Capt., Vermont
Herrington, Daniel	Pennsylvania
Herrod, William	Capt., Kentucky
Hersten, Peter	Capt., Virginia
Hester, Farel	North Carolina
Hicklin, Thomas	Capt., Virginia
Hickmon, Samuel	South Carolina
Higgins, George	Ensign, Virginia
Hill, John	Virginia
Hill, Roswell	North Carolina
Hinch, William	Ensign, Kentucky
Hinkle, Philip	Continental Line
Hinman, Timothy	Connecticut

Hobby, Thomas	Capt., Connecticut
Hodges, George	Capt., North Carolina
Hodges, John	South Carolina
Hogland, James	Capt., Kentucky
Holcombe, John	Col., Virginia
Holland, Thomas	Capt., Delaware
Holley, Francis	North Carolina
Holley, Francis	South Carolina
Holley, Jacob	North Carolina
Holmes, Asher	Col., New Jersey
Holmes, Jeremiah	New York
Hook, James	Capt., Virginia
Hopkins, John	Rhode Island
Hopkins, Joseph	Capt., Rhode Island
Hopkins, Stephen	Sea Service
Horbin, Joshua	North Carolina
Horner, Gustavus	Surgeon's Mate
Hosiac, David	Capt., Pennsylvania
Houston, Archibald	North Carolina
Howell, Arthur	Q. M., New Jersey
Hubbs, Jacob	Kentucky
Hughes, Joseph	Kentucky
Humphrey, Elijah	Capt., Connecticut
Hunt, William	New York
Hunter, Patrick	Ensign, Pennsylvania
Hunter, William	Pennsylvania Teamster
Hurlburt, Abriam	New York
Hutchins, William	Capt., Vermont
Hynes, Andrew	Capt., Kentucky
Ijams, Vachel	North Carolina
Ingram, James	Sea Service
Irish, Nathaniel	Capt., Artillery
Jack, Matthew	Lieut., Pennsylvania
Jackson, George	Capt., Pennsylvania
Jackson, John	Massachusetts
Jackson, William	Pennsylvania
Jacob, Edward	North Carolina
Jacobs, Samuel	Virginia
James, John	Virginia
Jarrett, Jospah	Capt., Pennsylvania

Miscellaneous List Other States

Johnson, Absalom	Pennsylvania
Johnson, Anderson	Virginia
Johnson, Benjamin	Capt., Virginia
Johnson, Colmon	Rhode Island
Johnson, James	Virginia
Johnson, Nathaniel	Connecticut
Johnson, Robert	Pennsylvania
Johnson, Samuel	Capt., North Carolina
Jones, Abel	Delaware
Jones, Cadwallader	Capt., Continental
Jones, Crain	Capt., South Carolina
Jones, Ebenezer	Delaware
Jones, Michael	Continental Line
Jones, Morgan	Ensign, Virginia
Jones, Samuel	Capt., North Carolina
Jones, Thomas	North Carolina
Jones, William	Capt., Virginia
Jordon, John	Capt., Artillery
Katt, George	Capt., Pennsylvania
Kaufman, John	Virginia
Kausler, John	Pennsylvania
Kearns, William	Virginia
Kellogg, Noah	Connecticut
Kelly, Alexander	Pennsylvania
Kelly, John	Capt., New Jersey
Kerby, Jesse	Virginia
Keyt, John	New Jersey
Kibbe, Lemuel	Connecticut
Kidd, Robert	North Carolina
Kimball, Jesse	Capt., Connecticut
Kincaid, Andrew	Pennsylvania
King, Jonah	Conn. & Mass.
Kingsbury, Lemuel	Corpl., Connecticut
Kinnison, David	Massachusetts
Kirkpatrick, Isaac	Pennsylvania
Kitchen, Zachary	South Carolina
Kitrick, John	Capt., Virginia
Knall, William	Capt., Virginia
Knight, John	Surgeon, Virginia
Kuster, Philip	Continental Line

Kyzer, Frederick	Kentucky
Lacy, Edward	Col., South Carolina
Laird, William	Col., Pennsylvania
Lamb, William	Pennsylvania
Lamson, Thomas	Massachusetts
Lane, Joseph	Col., Virginia
Lantz, Marb.	German Regiment
Latham, William	Capt., Connecticut
Lauck, Peter	Continental Line
Lavender, Hugh	South Carolina
Lawrence, Isaac	South Carolina
Layfield, Smullen	Sea Service
Layton, William	Delaware
Ledyard, William	Col., Connecticut
Lefever, William	Massachusetts
Leisure, Benjamin	Pennsylvania
Leisure, John	Pennsylvania
Lemon, Jacob	Virginia
Lemon, John	Pennsylvania
Leonard, James	Delaware
Letfridge, William	Capt., Virginia
Levi, Judas	Virginia
Lewis, Daniel	North Carolina
Lewis, Gager	Capt., North Carolina
Lewis, George	Virginia
Lewis Henry	Lieut., Pennsylvania
Lewis, Jesse	Virginia
Lewis, Samuel	Col., Virginia
Lewis, Willam	Capt., Virginia
Libby, William	Massachusetts
Lindsey, John	Pennsylvania
Lochrey, Archibald	Capt., Pennsylvania
Lockridge, Andrew	Capt., Virginia
Logan, David	Lieut., Pennsylvania
Long, Benjamin	Virginia
Long, Gabrill	Capt., Virginia
Long, Jonathan	Pennsylvania
Longwell, William	Pennsylvania
Lotman, Conrad	New Jersey
Loughrey, Jeremiah	Capt., Pennsylvania

Lowry, Jacob	Pennsylvania
Lowry, Michael	Pennsylvania
Loxley, John	Capt., Sea Service
Lucas, Thomas	Sea Service
Lucas, William	Virginia
Lungreen, Henry	Sea Service
Lynn, William	Col., Kentucky
Lyon, James	Surgeon's Mate, Continental
Lyon, Noah	Connecticut
McAdin, John	North Carolina
McAdoo, John	Capt., North Carolina
McBride, David	Virginia
McCackin, James	Pennsylvania
McCallister, James	Pennsylvania
McCaslin, Andrew	Pennsylvania
McCausland, Andrew	Lieut., Continental
McCausland, Andrew	Virginia
McCausland, Henry	Massachusetts
McCausland, James	Rhode Island
McClain, John	Sea Service
McClain, William	Pennsylvania
McClaskey, William	Capt., Pennsylvania
McCleery, William	Pennsylvania
McClellen, Sanil	Col., Connecticut
McClure, Nathaniel	Sea Service
McCormick, John	Pennsylvania
McCormick, William	Pennsylvania
McCoy, Alexander	Pennsylvania
McCoy, William	New York
McCracken, Joseph	Capt., New York
McDade, Philip	Continental Line
McDave, James	Capt., Pennsylvania
McDavit, Philip	Continental Line
McDonald, John	North Carolina
McDonald, William	Rhode Island
McDonald, William	Continental Line
McDowell, John	North Carolina
McElhattan, John	Pennsylvania
McFarlin, Daniel	Capt., Line Service
McFarlin, George	South Carolina

McFerrin, William	Virginia
McGaw, John	Capt., South Carolina
McGuire, Neley	Capt., North Carolina
McKaskey, William	Capt., Pennsylvania
McKee, Robert	Pennsylvania
Mackelroy, George	Capt., Sea Service
Mackey, Aeneas	Col., Pennsylvania
McKinney, Roderick	Sea Service
McKinzie, Moses	German Regiment
McMachen, James	Lieut., Virginia
McMachen, William	Capt., Virginia
McMann, William	Virginia
McMillin, Collin	Sea Service
McMillan, Samuel	Massachusetts
McMillan, William	Massachusetts
McNamara, Michael	Capt., Marines
Macon, Harrison	Capt., North Carolina
McPherson, Barton	Virginia
McRisit, John	Sea Service
Madison, George	Capt., Virginia
Major, Thomas	North Carolina
Mallery, Nathaniel	Connecticut
Mallery, Truman	Connecticut
Manley, John	Capt., Massachusetts
Mansfield, Thomas	Delaware
Marathy, Mathew	Sea Service
Markland, Edward	Lieut., Sea Service
Marsh, John	Virginia
Marshall, Robert	Pennsylvania
Martin, Charles	Virginia
Martin, Ennalls	Surgeon, Continental
Martin, Ephraim	Col., New Jersey
Martindale, John	Fifer
Matthews, Bennett	Sea Service
Matthews, Sampson	Col., Virginia
Maxwell, Adam	Lieut., Pennsylvania
Maxwell, John	Pennsylvania
Maxwell, Robert	Capt., South Carolina
Meigs, Return	Col., Connecticut
Merritt, Daniel	North Carolina

MISCELLANEOUS LIST OTHER STATES 145

Middleton, Gilbert	Capt., Sea Service
Middleton, William	Capt., Sea Service
Mifflin, Thomas	Q. M., Pennsylvania
Miles, William	Sea Service
Miller, George	Pennsylvania
Miller, George	New York
Miller, Nathan	Rhode Island
Miller, Peter	Continental Line
Miller, Samuel	Capt., Pennsylvania
Mills, Elijah	Pennsylvania
Mills, James	New York
Mills, Jeremiah	Lieut., New Jersey
Mills, Solomon	New York
Miner, Clem	Lieut., Connecticut
Mitchell, Solomon	North Carolina
Moler, Joseph	Georgia
Monroe, Lemuel	Massachusetts
Montague, Nathaniel	Vermont
Montgomery, Alexander	Pennsylvania
Montgomery, Angus	Pennsylvania
Montgomery, Hugh	Pennsylvania
Montgomery, John	Virginia
Moody, Joseph	Massachusetts
Moore, Abraham	Virginia
Moore, James	Lieut., Pennsylvania
Moore, Thomas	Capt., Virginia
Moore, Thomas	South Carolina
Moore, Thomas	Capt., Maryland
Moore, William	Col., North Carolina
Mopp, Frederick	German Regiment
Morgan, Jacquil	Virginia
Morgan, James	Virginia
Morgan, James	Capt., New Jersey
Morgan, John	Capt., North Carolina
Morgan, William	Virginia
Morris, Thomas	South Carolina
Morris, Zadock	Delaware
Morrison, James	Pennsylvania
Morrison, William	North Carolina
Morton, Josiah	Virginia

Morton, Samuel	Massachusetts
Moseley, Blackman	Capt., Virginia
Moseley, Joseph	Virginia
Moseley, Samuel	North Carolina
Moser, Christian	Pennsylvania
Moser, Michael	Pennsylvania
Mosier, Francis	North Carolina
Moss, Daniel	Connecticut
Moss, Nicholas	Continental Line
Moulton, John	Capt., North Carolina
Mulford, Benjamin	New Jersey
Mullens, John	Virginia
Munn, Francis	
Munny, Christopher	Virginia
Murdock, Benjamin	Capt., Continental
Murphy, Anthony	Capt., Virginia
Murphy, John	Lieut., North Carolina
Murphy, Philip	
Murphy, William	N. C. & Va.
Murray, Alexander	Sea Service
Murray, George	Pennsylvania
Murray, Richard	Pennsylvania
Muterspaw, Philip	Pennsylvania
Myers, John	Pennsylvania
Nanny, David	New York
Naramore, Asa	Massachusetts
Nash, Thomas	Capt., Connecticut
Nason, Joseph	Capt., Massachusetts
Nearing, John	Connecticut
Neese, Peter	Pennsylvania
Neill, John	Capt., Pennsylvania
Nelson, Robert	Pennsylvania
Nelson, Thomas	Virginia
Neves, William	Virginia
Nevil, John	Virginia
New, Anthony	Capt., Virginia
Nichols, David	Capt., Connecticut
Nichols, John	Sea Service
Nuper, Joseph	Pennsylvania
Nutter, Benjamin	Capt., Sea Service

MISCELLANEOUS LIST OTHER STATES 147

Oakes, John	Massachusetts
Oakes, John	Pennsylvania
Oard, William	Virginia
O'Daniel, John	Virginia
Odell, Stephen	Lieut., Virginia
Officer, James	Pennsylvania
Olds, Aaron	Connecticut
Oliver, John	Pennsylvania
O'Neal, Constantine	Pennsylvania
Oneal, John	Pennsylvania
Oram, Cooper	Pennsylvania
Orr, John	Pennsylvania
Orr, Robert	Capt., Pennsylvania
Overstreet, John	Major, Virginia
Paine, John	Sea Service
Palmer, Elijah	Capt., Connecticut
Palmer, Moses	Ensign, Connecticut
Palmer, Nathan	Capt., Connecticut
Parson, Hezekiah	Capt., Connecticut
Parson, James	Sea Service
Patterson, Peter	Pulaski Legion
Patton, Alexander	Virginia
Patton, James	Virginia
Patton, John	Pennsylvania
Patton, John	Virginia
Paul, James	Pennsylvania
Paxton, James	Q. M., New Jersey
Peace, John	South Carolina
Peirce, Samuel	Connecticut
Pendleton, Nathaniel	Capt., Virginia
Penniton, Abraham	Pennsylvania
Perkin, Daniel	Capt., Connecticut
Peter, John	Continental Line
Philips, David	Sergt., Connecticut
Phillip, John	Pennsylvania
Philipps, Philip	Lieut., Kentucky
Pickhem, Barber	Lieut., Rhode Island
Pike, Zebulon	Paymaster, Continental
Pittier, Lewis	Continental Line
Pitts, Richard	Connecticut

Plum, Jacob	Pennsylvania
Plummer, Elisha	Pennsylvania
Poinier, John	Capt., New York
Pollard, William	Capt., Virginia
Pollock, David	Pennsylvania
Pond, Timothy	Connecticut
Porter, Petter	Massachusetts
Porter, William	Lieut., Virginia
Potterf, Casper	Virginia
Pourroy, George	Capt., Kentucky
Prather, Henry	Capt., Kentucky
Prentice, Eleaser	Capt., Connecticut
Prentice, Jonas	Capt., Connecticut
Preston, John	Delaware
Price, Joseph	Continental
Pridmore, Jonathan	Pennsylvania
Pridmore, Theodore	Pennsylvania
Prior, Abner	Capt., Connecticut
Prior, Ebenezer	Connecticut
Purnell, Zedic	Patriot
Purseley, Peter	Delaware
Quarterman, John	Pennsylvania
Rain, Isaac	New Jersey
Ramsey, Dennis	Major, Virginia
Randoll, Roswell	Lieut., Connecticut
Randolph, Fitz	Capt., Pennsylvania
Randolph, John	Major, Continental
Randolph, Michael	Capt., Continental
Rankin, Robert	Capt., North Carolina
Ray, John	Kentucky
Read, David	New Jersey
Read, James	New Jersey
Read, James	Col., New Hampshire
Read, John	Surgeon's Mate
Read, Zalmon	Capt., Connecticut
Rector, Maxmillian	Virginia
Reece, Andrew	Pennsylvania
Reed, Andrew	Pennsylvania
Reed, Caspar	Capt., Pennsylvania
Reed, Edward	Sea Service

MISCELLANEOUS LIST OTHER STATES 149

Reed, Jacob	Col., Pennsylvania
Reed, James	Pennsylvania
Reed, Joseph	Pennsylvania
Reed, Philip	Col., Pennsylvania
Reed, Philip	Pennsylvania
Reed, William	Pennsylvania
Reese, James	Capt., North Carolina
Renfrow, John	Capt., North Carolina
Rhodes, John	Capt., Delaware
Rice, Nehemiah	Lieut., Connecticut
Rice, Randall	Ensign, Rhode Island
Richards, Benjamin	Lt. Col., Connecticut
Richards, Samuel	Connecticut
Richardson, Holt	Col., Virginia
Richardson, John	Virginia
Richardson, Thomas	North Carolina
Rickerson, Daniel	Capt., Virginia
Rickey, Joseph	Pennsylvania
Risker, George	Lieut., Virginia
Robert, Joseph	Lieut., Virginia
Roberts, Benjamin	Capt., Kentucky
Robeson, James	Sea Service
Robinson, David	Ensign, Virginia
Robinson, James	Pennsylvania
Robinson, James	New Jersey
Robinson, John	Virginia
Robinson, Stanley	Sea Service
Rock, John	Pulaski Legion
Rogers, David	New York
Rollens, Hannahiah	New Jersey
Rosamond, Samuel	Capt., South Carolina
Rossetter, Bryan	Connecticut
Runyan, Henry	New Jersey
Russel, Robert	Capt., Virginia
Ryan, John	Continental Line
Safley, Henry	Virginia
Samuels, Robert	Capt., Pennsylvania
Sanders, Adair	Capt., North Carolina
Sanders, Adams	Capt., North Carolina
Sanford, Edward	Lieut., Virginia

Sanford, Elihu	Connecticut
Sanford, John	Capt., Virginia
Savage, Benjamin	Capt., Pennsylvania
Saylor, George	Pennsylvania
Scott, Abraham	Pennsylvania
Scudder, Nathaniel	New Jersey
Scull, Edward	Capt., Pennsylvania
Seabrook, Thomas	New Jersey
Sears, Thomas	Lieut., New York
Seawell, Benjamin	Col., North Carolina
Selfrage, John	New York
Seltzer, Charles	Pennsylvania
Semple, Robert	Capt., Virginia
Sevier, Robert	Capt., North Carolina
Shade, Jacob	Virginia
Shaeffer, Peter	Capt., New Jersey
Shall, George	Pennsylvania
Shank, Christian	New Jersey
Shaw, Henry	Virginia
Sheifely, Mathias	Capt., Pennsylvania
Shelton, Leroy	Virginia
Shepard, Abraham	Col., North Carolina
Shepard, Colvin	Capt., New York
Sherburne, Henry	Col., Rhode Island
Sherman, John	Conn., Paymaster
Shields, John	Capt., Pennsylvania
Shoemaker, John	New Jersey
Shriner, John	Pennsylvania
Shrupp, Henry	Pennsylvania
Shumaker, John	North Carolina
Shutz, Frederick	Continental Line
Simpkins, Dickinson	Lieut., Pennsylvania
Simpson, Southy	Capt., Virginia
Skerrett, Clement	Lieut., Continental
Slate, Christian	Capt., Pennsylvania
Slaughter, Jacob	Pennsylvania
Sledham, Joseph	Capt., Delaware
Sloan, John	Pennsylvania
Sloan, William	Pennsylvania
Slocum, John	Rhode Island

Smiley, John	Pennsylvania
Smiley, Thomas	Ensign, Pennsylvania
Smith, Benjamin	Lieut., Virginia
Smith, Caleb	North Carolina
Smith, David	Capt., Continental
Smith, Henry	Lieut., Pennsylvania
Smith, James	Capt., North Carolina
Smith, James	Col., Pennsylvania
Smith, John C.	Capt., South Carolina
Smith, Nathan	Virginia
Smith, Oliver	Major, Continental
Smither, Ebeneran	Rhode Island
Smoot, James	Virginia
Smoot, John	Virginia
Snivley, Casper	Capt., Pennsylvania
Snowden, Benjamin	Surgeon's Mate, Continental
Snyder, Peter	Pennsylvania
Sollard, Thomas	Capt., Sea Service
Souther, Valentine	Va. & N. C.
Sparhawk, Nathan	Col., Massachusetts
Sparr, Richard	Virginia
Speake, George	Virginia
Spear, Samuel	————
Spicer, Samuel	Pennsylvania
Sprague, John	Rhode Island
Standift, Lemuel	————
Stanks, Thomas	North Carolina
Stansbury, Luke	North Carolina
Stansbury, Solomon	North Carolina
Staples, John	Virginia
Steele, John	Capt., Pennsylvania
Steele, John	Pennsylvania
Steers, Hugh	Pennsylvania
Stephens, William	Lieut., Virginia
Sterling, Henry	Virginia
Steven, John	Capt., Connecticut
Stevens, William	Virginia
Stevenson, James	Pennsylvania
Stevenson, James	South Carolina
Stewart, John	Pennsylvania

Stewart, Thomas	Ensign, Pennsylvania
Stinchcomb, Christopher	Delaware
Stith, John	Lieut., Continental
Stoddard, Nathan	Capt., Connecticut
Stokley, Thomas	Capt., Pennsylvania
Stoner, John	Pennsylvania
Storm, Peter	Capt., Pennsylvania
Stratton, Thomas	Connecticut
Stringer, James	Lieut., Kentucky
Stringer, Peter	Capt., Kentucky
Strother, John	Virginia
Stuart, William	Capt., Virginia
Stump, Jacob	New Jersey
Stump, John	New Jersey
Sullivan, Daniel	Pennsylvania
Sullivan, James	New York
Sutherland, Alexander	Virginia
Swan, Charles	Virginia
Swann, John	Capt., Continental
Swearingen, Van	Kentucky
Swift, Heman	Col., Connecticut
Sydars, Solomon	Virginia
Tallmadge, Benjamin	Major, Continental
Tedford, John	Virginia
Telford, Joseph	Virginia
Tennant, Gilbert	Surgeon, Continental
Tennant, James	Rhode Island
Tennehill, James	Kentucky
Terry, Ebenezer	Connecticut
Terry, Shadrach	Capt., Massachusetts
Terry, William	Capt., Virginia
Thompson, James	North Carolina
Thompson, William	Col., South Carolina
Throckmorton, Joseph	New Jersey
Tilden, Daniel	Capt., Continental
Tilton, James	Surgeon, Delaware
Timmons, Joshua	Delaware
Tobin, Jacob	Surgeon, Continental
Trafton, Joshua	Capt., Continental
Trammell, Sampson	Capt., Virginia

Miscellaneous List Other States

Tresler, Frederick	Pennsylvania
Trout, Henry	German Regiment
Truesdel, Samuel	New York
Trusdale, John	Pennsylvania
Tryer, Andrew	Pennsylvania
Tucker, Reuben	Virginia
Turner, Berryman	Capt., North Carolina
Turner, Henry	Sea Service
Tyler, Abraham	Capt., Massachusetts
Tyler, Daniel	Virginia
Tyler, George	Lieut., Virginia
Tyler, Samuel	Connecticut
Vallentine, George	Pennsylvania
Vallentine, George	Virginia
Van Buskirk, Abraham	New Jersey
Van Buskirk, Peter	New Jersey
Vance, Samuel	Capt., Virginia
Vaughan, Joseph	Col., Delaware
Vaughan, Noel	South Carolina
Vaughan, William	South Carolina
Veatch, Jeremiah	Pennsylvania
Vermillion, Samuel	North Carolina
Vickroy, Thomas	Pennsylvania
Wadsworth, Thomas	Pennsylvania
Walbridge, Joshua	Massachusetts
Walbridge, Peter	Massachusetts
Waldron, Charles	North Carolina
Waldron, David	Sea Service
Walker, George	Sea Service
Wall, John	Pennsylvania
Wallace, Adam	Capt., Virginia
Wallace, Michael	Capt., Virginia
Waller, John	Lieut., Virginia
Waples, Eli	Delaware
Ward, Andrew	Col., Connecticut
Warford, James	Capt., Pennsylvania
Warman, Thomas	Capt., Virginia
Washington, William	Col., Continental
Wasson, John	Virginia
Wasson, Joseph	North Carolina

Waterbury, David	Col., Connecticut
Waters, James	Virginia
Watts, Archibald	Pennsylvania
Watts, Thomas	Capt., Delaware
Wayt, William	Virginia
Weaver, Henry	Pennsylvania
Weaver, Jacob	Capt., Pennsylvania
Webbs, Henry	Pulaski Legion
Webb, Moses	Connecticut
Webb, Samuel	Col., Connecticut
Webster, Alexander	Col., New York
Weed, James	Delaware
Weeden, Thomas	Continental Line
Weldin, Jesse	Delaware
Wellfong, John	North Carolina
Wells, Charles	Pennsylvania
Wells, Charles	Virginia
Wells, Samuel	Capt., Kentucky
Welsh, Robert	Pennsylvania
Wendell, John	Capt., Continental
Wertz, George	Pennsylvania
Wharton, Joseph	Continental Line
Wheeler, Benjamin	Pennsylvania
Wheeler, Joshua	Pennsylvania
Wheeler, Samuel	Virginia
Whetstone, Daniel	North Carolina
White, Anthony	Continental Line
White, Richard	Lieut., Virginia
White, Thomas	Pennsylvania
White, Thomas	Tennessee
White, William	Capt., Massachusetts
Whithead, John	Capt., Virginia
Whiting, Samuel	Col., Connecticut
Whitlack, Bennett	Pennsylvania
Wicks, Amos	Capt., Virginia
Wideman, Adam	South Carolina
Wiley, Thomas	Capt., Continental Line
Wilkinson, John	Capt., Virginia
Williams, Daniel	New Jersey
Williams, Francis	

Williams, Gerard	Pennsylvania
Williams, James	Pennsylvania
Williams, John	Col., New York
Williams, John	Virginia
Williams, Joseph	Delaware
Williams, Lawrence	Pennsylvania
Williams, Nathan	Mass. & Vt.
Williams, William	Virginia
Williamson, Alexander	Pennsylvania
Williamson, Eleazer	Capt., Pennsylvania
Willis, Hezekiah	Col., Connecticut
Willis, Meshach	Georgia
Wilson, Andrew	Capt., North Carolina
Wilson, James	Capt., Pennsylvania
Wilson, John	New York
Wilson, William	Pennsylvania
Wimmer, John	Pennsylvania
Winds, William	Col., New Jersey
Witcher, William	Capt., Virginia
Withington, Martin	Pennsylvania
Wolf, David	Virginia
Wolf, Michael	Virginia
Wood, Aaron	North Carolina
Wood, Amos	Massachusetts
Wood, John	Va. & N. C.
Wood, Thomas	Capt., North Carolina
Woodworth, Joseph	Connecticut
Woolcott, Erastus	Col., Connecticut
Wright, Elijah	Pennsylvania
Wright, Nathan	Georgia
Wright, Robert	Virginia
Wyatt, John	Virginia
Yeat, John	Capt., Connecticut
York, Jeremiah	Connecticut
Young, Robert	Lieut., Virginia
Young, Thomas	Capt., Virginia
Younger, George	Sea Service
Younger, Kanard	Virginia
Yule, James	Massachusetts